SQUIRREL PIE

SQUIRREL PIE

Elisabeth Luard

B L O O M S B U R Y
LONDON · OXFORD · NEW YORK · NEW DELHI · SYDNEY

Bloomsbury Publishing
An imprint of Bloomsbury Publishing Plc

50 Bedford Square   1385 Broadway
London   New York
WC1B 3DP   NY 10018
UK   USA

www.bloomsbury.com

BLOOMSBURY and the Diana logo are trademarks of Bloomsbury Publishing Plc

First published in Great Britain 2016

British Library Cataloguing-in-Publication Data
A catalogue record for this book is available from the British Library.

Library of Congress Cataloguing-in-Publication data has been applied for.

ISBN: HB: 978-1-4088-4610-0
ePub: 978-1-4088-4609-4

2 4 6 8 10 9 7 5 3 1

Designed by Libanus Press

Typeset by Newgen Knowledge Works (P) Ltd, Chennai, India
Printed and bound in Great Britain by CPI Group (UK) Ltd, Croydon CR0 4YY

MIX
Paper from
responsible sources
FSC® C020471

To find out more about our authors and books visit www.bloomsbury.com.
Here you will find extracts, author interviews, details of forthcoming
events and the option to sign up for our newsletters.

For my grandchildren, Jessie, Bonnie, Harper, Iona, Orin, Sophie and Plum, who will inherit the care of our beautiful planet

CONTENTS

CONTENTS

Preface

AS A FOOD WRITER BY TRADE AND TRAVELLER
whenever I get the chance, my interest lies in how – and why and
what – the rest of the world prepares its daily dinner. While it's
possible to eat chips and caviar anywhere on the planet – Adelaide,
Rome, Mumbai or San Francisco – what we cook at home, the
dishes whose ingredients and method have their origin in necessity,
remains remarkably regional, particularly when we come together
to celebrate a festival or mark a rite of passage.

The composition of the dishes we cook to remind
ourselves of who we are is dictated by climate, geography,
latitude and trade routes. Of these four determining factors,
the most powerful is geography. The divisions in this book
reflect that islanders share a way of life with other islanders,
river-dwellers live like other river-dwellers, foresters have
much in common with their fellow foresters, desert-dwellers
live like other desert-dwellers.

Few of us still live as our ancestors did. Fewer still would
want to. And yet what's on sale in the marketplace – any marketplace – tells a different story, whether a few stalls heaped with
wild gathered leaves and roots by a roadside on the shores of
Lake Tana in the Ethiopian Highlands, or the gastronomic
splendours of the central market in Lyon in southern France, for

most of the world, the daily dinner begins with whatever's in season and fresh but above all familiar.

I came late to the tourist trail. Travel was never a possibility in the early years of family life, when four children needed me at home. Later, when my responsibilities as wife and mother had lightened, I seized every opportunity to take to the road. Journalists go wherever they're sent – usually in the low season, when life in whatever tourist destination is on the official list has returned to normal, whether this is a spa hotel on a paradise island in the Hawaiian archipelago or a bed-and-breakfast in a mud hut in the Great Rann of Kutch. Notes of my experiences along the way – as well as a lifetime spent poking around in other people's cooking pots – provided the raw material for the stories in this book. The recipes included at the end of each chapter are those borrowed or begged on my travels. The drawings – I was a natural history artist before I ever wrote a recipe – are derived from the watercolours in my sketchbooks.

As a child, I was no stranger to faraway places. Early school-days were spent in Montevideo, capital of Uruguay, a dozy harbour port on the River Plate. My brother and I were stepchildren, leftovers from a wartime marriage brought to an untimely end in the icy waters of the Atlantic in World War II. Our mother remarried a diplomat on the Latin American circuit and employed cooks and maids to run the household. Left more or less to our own devices after school, we would join our schoolmates on the quayside to catch bony little flatfish for our mother's cook to fry for our supper. Children are valued and spoiled among the Latins and language was no problem. I already spoke French, the diplomatic language, and Spanish easily followed. The kitchen, with its bubbling cooking pots and delicious scents of garlic and herbs, quickly became my refuge. Sometimes, I was even allowed to go home with one of the young maids at the weekend. Her mother cooked thick bean stews fiery with chilli and I fell asleep on an old bus-seat with never a thought for my own soft bed. By the time I was dispatched to a dismal English boarding school to finish my erratic education, I already understood – if only by instinct – that home is a state of mind, portable as a penknife, the most useful item in a child's pocket, and just as likely to be lost.

Married at twenty-one and a mother soon after, I had little time to enjoy the freedoms of a young woman in London in the newly liberated sixties, let alone establish a career for which I was, in any event, equipped with little more than secretarial skills and a year or two at art college. Life with husband Nicholas – at the time of our marriage, proprietor of *Private Eye* and owner, with his friend Peter Cook, of a satirical nightclub in Soho – was never likely to be easy. And so it proved when the breadwinner of the family took up a new career as a novelist.

Writing is an uncertain business, and money was always short. So I uprooted husband and family to spend the early school years in a remote valley in Andalusia in southern Spain, among the Latins in a place where I felt at home. There was a chance, too, to augment the family income by selling my work as a natural history artist in the new tourist boutiques opening further up the coast.

There was much to be learned from the self-sufficient farming community in the valley, and my neighbours, taking pity on the ignorance of a vulnerable young mother whose saving grace was fluent Spanish, took it upon themselves to instruct me in the household essentials. How was it that a mother responsible for four small children had never learned how to salt down the meat of the household pig? Had my own mother taught me nothing? I soon learned how to slaughter and skin a rabbit for the Sunday paella and soothe my children's sniffles with snail broth flavoured with pennyroyal. As a matter of urgency, a sty-pig was installed in a stone-walled enclosure behind the house, and an elderly donkey provided to carry the children to the local school.

Memories of civil war and the brutal dictatorship that followed made the valley-dwellers wary of change. Self-sufficiency, the product of back breaking labour and a willingness to endure hardship, delivered a measure of independence. Most of the necessities of life were available without charge. Every household milked two or three goats and made their own cheese, kept chickens for eggs and meat, fattened up a sty-pig on the kitchen leftovers, grew enough vegetables to see them through the summer and dried their own pulses to carry them through the winter. One or two households ground their own grain in the mill by the stream and baked their own bread, while the forested upper slopes provided a little money from the sale of the cork bark stripped from the cork oaks every seven years, fodder for semi-wild herds of Iberico pigs and charcoal for cooking fires.

When change came, the pace was rapid. With the dictatorship replaced by democracy, the young moved to the towns for wages and only the old folks were left in the whitewashed farmsteads to milk the goats and prepare the cheese with rennet from the stomach of a newborn kid. By the time we left our life in the valley, knowledge that sustained an ancient way of life was already vanishing as fast as snow in summer.

The valley-dwellers had good reason to abandon the old ways. Few, given a choice, would want or even be capable of such a life, romantic though it may seem. To those of us fortunate enough to live in a world of plenty, it might seem unnecessary – even archaic – to look beyond the narrow confines of science and nutrition and take account of the diet of necessity. And yet if we abandon the ancestral hearth-fire, forget what our forefathers learned over the millennia, we deprive ourselves of a store of knowledge we can ill afford to lose.

Introduction

Vic Cherikoff, huntsman, TV chef and rugged frontman for the bush-tucker craze sweeping Australia like a flashfire through a eucalyptus grove, inspects his sell-out audience through narrowed eyes. The scent of raw meat and fear hangs in the air.

We've been warned to expect surprise, and it seems from the uneasy shifting around me that I'm not the only one who has yet to experience kangaroo in the form suggested by the furry corpse on the counter. In 1990 – while I've been skinning rabbits and gutting fish since a rough-and-ready childhood escaping adult supervision in the wilds of Uruguay, where my mother's second husband had been posted to the embassy in Montevideo – this looked a lot too much like Christopher Robin's friend Kanga in *Winnie the Pooh*.

A hand rises tentatively from the crowd.

'My grandpa used to feed it to the dog.'

'Yeah,' said Vic. 'That would be about right, mate. Ready to be surprised?'

Surprise has just been wheeled on stage by two men in white coats, much as a road-crash victim is trolleyed into the operating theatre in a medical sitcom. And Vic – mahogany-tanned, shirt-sleeves rolled to reveal muscular biceps – tips his trademark Akubra hat to the back of his head, thrusts a pair of hairy thumbs into the rugged leather strap threaded through the loops of well-worn khaki shorts, fixes the front row with a gimlet eye and begins his examination.

'Wallaroo,' he announces, stroking the speckled fur with a gentle hand. 'Your average wallaroo is half the body-weight of the big red. My Aboriginal friends tell me it's the meat of their forefathers – apologies due.' Acknowledgement of ancestral wrongdoing is required of anyone making public reference to the original inhabitants. Vic has stripped the apology down to its bare essentials, much as he is preparing to do with the corpse.

There's no room here for sentimentality. I tell myself that meat is meat, whether or not it carries its babies in a pouch and is an adorable reminder of caring motherhood. I inspect the corpse, with its long grey tail of surprising thickness which disappears into soft fur sprinkled with dun-coloured freckles and ends in a pointy dog-like face with large semi-transparent ears and thick black lashes half closed over what we all instinctively know must be big brown eyes. Big brown eyes are a problem. They always are. Even though I kept a household pig to eat up the kitchen scraps when I lived with my own young family in a remote valley in southern Spain, pig-dispatch and dismembering was reckoned men's business – women and children exempt – and anyway an adult porker, particularly one of the semi-wild Iberico breed, can never be considered cuddly.

Rabbits and barnyard birds were women's business in the valley, and I kept both and did the deed myself. But that was the 1960s, when a degree of self-sufficiency was a natural part of what was expected of a woman running a household in a region where famine was a recent memory. Andalusia had suffered terrible deprivations during the Civil War, and good house-keeping – the reason for keeping a sty-pig and feeding kitchen scraps to the hens – was a moral obligation.

But this is a theatrical event and Vic is a showman. Curiosity is why most of us are here – me too. Never mind the message, the moral imperative to make good use of a national emblem otherwise classed as a pest. Cattle and sheep imported by the settlers pushed the native fauna off the menu, turning the natural world on its head. Kangaroo steaks are one thing when presented on a plastic tray in the supermarket as exotic meats, quite another when still encased in a beautiful furry coat and about to go under the knife.

'Here's how it works,' continues Vic, glancing around his audience as he sharpens the blade. 'First the nice folk, which are you and me, don't eat people. Then we don't eat pets, then we don't eat anything that looks at us over the fence or bounces around the bush in a furry jacket – unless, of course, we don't have to look at it till it looks like something we don't recognise so we don't have to do all the messy stuff.'

This is about to change. We are here to experience the messy stuff, and if that puts some of us off eating meat for good, that's our choice.

'Isn't he gorgeous?' breathes the matron to my left – and she doesn't mean the 'roo.

The attraction of the hunter, whether in person or on TV, is animal magnetism. There's no doubt that the object of her admiration has magnetism in spades. It's caveman stuff. If a taste for kangaroo is the beginning of a beautiful relationship, who needs the wheatgrass smoothie?

'Your average bush-tucker chow,' continues Vic, applying flint to steel with a casual twist of the wrist, 'can be skinned like a rabbit.'

Few of us, I'd guess from the neat hairdos and manicured nails, have ever skinned a rabbit. I, on the other hand, find myself wondering if 'roo pelt, properly treated by scraping and salting as for a rabbit-skin jerkin, would make a nice warm winter jacket.

'A tender young 'roo such as this,' Vic advises, slipping sharpened blade between fur and flesh to expose the meat of a muscular thigh, 'yields forty kilos of storable protein when prepared in the form of biltong, enough to carry an Aboriginal family (apologies due) into the next hunting season.' When the beast is hefted back to the homestead, he tells us – an event that takes place after eviscerating the animal in situ – an adult wal-laroo is enough to feed a settler-family for a month. 'When cleanly killed and properly butchered,' he continues, 'bushmeat is the leanest, healthiest meat on the planet.'

With surprising delicacy, Vic lifts the transparent blue-grey membrane that lies between the furry coat and the meat. 'See this?' he enquires, demonstrating the membrane's strength by stretch-ing it between finger and thumb. 'You have to strip this off before preparing your bushmeat for drying. Easy does it. Just cut it in strips and hang it over a thorn bush and keep away the blowflies till it's all dried out and it'll still be good as new in ten years' time. Which is more than you can say for us blokes – sheilas excepted.'

The audience laughs.

Vic finishes skinning the 'roo, piles the fur on the side, and starts to joint the meat.

'No need for the ten-year wait, ladies,' he adds, holding up a neat ribbon of perfectly carved pale-pink flesh. 'Just flip it on the barbie and send the hubby to crack open a tinny.'

The audience relaxes. 'Roo is beginning to look more like dinner. After the talk of biltong, blowflies and ten-year waits, mention of 'roo meat's suitability for Australia's cherished Sun-day ritual is as reassuring as a cold fistful of beer after a long hot morning shark-dodging on Bondi Beach.

'A word for all you bush-tucker beginners,' Vic continues. 'Bush-tucker meat comes in all sizes. Start with your average small reptile – plenty of those in the bush and plenty more in your average Sydney or Melbourne backyard.'

The suggestion introduces a note of danger.

Most of us are city-dwellers who had never thought of reptile-infested backyards as potential hunting grounds. Not me. My brother – eight when I was seven – caught a grass snake in our garden in Uruguay and our mother's cook prepared it with sweetcorn for our supper. And I remember frill-collared, leathery-skinned iguanas tethered to the wrists of their captors and sold live from the roadside when we lived in Mexico – another diplomatic posting – reappearing in the market as the stuffing in my favourite street snack, *tamales*, cornmeal dumplings steamed in maize-leaf. Iguana was indistinguishable from chicken-neck, another favourite stuffing, and came with a dab of chocolate-thickened chilli sauce.

'Take your armadillo,' announces Vic calmly as he dusts the 'roo joints through seasoned flour. 'No need to skin your average armadillo – just gut it and shove it under the coals for half an hour. If you strip it out and shove the meat in a bun nobody will know it from chicken. Goanna tail, too – no need to bother with the rest of it. With your average meat-sized lizard, the tail is the best bit. For a gourmet dish – which is what we're here for, ladies and gentlemen – peel your goanna tail and smash the backbone between a couple of planks to force the fat into the meat and crush in the calcium and phosphates from the bones. The Aboriginals knew a thing or two about nutrition. Treat it like that and the meat is as tender as minced chicken. Great for hamburgers.'

The audience contemplates this nutritional, cultural and gastronomic advice in awed silence.

I stick my hand up to enquire whether snake is suitable for the plank-crushing treatment, thereby blowing my cover as a non-native.

Vic explains that if there are any snakes left in the Old Country – this being unlikely since most of them have probably emigrated to Oz and are currently holding political office in Canberra – you can cook them in just the same way, as long as you cut off the head first so you're OK against the poison. Being OK against the poison applies to a fair proportion of bush-tucker – more native knowledge which was frequently ignored by English colonists.

The lady on my left rattles her bracelets as she sticks up her hand to enquire after crocodile. Vic grins. Crocodile is selling like hot cakes in Sydney's fashionable watering-holes, and the question is welcome.

'Take your average crocodile – and you'll only find 'em north of the Tropic of Capricorn – they're best in the dry season which is right now, October and November. The only piece worth eating is the last couple of feet of the tail, though you can bake even a big bastard whole in its skin in a ground oven.'

My neighbour sighs with satisfaction. Real-man talk is what she came for and the ground oven, a pit dug in soft sand with heated stones as the power source, is the realest of man talk.

'When wrapping your bush-tucker for the pit-barbie,' continues Vic, expertly chopping 'roo tail by slipping a murderous-looking meat cleaver through the joints with the delicacy of a manicurist painting fingernails, 'use eucalyptus bark instead of that plastic-coated rubbish they sell as foil.'

He unrolls a package of paper-thin material and begins to enclose the little pink back fillets from the 'roo. 'Chef's perk,' he says with a grin, slipping the packages under the counter.

There's no question that Vic is master of his craft. In about the same time as it would take me to skin and joint a rabbit – and I'm no slouch at bunny-skinning – Vic has reduced forty kilos of recently deceased, fully grown marsupial to a pile of stripped-out bones, chopped-up tail, neatly folded bundle of speckled brown fur and a bucketful of pinkish chunks of flesh. Bushmeat is particularly suitable for long slow cooking in an earth oven, since the meat cooks in its own steam, a process that has much the same effect as a pressure cooker, though the tenderising takes rather longer.

'Wouldn't you just love to pick him up and take him home?' whispers my bosom-heaving neighbour.

Not really. Vic doesn't strike me as a homebody.

The demonstration comes to a triumphant conclusion as Vic chucks the tail joints and meat chunks into an empty beer-keg and adds the contents of a Fosters six-pack, a handful of greeny-yellow desert limes still frosty from the freezer, a generous dusting of reddish salt crystals from the Murray River and a fistful of Tasmanian mountain pepper-berries which he stirs in with the skinning knife.

He finishes with a flourish, thrusting the knife back into the holster on his belt as the white-coated operatives reappear with the trolley, this time laden with a stew-pot from which rises the appetising scent of slow-cooked bushmeat fragrant with herbs and citrus.

The operatives exchange one container for the other and wheel the newly filled barrel away, presumably for burial in Vic's personal backyard earth oven. A day and a night is what it takes, which is why we'll not be able to fully experience this particular wallaroo but are invited to appreciate the very same taste and flavour in the form of one that Vic, in true TV-chef style, has prepared earlier.

The audience claps and cheers. Some of us are awaiting direct experience of what we have just observed; some of us, relieved by the safe conclusion of an ordeal, are preparing to slip away unnoticed.

Vic will have none of it. 'Not so fast, ladies and gentlemen!'

Vic, quite apart from his remarkable knife skills, is – or was until last year, when he set up his own bush-tucker supply chain – the resident expert on bush-food at the Human Nutrition Unit at the University of Sydney. He has just published *The Bushfood Handbook*, a distillation of a couple of decades of hands-on experience. Not only does he give a wealth of information on plant-foods used by the indigenous population, with identification, growing-habits, tasting notes and culinary uses both ancient and modern, he delivers an impassioned plea for the health of the planet.

His mission, Vic explains as his helpers pass out tasting portions of bush-tucker stew, is to transform what it means to cook Australian, from its current settler-led Euro-Asian gastronomic style to something more closely resembling indigenous cooking, at least in the use and understanding of native ingredients. The problem with this is that the scarcity of vegetation in Australia's desert regions – most of the landmass – means it's no longer morally acceptable to gather plant-foods from the wild. It is, however, more than possible to harvest a wide variety of edible fruits and nuts from municipal plantings in city streets and parks.

In addition, he continues, any city-dweller with access to the smallest patch of garden, balcony or window box can do themselves and the planet a favour by restoring the indigenous national larder and growing their own. Full instructions and garden knowhow are in the book.

The scent from the cooking pot is appetisingly rich and the flavour, when finally tasted, deliciously gamey. The more squeamish among us have lost their appetite, which is a shame since stewed wallaroo turns out to be very good indeed. The meat is as tender as anyone might wish, bathed in fragrant juices, sticky and gelatinous, thickened by the inclusion of the tail joints in much the same way as oxtail soup. I scoop up the scraps with a chunk of damper – campfire bread – while Vic unloads a trayful of bush-tucker treats for our inspection. Lillipilli fruits, Kakadu plums, quandongs and wattle-seeds are as unfamiliar to the audience as they are to me. Some of us linger at the counter for a taste. The flavours of the fruits are strong and sour, and the wattle-seeds nutty but gritty.

By now Vic is busy signing copies of his book. Hot off the presses, the publicity is the reason I'm here. I join the queue for

signing. As a food and travel writer, my brief is to report on what's new and exciting in Australia's gastronomic capital and Vic is riding the wave. He writes my name on the flyleaf and adds a dedication in appreciation of my consuming passion for food and wild things. He's right.

Later, back in my hotel room with sketchbook and notes, I flip through the pages of his lavishly illustrated tome. Vic has gathered an astonishing amount of useful information on the diet of the original inhabitants – hard to come by, since few are willing to discuss their secrets.

A handful of recipes by famous chefs modernise the text, but the story is of a world long vanished, interviews with men and women whose way of life depended on an intimate under-standing of the land that was once their birthright, a record of what's already lost and cannot be regained. Sheep and cattle graze the desert grasslands through which the song-lines ran; the people who lived and thrived in a land of plenty are gone, replaced by an alien culture – my own.

I am an outsider here, as any visitor in a strange land must be. And yet I have long been aware that my paternal grand-father, a member of that alien race who claimed the land as their own, was born on a sheep station south of Sydney. His memoir of early life includes a photograph of a solemn little boy of three or four standing on the porch of a tin-roofed shack with one small fist thrust into the hand of a young woman in late-Victorian dress, formal and buttoned up to the neck, with curly dark hair piled on top of her head. I look a lot like her at the same age. She is my great-grandmother, Janet Murray. She was just twenty when she married my great-grandfather, a Lloyds underwriter, and the pair boarded ship for a new life rearing sheep in New South Wales.

Their son, my grandfather, was born on the sheep farm in 1885. Thereafter there was a scandal or tragedy (the story is unclear): twins who either died at birth or were born of the wrong father, a Maori chieftain on his way through Sydney to pay his respects to the Queen Empress. The chieftain, one version of the story goes, was presented with the fruits of his dalliance on his way home.

Whichever story is true, mother and son returned home alone in 1892 and resumed a respectable life in East Anglia. At the tender age of fourteen, the boy, my grandfather and the author of the memoir, enlisted as a naval cadet. There is mention of naval catering – Devonshire cream teas with strawberry jam – supplemented with illicit trout caught in the river Dart cooked by a friendly pub landlady. By the outbreak of the Great War, the young man had earned his airman's wings and found himself a wife, my grandmother, Marjorie Maitland of Edinburgh, who received as a wedding present from her by-now respectable mother-in-law a revised and updated 1912 edition of Mrs Beeton's *Book of Household Management*.

In due course the volume, more than a thousand pages in length and by now fragile and lacking a spine, was passed to me as the eldest granddaughter. So I bundled it up with string and tucked it away on a shelf, opening the pages only occasionally out of curiosity, thinking it irrelevant to life in the Andalusian valley where we lived as a family throughout the early years of our children's schooling.

Later, as my own career as a food writer led me to explore the culinary traditions of Europe's remaining self-sufficient peasantry, Mrs Beeton's instructions on the proper conduct of a Victorian household seemed scarcely relevant. And so the book remained neglected and unopened until, returning from my travels in the land of my grandfather's birth, I retrieved the volume from the back of the shelf and turned the pages.

Sure enough, under 'typical Australian dishes', a recipe for kangaroo-tail soup carries a pencilled note recording that the dish is good enough but can be improved by a dram of whisky just before serving. A dozen words, no more. Not much in which to read the story of a lifetime; not much is all it takes.

I've never forgotten the lessons I learned that day with Bushtucker Vic and the ladies of Sydney. Not least the excellence of wallaroo stew eaten with dugong-moth damper and the advisability of adding a dram of whisky when finishing off a gravy.

But the underlying message – and the reason I gathered the threads of my travels into the stories in this book – is the extraordinary number and diversity of foodstuffs available to our hunter-gathering ancestors. When the first settlers dropped anchor in Botany Bay, they found a peaceful, well-organised, hunter-gathering society in a land unaltered by cultivation for seventy thousand years. Bush-foods available in 1770 to Australia's indigenous inhabitants – largely overlooked by their colonisers – are estimated at ten thousand different species. At the time of first contact with Europeans, around a million people survived and thrived on what nature provides – nuts, blossoms, seeds, leaves, roots, insects, reptiles and molluscs, supplemented by modest amounts of fish, meat and grains. For the past ten thousand years or so – which is roughly when our ancestors began to bring livestock and grain foods into semi-cultivation – the population of the developed world has increased in direct proportion to its ability to fill the belly. We must eat to live, whatever the cost to ourselves or the planet.

If fear of famine still dictates the way we live, then fear of famine explains the way we produce our food and carries on right down to the laden supermarket trolleys wheeled past overstocked shelves and the panic engendered by the threat of a shortage, say, of sliced bread. I've always been happiest when I could dig my own potato patch or pickle my own olives or decide for myself what food I set on the table. This, naturally enough, sets me outside the usual run of things when reporting for newspapers or magazines on the man-made pleasures of travel – restaurants, hotels, museums, architecture – but leaves me free to search out the people and places where life continues more or less as it always has. While the hunter-gatherers – all but a few – are long gone from our planet, the principles that sustained them are still observable among rural communities who haven't yet been absorbed into the life of the city for whatever reason, whether practical or philosophical.

FORESTS

HIGH IN THE FOOTHILLS OF THE CAMBRIANS IN far west Wales, where I have lived for more than twenty years, the last of the oak trees of the ancient Caledonian forest unfurl tight-rolled tassels of tender green as soon as the days lengthen in spring. The leaves spread and darken to form a dense canopy of shade in summer, refuge for insects, birds and mammals. In autumn their seeds, fat golden acorns once eaten by man as well as beast, provide food for squirrels and hedgehogs and other woodland creatures. In winter, when the leaves fall to form a rich brown carpet underfoot, burrowing creatures and wood-land fungi set to work to convert a rich source of nourishment into loam.

While the oaks are king of the forest, lesser companions in the wildwood that once linked valley to valley from Cardigan Bay to the English border are willow, birch and ash. The trees come into leaf in no particular order, though the shepherds and farmers who earn a living in these uplands take the greening of ash before oak as a warning of bad weather to come. Hazel, rowan and elder share the hedgerows with hawthorn, crab apple and blackthorn, a source of food for forest creatures as well as fruits, berries and leaves that supplied country-dwellers with food for free. When children no longer walked to school and those who worked the land were forbidden access to forest gleanings, knowledge was lost and, with it, the memory of why the wildwood mattered.

Our ancestors moved barefoot and silent through the wildwood, reading changes in the contours of the forest floor that indicate the presence of edible roots and tubers ready for gathering, attending to the rustlings in the undergrowth that betray the movements of forest creatures, whether predator or prey. Hunters and hunted share a common understanding, and one can become the other. There was a time when the green-wood was our home, when the forest – far from the stuff of children's nightmares – was the benevolent provider of food and shelter and safety from harm. At different times in different places, hunter became herdsman, gatherer became farmer and the wildwood, such of it as had escaped the woodsman's axe, was turned into a pleasure playground for the few.

Although meat is the prize – the hunter's reward for patience and skill – crops of value to the gatherer include the precious subterranean truffle and a whole larderful of those multicoloured edible fungi traditionally sold to the rich by the poor. The resources of the forest, once available to all, are soon forgotten when the path through the woods remains untrodden. Those who had business in the forest – charcoal-burners, swineherds, wood-cutters – understood where and when the nuts and berries and fungi came to maturity. Children driven to school by bus are deprived of the knowledge of what to pick and eat in the hedgerows.

My own children, walking to school through an Andalusian cork forest, learned to suck the lemony stalks of wood sorrel and gather the cork-oak acorns that taste like chestnuts when fresh and sweet. There were, too, almonds to be gathered green before the shells hardened and the nuts were still soft and jelly-like, with furry skins that scratched your tongue. The Sunday paella was prepared with forest gleanings – rabbit from the cistus scrub and crayfish caught in the stream.

Our ancestors wrote the story of who they were and how they lived on the rough walls of the caves where they laid their bones. The creatures they hunted – even the foods they gathered – are long vanished from the wildwood. Yet the memory remains. And if you walk the woods of Maine with the hunters under a bluebird sky, or follow the grey-backed black-foot pigs of Extremadura through the scrub oak with their herdsman, if you hush the talk and listen to the silence, you'll hear the voice of the earth when the world was young.

Maine

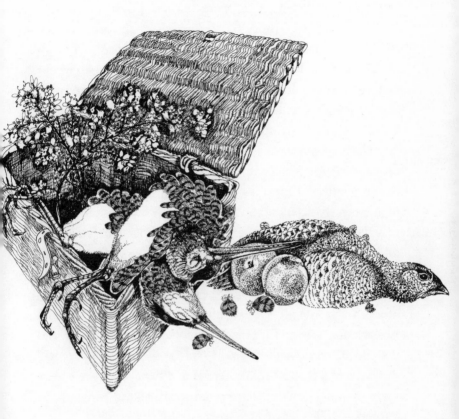

IT'S OCTOBER AND THE FALL COLOURS ARE ALL ablaze in the forests of New England, where the *Mayflower* unloaded her rebel cargo of Pilgrim Fathers on the wooded shores of Massachusetts Bay. The year is 2006, and I have stolen a few days from a literary engagement in Boston to join George and Lucie Semler for the start of the hunting season.

What I have in mind is squirrel pie. Not, I hasten to add, Beatrix Potter's cheeky, red-coated Squirrel Nutkin of European woods, but the fierce American grey, classed as a pest in Britain, ring-barker of trees and robber of wild birds' nests, a New World interloper that has pushed the red to near-extinction. For a half-orphaned, London-born child as I was, Beatrix Potter's stories and exquisite watercolours were magical places to explore. Later, as a natural history painter myself in an earlier career, Beatrix remained my heroine as both artist and cook – not least in her popping of Peter Rabbit's father in a pie. As a writer for children – and a shepherdess in later life – her views on what was or wasn't a suitable candidate for the pot were robustly unsentimental, as are mine.

The main purpose of my presence in the woods of Maine is because George Semler is a man who hunts for the pot rather than primarily for sport, as is usual in my homeland. I'm not a hunter myself – couldn't hit a barn door if I was close enough to turn the handle – but I come from hunting stock. My father, I'm told, was an excellent shot more than capable of filling the pot from the Norfolk Broads where he set up home in the early 1940s with my mother, but since he vanished into the cold waters of the North Atlantic not long after my birth, he wasn't around to teach me. True to the female stereotype, I'm a gatherer, and the undergrowth of the Maine woods at this time of year will surely yield a crop of edible berries and fungi – maybe even a skein of sunny yellow chanterelles or a handful of charcoal-burners – while I leave the important stuff to George.

Walking the wildwood with a huntsman such as George is about as far as a person can get from my own experience of walking up – the name given to the activities of the beaters for the benefit of the guns – hand-reared pheasants from a Hampshire beech-copse, or crouching in a windy butt on a Yorkshire grouse moor where the gamekeeper dictates the bag and the paying punters leave the pick-up to hired help and go home for roast beef and claret.

But in the woods of Maine, where the hunter's bag is whatever's in season and comes to hand, meat from the wild was once

the only fresh food available to a settler household when the land lay fallow under snow, the fishing harbours were closed by ice and everything that fell to the guns went into the pot. There are open and closed seasons, taking account of the breeding season, but the general rule is feathered before Christmas and furred thereafter. At this time of year, the hope is for the most prized of America's game birds, woodcock and grouse, for which squirrel and rabbit are just a by-blow.

Lucie and George Semler live in the last house on Peter's Cove, six-tenths of a mile from our evening's destination, the Fishnet Diner, where you can crack lobster claws and suck a steaming bucketful of littleneck clams while admiring the shimmering waters of Blue Hill Bay as the sun sinks in the west. The deal is takeaway or eat-in. On offer on the evening of my arrival, along with the lobsters scooped to order from the tank and freshly cooked, are hamburgers and ice cream. Clams and crustaceans are just about the only regular income for the fishermen who remain to scratch a living from the sea. The hamburgers – well, if you must have America's national fast food, you take what you get, with pickles and chips, followed by ice cream for the kids. This says as much about the easygoing Maine way of life for the well-heeled city families who flock to the beaches in summer as does the news just published in the local paper that Maine ranks as the second-poorest state in the Union.

Tomorrow, as is the way in a comfortable neighbourly community such as Blue Hill, we will be a dozen or more at table. The community is close-knit, accustomed to dropping in and out of each other's houses. Lucie is in charge of good fellowship and the guest list. George fills the pot and cooks the dinner.

⁓

Yesterday, when George went out for an early-morning wander to inspect the marshes at the edge of the sea for migrating duck, the casualty count on the road was a couple of grey squirrels, perfectly fresh and without a scratch. This morning, in the sunlight on the porch, he's skinning the little fellows into a bucket.

This is exactly what I was hoping for, though I hadn't imagined the catch would be so easily obtained, still less that George would have gone to the trouble of skinning and paunching without my encouragement, and I am anxious to discover how he cooks what is classed in Britain as a pest.

'What'll you do with those?'

George glances up from his work with a grin. 'Same as anyone else with any sense – cook 'em up and eat 'em.'

I explain my interest in what, in my view, would be a useful addition to the culinary habits of my native land. Our own red squirrel, as far as I can ascertain, has never featured on the menu in Britain, unless as the raw material for a hat. And with the American grey now outnumbering the red at a ratio of eighty-five to one, and the meat beginning to appear on high-class restaurant menus, well: waste not, want not.

'Sounds good to me,' says George. 'We might pick up a couple more on the hunt tomorrow.'

Squirrels are rodents, members of the rat family, of which a good many are considered fit for the pot. The squirrel family is distributed all over the world, some more gastronomically rewarding than others. In London parks, the American grey is lord of all it surveys, bouncing from branch to branch or poised motionless on a pathway, balanced on hind legs with front legs tucked daintily beneath its chin. Its big brown eyes, dear little ear tufts, a long bushy tail and soft grey fur with a smudge of reddish fur between the shoulders present the very picture of innocent adorability.

The red, meanwhile, is a retiring little fellow, rarely seen even in the few woodlands where it clings on by its toenails. Not only shyer but noticeably smaller and lighter than the grey, the red has even longer ear tufts, an even bushier tail, and its fur is a warm and cuddly russet-brown. The native red may have all but vanished in southern England, but happily for its survival in the Scottish Highlands, it is the grey which has attracted the attention of the ferocious little polecat, a voracious meat-eater, who noticed that the American interloper is meatier and altogether more of a mouthful than the red, and is clearly visible among the bare branches when the leaves fall from the trees.

Thinking my own thoughts, I watch George's squirrel-skinning with professional interest.

'There's a smelly little scent gland behind the forelegs,' he explains, nicking off the offending part with the point of the knife. 'If you leave it in place, it spoils the meat.'

The pelts come off like a glove, much like skinning a rabbit. I've had considerable experience in skinning rabbits. There's a tradition of ferreting in the uplands of Wales, but no one wants to bother with skinning, so the furry bodies sometimes land on my kitchen table. And we kept our own free-ranging hutch-rabbits when we lived in Andalusia, where they regularly escaped and bred with such enthusiasm that most of them ended up in the pot.

I have not yet 'experienced' squirrel, as Vic Cherikoff would define the process of cooking and eating kangaroo. Perhaps there might be similar marketing opportunities available for squirrel. Biltong springs to mind: chewable sticks of protein popular even with non-appreciators of game as a low-fat, unsugared snack.

Or perhaps not, considering, as I do now, the paucity of meat on the little pink carcasses.

'Any ideas?' asks George, casually bundling up the furry-tailed overcoats in much the same way as Vic rolled up his 'roo skin.

Not really, I reply. American cooks are the experts. In the household books of the early settlers, squirrel is recommended as excellent eating, being tender and well flavoured and much like young rabbit. The little fellows are the diagnostic ingredient in Brunswick stew, an all-in bean-pot from the plantations of Virginia, and in Burgoo, a dish of similar composition popular in the Appalachians and on the prairies of Kentucky, the Bluegrass State, in which okra, an African import, thickens the juices.

I inspect the raw material, now neatly jointed. 'Might be good in a pie?'

George considers the suggestion. 'How do you feel about pastry?'

I feel good about pastry. Pastry-making is a skill I learned at my mother's knee – or would have, had my mother ever offered a knee at which to learn. Instead she shipped me off at the tender age of sweet sixteen to learn domestic skills at the Eastbourne School of Domestic Economy, since these accomplishments, she felt, would be more likely to catch a suitable husband than a university degree. She may well have been right. The kitchen has always been my comfort zone – in wedlock and without. Nothing in my life has ever done what it's told with such blind obedience or led to such a satisfactory outcome as throwing up a batch of pastry, preferably along with a chilled glass of whatever comes to hand.

'This can be arranged,' says George.

Next morning, Lucie and I are on our way to a coffee morning with Lucie's mother, Dorothy Hayes. Coffee mornings, she explains as we leave George to his responsibilities to the game-larder, are a declaration of open house, an old New England tradition that once provided an opportunity for a quilting-bee and a gossip.

The Hayes are among the few old settler families who still live on Blue Hill Bay. There are far fewer residents along the bay in the winter than there were a century ago, when a self-sufficient farming community could make an extra income by setting lobster pots and inshore fishing. Open-house events such as coffee mornings and pot-luck suppers, when everyone contributes a single dish sufficient for the number of guests, is a tradition established by the early settlers when the arrival of extra mouths to feed – let alone a party – could empty the winter store cupboard, leaving the family unable to refill it until spring.

Our journey of a mile and a half round the bay takes three times as long as it should, since one of the residents has decided to roll his house on a low-loader to a new location just down the road, a situation accepted with good grace and jovial advice by those obliged to wait.

As a result we are an hour late for arrival at the Hayes family dwelling, stately as a sailing ship, riding high on the lip of the bay. The buildings and barns are the work of carpenters rather than bricklayers – clapboarded, shingled roof, with a glassed-in wooden deck painted in gunmetal grey and bird's-egg blue. Sash windows – six panes up and six panes down – are open to the ocean but lined with mosquito mesh. In winter, removable storm-shutters are clipped in place to protect from the cold when the temperature drops well below freezing. The changeover from mosquito-netting to shutters is an annual chore with which Lucie has promised to help her mother.

'This is my mother's favourite time of year for cooking,' says Lucie as we draw into the driveway. 'She loves all that bottling and preserving when the plums and apples are ripe. I think it reminds her of her childhood.'

Lucie's mother greets us at the door with a kiss on the cheek for her daughter and a formal handshake for me.

'Come in and make yourself at home, my dear, while Lucie hangs the shutters.'

The Hayes are of old New England stock and Dorothy is tall by the standards of her generation, quietly elegant in well-tailored slacks and cashmere jumper.

'I'm afraid you've just missed the rest of the party, which gives us time for a chat about the good old days, which is what I think you've come for, isn't that so?'

Not so much the good old days, I add with a smile, as what life was like when the farming communities of the bay filled their own store cupboards, at least in part.

Dorothy's face lights up with affection and amusement. 'I guess my daughter thinks I'm old enough to remember how Mrs Noah stocked the Ark. But it's true that when I first came here to live with my maiden aunts when I was a child, we made our own jams and jellies and bottled and pickled whatever we grew.'

She walks over to the window. The view towards the shore and the ocean beyond is of mown pasture, trimmed hedges and orchard trees planted in neat rows.

'It's been a good year for apples and plums. I bottle and freeze all through the summer, but there's always too much. It wouldn't be right to say we live as our grandparents did – not that anyone would want to – but some things are too good to lose.'

Spacious and comfortable, the house is full of mementos from the days when Dorothy and her husband were employed by the Rockefeller Foundation to oversee their medical programme. Artefacts and photographs from forty years travelling in Africa and Asia sit comfortably among carved narwhal horns and treasures found by grandchildren along the shore.

The table in the dining room has been laid with pretty bone china cups and plates, with the remains of a ring-cake, Dorothy's apple pecan coffee cake, set in pride of place. The scent is buttery and nutty and, as far as I can tell, doesn't involve coffee.

Dorothy nods in answer to my question.

'You're right – there's no coffee in the cake. It's called a coffee cake because it's the cake you have with coffee. It's an old family recipe and it's really the only cake I ever bake.'

The reason for our lateness explains much about how people lived in the old days – and still do. Wooden houses are easy to move and a lot less trouble than building a new house. If someone wanted to move, they didn't pack up their possessions, they just shoved rollers under the floorboards and moved the whole house.

'I remember one winter when I was a child, the bay was frozen over and they dragged one of the big houses – two storeys and a porch – right across the ice to get it from one side to the other. It was very exciting. They had to wait until the water was solid to drag it across, and even then they weren't sure the ice would hold. We children rather hoped it wouldn't.'

Dorothy laughs, reliving the moment as a mischievous little girl who hoped the grown-ups would somehow get it wrong.

She shakes her head, smiling. 'Come with me. We'll leave Lucie to hang the shutters and go down to the shore so you can see the marks on the rocks where the house got stuck. It was quite a sight!'

As we walk together towards the ocean, I sense that Dorothy is happy to share her childhood memories with a stranger. Widowhood, as I know myself, can be a lonely place. Friends as well as children get bored of talk of the old days, good or bad.

I return to Dorothy's throwaway comment about her childhood. Was there a reason why she was sent to live with her maiden aunts?

'None was needed. My family lived in Portland and my parents didn't want their children growing up in the city. It happened quite a lot in those days – children sent to relatives to be brought up in the countryside, where it was safe.'

She pauses for a moment, gathering her thoughts.

'If you want to know what was good about the old days, the most important thing was neighbourliness – you had to look after others. At that time most of the land was farmed and the roads were closed in winter because of the snow. Every household had to see to it that there was enough food in the cellar to last until the weather warmed up, and if one family was in difficulties, we had to help each other out. My aunts always saw to it that there was plenty of home-made wine for the grown-ups, and the most delicious preserves for the children. My favourite was rosehip jelly – you shall try it when we return.'

Another pause and a faraway look.

'But my favourite time of year was winter, when there was always a big jar of mincemeat – fruit and meat and brandy all mixed together and kept in the corner cupboard ready for Christmas and Thanksgiving. It was always made with deermeat, because that was what we had. The jar was never emptied: we just added fruit and meat as it came in – peaches and apples and cherries when they were in season, and shop-bought dried figs and prunes and raisins, and it was all kept covered with homemade brandy. It was quite delicious.'

Dorothy's face lights up with a smile of pure delight, once again a bright-eyed child savouring the most delicious mouthful she ever tasted. 'I remember baking a mincemeat pie for Thanksgiving when I was a young bride, and it was so perfect I never risked it again.'

Another pause and a shake of the head. 'I was just married and we were invited by some very grand neighbours for Thanksgiving, and it was up to me to bring the dessert. You might think it crazy – I know the English adore their pies – but I had no idea how to make pastry. So I got out a cookbook and looked up the recipe and followed it exactly, weighing everything and mixing and rolling just as the book told me. It was a disaster. I made the dough and rolled it out and it shrank back. I rolled it out harder and it shrank back. So I threw it at my husband and shouted: "You do it."'

She glances across at me. 'Does that shock you? No? I thought not. We women were never as downtrodden as some people think. You can bet your boots my husband did what he was told. And it worked. So I laid the pastry in the tin and filled it with mincemeat and put a lattice on top and baked it just as it said in the book. When it came out of the oven, it looked and smelled just right. When we got to where we were going, I could scarcely swallow my food for worrying. But when it came to eating the pie, it was truly delicious.'

Another glance, this time more speculative. 'It might surprise you to know that I knew very little about cooking when I was first married. The aunts made everything at home, but I was never really interested. They weren't at all strict. I was free as a bird as long as I did what had to be done in school. So straight after class, I'd run down to the shore and row out and drop a line over the side of a raft moored to the rocks over there and catch a bucketful of fish for supper.'

The curve of the bay at the edge of the Hayes property ends in a rocky promontory crusted with blue-black mussels and shiny with seaweed. An iron ring hammered into the rock is all that's left of the mooring. Dorothy walks over to the rocks and looks out over the sparkling blue water.

'In those days the bay was so full of fish even a child could catch them. If you had a line, a hook and a worm, in less than an hour you had more than enough to feed all twelve of us, which was everyone in the house. We caught flounder, sculpin and cunny, and picked clams and quahogs from the beach and set traps for lobsters. We always had plenty of lobsters — enough for the neighbours, too, and everyone came round for our lobster suppers. A Maine lobster supper – well, there's nothing like it in all the world.'

Along the shore, a line of cork balls mark where a few lobster pots have been set. A breeze is rising, roughening the surface of the bay, rolling white-tipped wavelets towards the rocks, warning of the storms of winter.

There's sadness as well as pleasure in talk of the past – in a recipe for mincemeat, the taste of rose-petal jam. For me, it's the scent of wood-smoke from a cooking fire that takes me back to an Andalusian hillside where four children gathered crayfish from the stream and we cooked rice with saffron and ate with our fingers from the pan. The reminder, as so often for me, is of the eldest of my three daughters, now gone these past twenty years from the planet. Their father, too, ten years ago. What's done is done and cannot be undone. With the company of seven grandchildren to bring sunshine back to my life, new memories gather.

Meanwhile Dorothy, lost in her own thoughts, bends to gather a handful of sea-scrubbed pebbles, opens her fist, and lets them drop. There's loss in both our lives, a bond between those of us who remember the sunny days of childhood – our children's and our own.

'Must be time for coffee cake,' says Dorothy briskly.

Back in the Semler abode, George has turned his attention to dry-plucking a couple of mallard bagged yesterday by the shore, producing a bucketful of pillowy down to join the squirrel pelts. Beyond the kitchen window a pair of waterbirds – little grebe, if my bird-painter's eye is not mistaken – dib-dab at the stream's mouth in a tidal rush of sweet-salt water, the undersides of their tails flashing milk-white. At the edge of the reed beds beyond, another dark-feathered waterbird moves out and upends itself in an inky pool frothed with white bubbles from the falls above.

'Black duck,' says George, following my line of sight. 'Not so good as mallard. A rare visitor. We'll head over this evening and tell Cousin Chrissie.'

Cousin Chrissie, George's first cousin, lives in a clapboard house on her own at the end of a long dirt road which meanders through pinewood thick with berry bushes. Boundaries in the woods are unmarked. Dwellings passed on the way are of rough-hewn timber, log cabins little more than shacks for summertime. Those that are lived in all year are huddled together as semi-trailer parks rimmed with old fridges, broken cars, dismantled bits and pieces of no use to anyone but kept just in case.

The cousins grew up together, and Chrissie is the closest George has to a sister. As so often happens in families when one child doesn't want to compete with another, Chrissie, George explains as we bump along the track in his battered four-wheeler, is as knowledgeable a gatherer as George is a hunter.

Preliminary introductions over, Chrissie turns her attention to her cousin. 'Glad you stopped by, George. I saw a black duck on the pool by the road alongside you. Hope they haven't shot it.'

George, unfazed by the implication that he might be responsible, laughs and shakes his head.

'No chance, Chrissie.'

Chrissie nods. The cousins, self-evidently, don't see eye to eye on what is suitable for the pot, but they're family, and nobody wants to quarrel with family.

'How's the blueberry harvest going?' Blueberries are less contentious.

'Pretty much over. Not so many pickers this year. Guess it's not worth the money.'

We are midway through October and the leaves on the maples blaze scarlet and gold under a cloudless sky. While the canopy of aspen and birch around the bay is still green, on Blue Mountain the slopes are bright with swathes of carmine and russet slashed with shimmering ribbons of crop-lines, evidence the pickers have done their work.

When Chrissie was a girl, children were let out from class to gather the crop, and for the pickers and their families, the blueberry harvest was – still is – the only reliable source of income available to the poor. The pickers were paid by weight and each family was allotted a line, raking from top to bottom. Once you'd filled a half-bushel basket, you took it to the blower for the leaves to be blown off before it was weighed and paid for. The faster and cleaner a picker could rake, the more he or she could earn. The work was never well paid, but money is money.

'If you raked well, you could earn twenty dollars in a day. Fifty years ago it was worth the energy, maybe not now. Boys and men and girls all took the work – youngsters earning pocket money, families earning a living.'

Earning a living is not easy for those obliged to pay cash for necessities. Chrissie lives frugally, but there's family back-up and others are not so fortunate. Maine has poverty in the blood. 'Study says "Maine poverty pervasive",' announces the headline in today's *Bangor Daily News*, spread out on Chrissie's kitchen table. 'The number of Mainers using food stamps has increased sharply, a jump from last year in the number of homes using federal low-income heating assistance.'

No one in the trailer parks collects firewood or knows how to crop the wild. And even so, there are rules and regulations in place that discourage such activities. There's work to be found in the tourist industry, but it's seasonal and the pay is low. Much of what the early settlers cleared for farmland is gone, returned to wildwood in a single season. Abandoned orchards are the only evidence of their passing.

Self-sufficiency, even for those with practical knowledge like Chrissie's, is no longer a way of life but a choice. The hunters – even the gatherers – are a privileged few.

⚜

The following morning, I am issued with stout boots and a sturdy hat. Protection of vulnerable extremities is an obligation and a duty. No one wants to have to carry anyone home on their back.

The hunters – three stout fellows including George, along with a pointy-nosed retriever – assemble on the porch. Introductions are effected. Hunters are cautious of strangers, but George gives me an undeserved write-up as a seasoned hunt-follower, and all is well.

Today is what Mainers call a bluebird day. The air is clear as glass, cold as winter, and the arch of the heavens is cobalt blue. We set off, empty game-bags slung over camouflage-clad shoulders and guns held broken-breeched, walking silently in single file along the edge of the steep bank of a narrow stream along the remnants of a track.

For half an hour we walk steadily upwards, working our way round the hillside towards the blueberry barrens and the wildwood beyond.

Silence sharpens the senses to rustlings and murmurings and the sound of falling water. Maine woodland is unkempt and thick with undergrowth tangled with berry bushes spiked with thorns. The stream vanishes and reappears, diamond bright or ink dark, crisscrossed with fallen saplings or dry branches that crackle underfoot, rimmed with half-capsized saplings of birch and willow and creeper-vines hung with waxy fruits in carmine and saffron and cream.

Once into the uplands, tall trees give way to open sky and scrubland littered with glittering granite boulders dumped in heaps by the movement of prehistoric glaciers. We are among the blueberry barrens. The bushes are low to the ground, streaked with ribbons of quaking grass hung with dewdrops to mark the lines of the raking. A blueberry rake is made of wood – there'd been one stacked against the railing on Chrissie's porch, T-shaped with a short handle and a long bar with a line of sharpened wooden pegs.

The guns huddle together in conference while the gun dogs wait patiently with lolling tongues. George beckons me over.

'You're on bird-dog duty. Stay close, follow the path, keep up with the guns and mark the quarry where it falls.'

Bird-dog rules apply to dogs as well as humans – we follow a downed bird as far as pick-up for as long as it takes. While a walker-up is useful for the guns in open country, in the wildwood where the light is low and the shots are long, a bird is easily lost and the hunter is only as good as his back-up.

'Don't think you'll have it easy,' says George, handing me a mugful of steaming coffee from a flask. 'The pick-up can be just as dramatic as the shot. In woodland, failure is a lot more likely after the bird is down – the problem is always the find.' A lost bird is worse than no bird at all. No responsible hunter will quit the find until the quarry is in the bag.

The hunters, sipping steaming mugs, embark on a discussion of the important matter of what to do with the contents of the bag when you get it home – assuming, that is, that there's anything in the bag to do something with. The American woodcock, *Scolopax minor*, though smaller than the European *S. rusticola*, belongs to the same species and has the same habits as its relative, in that both species empty their digestive system of unwanted matter as they fly, so the innards – the trail – are always sweet and fresh and suitable for leaving in place when the bird is roasted at a high heat with butter.

Thereafter, says George, the trail can be mashed up with a little brandy and butter to spread on toast. When spread on a crunchy piece of bread, continues George, this is the very best part of a woodcock, with a flavour more intense than even the bird itself. And since a woodcock is barely enough for one, it just about doubles the pleasure.

Food-talk is making the hunters hungry in much the same way as the thought of a mouse encourages a cat. I imagine this is George's intent and the mood has changed. We are no longer a bunch of casual ramblers out for a morning stroll. The hunters ignore the path, separating into a line and walking abreast ten yards apart, pushing steadily through the undergrowth.

'Follow closely, keep out of the line of sight of the guns, watch where the quarry falls and don't chatter.'

I obey as best I can, but the terrain is rough and the light dim.

An unwary stumble releases a waft of rancid scent. 'Dead porcupine,' says George, turning to prod the undergrowth. Or possibly, since the prints of whitetail deer are fresh in the earth, a rutting stag marking his territory with musk. Deer is prohibited as game from the beginning to end of the breeding season.

From now on, George keeps up a gentle commentary on what it has meant to him to hunt the wildwood since boyhood. 'My father took me out with him as soon as I could walk a yard or two without landing on my butt. But he never went out into the woods as we are now – his idea of hunting was to walk down the rides and hope for a left and a right.'

Rides are the paths cut to allow two horsemen to ride abreast – carriages, too, in the old days. A left and right –

downing two birds from a double-barrelled shotgun without the need to reload – is something to boast about in the gun room after the shoot.

Instruction in gun etiquette follows. You can put a shot through the head but never into the body or the cook won't thank you for spoiling her dinner – this with a sideways glance and a smile. Keep your eyes down as well as up and read the signs. Grouse are berry-eaters. Picked-over crab apples on the ground are a sign the grouse have been feeding. When the windfall crabs are bruised and softened by the fall, they'll stuff themselves to bursting before heading up to roost in the pines. A grouse with a well-stuffed crop won't move without good reason, and then it hurtles through the branches like a drunken sailor, confusing the guns. Confusing the guns means the bird goes free.

'You can put a bird up four, five – ten times until you fire a shot. And you don't shoot at all till you're sure of the fall.'

Right on cue, a shot rings out to our right. From the way the bird falls, the kill is clean and we have at least one wood-grouse in the bag. Next into the bag is a plump little woodcock with beautiful speckled feathers – Miss Potter, I muse as I retrieve the bird from the undergrowth, would have sat down on a log and made a sketch, but for me, paper and paints must wait till the hunt is over.

Another crash to our left and a second grouse is in the bag. A fall from a clean shot is easy to locate, even by me – though the dogs are on it immediately, soft mouths carrying the quarry back to the huntsman.

If a bird is wounded, George explains in a gentle aside, this is a failure of marksmanship much frowned upon in company such as this, and the bird must be followed until found. There are no shortcuts and the dogs are trained to follow as keenly as the hunters.

Still no clear view of the quarry for George. First one and then another apple-sated grouse blunders away in the distance, securely out of sight. Another crash in the treetops just ahead and George raises the gun, then lowers it without a shot. The line of sight is still unclear. But the bird has roosted again not far away. George breaks the breech and, never letting the quarry out of his sight, moves steadily off in its wake. The bird lifts again and settles once more. In the excitement of the chase, I find that I can move as silently and surely as the most seasoned hunter. And when the quarry finally falls at the edge of blueberry barrens from a perfect shot to the head, I am, if not first on the scene, at least a respectable runner-up to a canine rival.

In the wildwood of Maine, chances are that even the keenest marksman will return home empty-handed. For every bird downed, as far as I can count them, three fly free. By the end of the day, between all three guns, our achievement is four fine fat wood-grouse, six plump little woodcock, a rabbit and a couple of extra squirrels, just for me.

George's enthusiasm for the chase is more than matched by his happiness when skinning, gutting, de-feathering and discussing the possibilities raised by the contents of the hunter's bag.

The woodcock, once claws and beaks have been inspected for elasticity – a sign of a first-year bird – are declared candidates for roasting. How, he enquires, do I like to serve my birds when roasted? Bloody or well done? I know better than to choose the latter. Quite right, he agrees. The meat of any game animal, while tender when young, is lean and inclined to dry out in the oven unless cooked rare.

On the contentious subject of whether to hang game birds, as is usual in Britain – with the exception of waterbirds, which must be plucked, drawn and cooked as soon as possible – I have always found opinions divided among those who hunt for the pot. Other hunting fraternities – those of France, Italy, Spain and Germany – consider the birds should be cooked fresh.

If there is any rule to be followed, it is that all game birds can be cooked within a few hours, when the meat will be tender and the flavour delicate, but if the birds have had time to cool and stiffen before being brought home, the meat will be tough and the flavour unpleasantly strong unless they are left, undrawn in feather and hung on a hook in a cool larder, until the fibres relax and the meat returns to its original tenderness.

George is a man for tenderising on the hook. 'I give them a week in winter and half the time in autumn,' he says, plucking one of the grouse into the bucket between his knees. I like to pluck wet in the sink so the feathers don't fly all over the kitchen, which turns out to be a mistake as the down sticks to my finger-tips like fat little thimbles. George plucks twice as fast as me – two birds de-feathered to my one – but then, I comfort myself, he's had plenty of practice.

Dinner is on the way. Most of the day's bag, says George, will go in the freezer as winter stores. Wild meat is strong and well flavoured, and you don't need much to make a dish to feed many.

I volunteer for squirrel duty and gratefully accept, considering the number of guests expected for dinner, the addition of rabbit. Squirrels are lean little creatures, and bony. Only the haunches are meaty enough to be worth the trouble of roasting, while the fore-quarters and saddle – two tiny fillets not worth lifting from the rack – yield flavour but little nourishment. Had we been discussing rabbit alone, I'd have suggested a finishing lick of cream and mus-tard, as they cook it in France, or as in Spain, in olive oil with garlic and the dry white wines of Jerez. However, the kitchen cabinet, swollen by now with new arrivals keen to contribute opinions, consider my suggestions with respect and polite rejection.

The squirrels are declared suitable for gentle braising with a few scraps of home-cured bacon from the freezer as the basis for squirrel pot pie. Pot pie, I learn, is a declaration of national identity in much the same way as hoisting the Stars-and-Stripes on the flagpole to tell the neighbours you're at home. It differs from the English pastry-topped savoury pie in that the filling is left in the pot in which it's cooked – or was, whenever anyone observed such nice distinctions. The reason for the lid – a rolled-out piece of bread dough in the old days when pastry made with butter was a luxury – is to avoid the gravy slopping all over the place when the stew is transported elsewhere, say, for a church gathering or a pot-luck supper, as today.

With choice of ingredients and cooking method agreed, I proceed with caution as the bones are semi-transparent and sharp as needles. Once jointed, I set the pieces to simmer in home-pressed cider with thyme and juniper.

Now for the pastry. Pastry cooks need cool hands, a quiet corner and patience – hence the tradition in professional kitchens that pastry-making is woman's work. I clear a space, sift flour and rub in butter with the tips of my fingers, then settle down with my sketchbook and paints to listen to the talk and sip my glass of wine.

The lessons to be drawn from our day in the woods of Maine, there's general agreement among the hunters, is that where the balance of nature remains unaltered – Maine has lost her wolves, bears are few and only the two-legged hunters remain at the top of the food chain – we may well have a blueprint for the future, as long as predator and prey are kept in balance.

Listening quietly as the discussion rolls back and forth, I finish my sketch of the exquisitely patterned feathers from the plucking, before finishing the pastry-rolling and de-boning the squirrel meat, tender from an hour or two's slow simmering with vegetables and herbs. Soon the pie is in the oven and the layers of buttery pastry, glimpsed through the glass, begin to puff.

The guests are at table, night has fallen, glasses are filled and we're ready to eat. A single wood-grouse has been buried in a Boston bean-pot, the best way, explains George, to ensure that everyone has a chance to appreciate the fruits of the chase and leave more for tomorrow. The mallards and everything else from the day's hunting – all but a brace of woodcock – have been packed away in the freezer to keep the household fed through the winter. Meat from the wild is a precious resource, used sparingly as much for flavour as for nourishment.

The pie is baked and smells delicious, the bean-pot is emitting puffs of fragrant wood-grouse-scented steam and George is ready to roast the brace of woodcock to serve on toasts.

Woodcock meat, he explains, is red and dark and needs high heat briefly applied, while grouse benefits from a gentle heat applied at leisure, as in the bean-pot.

'With woodcock, the only unforgivable sin is overcooking,' continues George, patting little bits of butter along the breasts of the birds and settling them gently in their roasting tray. 'It's a tragedy if they're not served pink and bloody.'

He adjusts the oven heat and slips the tray on the rack.

'So that's about it. Heat 'em up and eat 'em.'

And then, as is proper among the fellowship of the hunt, conversation falters as the guests turn their attention to the feast on the table. The guests have brought freshly baked bread and big bowls of salad leaves, last of the season. The woodcock, no more than a morsel per person, is dark and delicate, while the trail spread on the toast has a flavour of forest berries. My pie, finished with cream and mushrooms and flavoured with juniper, is juicy and rich in its casing of buttery crust. But the star of the show, all are agreed, is the dish of slow-simmered oven-baked beans – prepared to a family recipe sweetened and flavoured with maple syrup – which has soaked up the fragrance of wood-grouse.

After every delicious scrap has been mopped from plates, talk turns, as happens among friends, to a subject of interest to all – the relationship between Old World and New and the role of imperialism in shaping the politics of modern America. Some of us are Republicans and some are Democrats, but common cause can found in the desire for freedom. The right to carry a gun and hunt for the pot meant life or death to the early settlers, forbidden to hunt the king's forest in their land of origin. And while the record thereafter shows how this right can be abused, that too was part of the freedoms claimed when the Redcoats were sent in by the British Crown to teach the tea-drinkers of Boston a lesson in paying their taxes.

If the settlers' muskets delivered the final victory, the Redcoats were defeated by the forest long before battle lines were drawn. Sent into battle through an untamed wilderness, lacking supply lines, wading through fallen tree trunks, up to their armpits in peat-water, weighed down by sodden uniforms, flesh ripped to ribbons on thorn bushes, they were hungry and dispirited long before the fight even began.

For myself, I add in my capacity as the only non-native at table, I feel common cause with the rebels. My mother's side of the family are American-born and-bred, descendants of escapees from religious persecution on the Polish-Russian border in the 1890s. Grateful for sanctuary in the city of Baltimore, the family made a modest fortune in trade – tobacco and tailoring – and sent a favoured son, my great-grandfather, to London to expand the business and make a very considerable fortune. That it didn't have a chance to trickle down to me was a blessing in disguise, said my father's forthright sister, since it saved me from a life of idle luxury like my mother's.

Idle luxury wouldn't cut the mustard among the company I'm keeping. Our group includes the Semlers' neighbours and friends, Daniel and Susan Dennett. Dr Dennett is the grand old man of the philosophical movement that emerged half a century ago to alert the world to the dangers of ecological irresponsibility with Rachel Carson's *Silent Spring*. Dr Dennett's own contribution to the debate that has raged ever since, *Darwin's Dangerous Idea* – a call to stop relying on fairy stories and take responsibility for our beautiful world – delivered the author a Pulitzer Prize. Like his revolutionary predecessor, Dr Dennett's answer is to take a look around your own backyard and draw your own conclusions.

The meal concludes with enthusiastic toasts drunk in generous tumblerfuls of Dr Dennett's home-made blueberry fire-water. Thereafter my appreciation of the conversation raging round the table, however brilliant and contentious, fades into benevolent contentment as I retire to my bed in the attic to listen to the owls hunting the wildwood and the faint sounds of the world being set to rights below.

There are no easy answers to the omnivore's perennial dilemma – how to feed the world without destroying the nature of our precious planet – though here, in the wildwood where our ancestors lived their lives in harmony with their surroundings, is as good a place to start as any.

BRUNSWICK STEW

A hunters' stew named for Brunswick County, Virginia, but popular throughout the Southern States. Other ingredients vary but squirrel is unarguable, though there are those who substitute wild rabbit. Bernard Clayton, an authority on American traditional cooking, describes it as 'a large dish for a number of robust eaters which is not worth making in reduced quantities'. It is, however, endlessly recyclable in pies and pasties and can be cooked right down in a frying pan to a hash.

Serves 6–8
4 grey squirrels, skinned, cleaned and quartered
2 tablespoons plain flour, seasoned with salt and pepper, for dusting
3 tablespoons butter or lard
150 g salt pork or streaky bacon, diced
3 medium onions, peeled and finely chopped
2 red peppers, de-seeded and diced
1 kg ripe tomatoes, skinned and chopped (or tinned)
2 tablespoons tomato purée
1 large glass red wine
salt and pepper

To finish
2 large potatoes, peeled and diced
250 g fresh or frozen sweetcorn kernels
250 g ready-cooked butter beans
Tabasco, to taste
Worcestershire sauce, to taste

Check the squirrel joints for stray shot, nick out the little scent glands behind the front legs and trim off any bruises, then leave to soak in salted water for 1–2 hours.

Drain the squirrel joints, pat dry and dust with the seasoned flour.

Heat the lard or butter in a large casserole and fry the joints until they take a little colour. Remove from the heat and reserve.

Fry the pork or bacon in the drippings in the casserole until the fat runs, then add the onion and fry gently until it softens and takes a little colour. Add the diced pepper and fry for a minute or two. Add the tomatoes and tomato purée, bring to the boil and squish to soften.

Return the squirrel joints to the pan, add the wine and just enough water to cover, and season. Bring the pot up to the boil, turn down the heat, cover with a close-fitting lid and leave to simmer gently, either on the stove or in a low oven, 150°C/Gas 2, until the meat is perfectly tender – around 1–1½ hours (check and add more water if necessary).

To finish, add the potatoes, sweetcorn and butter beans, and just enough water to cover. Bring the casserole back to the boil, cover with the lid and simmer for another 30 minutes, until the potato is tender. Remove the lid and let the stew bubble to concentrate the juices – the dish should be juicy but not soupy. Taste and correct the seasoning and finish with a dash of Tabasco and a shake of Worcestershire sauce.

The traditional accompaniment is cornbread, but soft polenta or cornmeal mush is almost as good.

SQUIRREL POT PIE WITH CIDER, APPLES AND CREAM

Novelist Annie Proulx recommends cooking the American grey Southern-style, in cider with cream, and advises those undertaking preliminaries to be sure to remove the smelly glands from behind the forelegs and give the joints a soaking in cold salt water. The pot pie is a deep-dish pie, covered in a crust for ease of transportation to pot-luck suppers or church gatherings.

Serves 4
4 grey squirrels, skinned, paunched and jointed
2 tablespoons plain flour, seasoned with salt and pepper, for dusting
1 tablespoon butter
2–3 bacon rashers, diced
1 teaspoon juniper berries, crushed (optional)
1 litre dry cider

To finish
2–3 large cooking apples, peeled, cored and cut into chunks
1 tablespoon butter
1 tablespoon plain flour
250 ml double cream

For the flaky pastry
300 g plain flour
½ teaspoon salt
250 g cold unsalted butter
5–6 tablespoons cold water

Trim the joints of any little bone splinters or traces of fur, and dust them through the seasoned flour (or drop flour and joints in a bag and shake well). Reserve.

Melt the butter in a casserole and fry the bacon until the fat runs. Add the squirrel joints and juniper berries, if using, and fry until the meat browns a little.

Add the cider and just enough water to submerge everything. Bring the pot to the boil, cover tightly and cook either slowly on the stove or in a gentle oven, preheated to 150°C/Gas 2, until the meat is dropping off the bone – allow 1–1½ hours, depending on the age of the squirrels. Check and add more water if it looks like drying out – there should always be enough liquid to cover the meat. Debone the meat and reserve the juices.

Meanwhile, make the flaky pastry and heat the oven to 220°C/Gas 7. Sift the flour with the salt in a large bowl. Chop the butter into walnut-sized pieces and mix it into the flour, leaving it lumpy. Add enough water to make a fairly firm dough. Cover and chill for 10 minutes. Roll out on a floured board into a strip 15 cm wide and about 2.5 cm thick. Fold the pastry into three, like a napkin. Give it a quarter-turn to bring the open end towards you. Roll it out to a thickness of about 1 cm, fold again into three and set aside for another 10 minutes. Repeat the process with the folds in the opposite

(recipe continued overleaf)

direction. Set aside for 10 minutes. By now the pastry should show no sign of streakiness.

To finish the pie filling, fry the apple chunks in hot butter until they take a little colour (don't let them soften), then remove them and add to the de-boned meat. Sprinkle the flour into the hot butter, wait until it froths, add the reserved cider juice and bring up to the boil, scraping in the little sticky brown bits. Add the cream and let it bubble up until the sauce thickens a little, then pour it over the meat and apple pieces in a round pie-dish. Leave to cool completely while you roll the pastry.

Roll out the pastry to fit a deep pie-dish, using the trimmings to make a double edge and running a damp finger round the rim so the lid stays in place. Before laying over the pastry, pop an upturned eggcup on top of the stew to make sure the pastry stays domed. Cut a cross in the middle to let out the steam and mark the edge with a fork to make a rim.

Bake in the hot oven for 20–30 minutes, until the pastry is well risen, crisp and golden.

BOSTON BEAN-POT WITH GROUSE

For a traditional Boston bean-pot, the beans are cooked in a closed pot with maple syrup and mustard, taking on the flavour of the grouse.

Serves 4–6
1 wood-grouse, plucked and gutted
100 g fatty bacon or salt pork, diced
350 g white haricot beans, soaked overnight in cold water
½ teaspoon peppercorns, crushed or ready-cracked
1–2 bay leaves
2–3 cloves
1 generous tablespoon maple syrup or brown sugar
1 teaspoon strong English mustard
salt

Preheat the oven to 150°C/Gas 2.

Wipe over the grouse and trim off any stray feathers. Fry the bacon in a large casserole until the fat runs, then brown the bird on all sides in the oily drippings. Remove from the heat.

Meanwhile, drain the beans and transfer to a saucepan. Add about a litre of cold water – enough to cover the beans generously – along with the peppercorns, bay leaves and cloves, and bring to the boil. Skim off any white foam that rises, turn down the heat, cover loosely with a lid and bubble gently for 40–50 minutes until the beans have softened but are still firm. Check and add more boiling water if the pot looks like it is drying out.

Remove the bay leaves and cloves (if you can find them – if not, no matter) and stir in the syrup or sugar, the mustard and a level teaspoon of salt. Tip the beans into the casserole with the grouse and bacon, and add enough boiling water to submerge everything completely. Cover and cook in the oven for at least 1 hour, until the beans are perfectly tender and the meat is dropping off the bone. Check the seasoning and add more salt if necessary. Serve with a crisp green salad of winter leaves – endive, chicory and dandelion.

WOODCOCK TOASTS

Woodcock and snipe are the most delicious of all game birds and need only the briefest roasting in butter. Both can be cooked undrawn – innards left in – fresh from the woods, or hung in feather undrawn for a day or two. If you find the flavour of the trail too strong in ungutted cooked birds, mash the innards straight into hot butter, though the woodcock will not be as juicy and fragrant.

Serves 4 as a starter
1 brace of woodcock (i.e. a male and a female bird), plucked
50 g unsalted butter
½ teaspoon freshly ground pepper
½ teaspoon thyme leaves

(recipe continued overleaf)

49

For the toasts
75 g unsalted butter
4 thick, woodcock-sized rounds of sourdough bread
2 tablespoons brandy
1 tablespoon lemon juice
salt and pepper

Preheat the oven to 220°C/Gas 7.

To truss the little birds for the oven, leave the head on, turn the beak sideways and poke it through the crossed-over drumsticks so that the bird holds its shape. Spread the breasts with butter mashed with freshly ground black pepper and a pinch of thyme. Roast for 15–18 minutes to cook rare, which is how they should be served.

Set the birds to rest in a warm place while you prepare the toasts.

Melt half the butter in a small pan and add the juices from the roasting tin. Fry the bread rounds on both sides until crisp and lightly browned, then remove to a warm serving dish.

Reheat the pan to melt the rest of the butter, and mash in the trail from the birds' cavities. As soon as it's really hot, add the brandy, lemon juice, salt and pepper and toss over a high heat for 2–3 minutes. Spread the trail on the toasts, quarter the little birds and top each round with a leg, a wing and the buttery juices.

Note: If you're out of luck with the birds themselves, replace with Scotch Woodcock: scrambled eggs and anchovies on toast, one of the little tidbits served as a savoury instead of cheese at the end of a formal dinner in grand country houses of Britain until the 1970s.

DOROTHY'S ROSEHIP JELLY
Dorothy advises gathering the hips for jelly after the first frost, so that the skins and flesh have softened. All varieties of rosehip – wild or garden – are suitable for jelly and have enough pectin to set perfectly.

Enough to fill 3–4 jam jars
1 kg rosehips, picked on a dry day
approx. 1 kg caster or granulated sugar

Rinse the hips and shake them dry. Transfer to a heavy pan with enough cold water to cover. Bring to the boil, turn down the heat and cook until the fruit is mushy and soft – about 15–20 minutes.

Strain the juice through a cheesecloth (if convenient, hang the bundle on a hook over a basin and leave it to drip overnight).

Measure the juice and return it to the pan with its own volume of sugar. Bring back to the boil, turn down the heat and bubble until setting point is reached – about 20 minutes or so. Test the jelly by placing a drop on a cold saucer – if you push it with your fingertip and it wrinkles, it's ready. If not, bubble the mixture for a little longer and test again. Sterilise the jars by heating them in a low oven for 10 minutes or so before ladling in the jelly, allow to cool and secure the lid tightly, or cover the surface of the jelly with a round of greaseproof paper, then seal the jars under a cellophane covering secured with a rubber band or string. Store in a cool dark place and serve with game.

APPLE PECAN COFFEE CAKE

A coffee cake is not actually flavoured with coffee but is a cake for dipping into coffee at a coffee morning. The streusel topping is Austrian and the cake is baked in a ring mould, the traditional *kugelhopf* tin, which makes it much easier for cutting and sharing.

Serves 12
For the streusel topping and filling
200 g shelled pecans
350 g soft brown sugar
1 tablespoon ground cinnamon
100 g cold butter, cut into small dice

(recipe continued overleaf)

For the cake batter

60 g butter, at room temperature

250 g granulated sugar

2 teaspoons vanilla extract

4 large eggs

300 g plain flour

½ teaspoon salt

2 level teaspoons baking powder

250 g apple purée

Preheat the oven to 180°C/Gas 4.

First, prepare the streusel. Chop the pecans roughly – you need them to be quite chunky. Add these to a bowl, along with the other streusel ingredients, and chop everything together with a knife until the mixture looks like very rough breadcrumbs – lumps are essential. Reserve.

Beat the butter to soften, add the sugar and vanilla and beat vigorously by hand or in a mixer until light and pale. Crack in the eggs one at a time, still beating enthusiastically.

Sift the flour with the salt and baking powder, and fold alternate spoonfuls of flour and apple purée into the egg mixture. When everything is in, you should have a soft, sludgy, almost runny batter which drops easily from the spoon (add a little milk if it's not runny enough).

Butter a large ring mould and spoon in half the cake batter. Sprinkle half the streusel mixture over the top. Spoon in the rest of the batter and finish with the remaining streusel mixture.

Bake the cake for 1½–2 hours, or until the topping is crispy and flecked with dark brown burnt sugar. Check the cake for doneness with a skewer – there should be no sign of liquid batter, but expect to see runny brown sugar. Allow to cool for an hour before you loosen it with a spatula and flip it out of its mould. That's it.

Extremadura

THE HUMPBACKED BLACK-FOOT PIGS OF THE Iberian peninsula, last of the semi-wild foraging herds of Europe, fatten in autumn on the acorns of the scrub oaks of the *dehesa* in Extremadura, the dry lands, red and hot, that run down the Portuguese border. Their haunches, lean and muscular, are used to prepare *pata negra*, the salt-cured, wind-dried mountain hams of the region.

These herds, it's fair to assume, survived in the forests of Iberia largely because of the prohibitions on the eating of pig meat during seven centuries of Muslim ascendancy. The followers of the Prophet crossed from the deserts of the Maghreb to the fertile shores of Andalusia, and set up home until the caliphate of Granada fell in 1492 to the combined might of Isabel of Castile and Ferdinand of Aragon.

Thereafter Christian pork replaced Muslim lamb in the cooking pots of Al-Andaluz – and if it didn't, the Inquisition would want to know the reason why. Religious backsliding could be identified by an unwillingness to stock the store cupboard with chorizo, ham and all the other pork products used for flavour and richness in winter stews. Many of the questions recorded in the Inquisition's meticulous records held in Seville and Madrid have to do with the composition of the contents of the cooking pot. Questions were subtle enough to include method as well as ingredients – whether or not the meat was fried before the addition of a liquid. Until the arrival of the Moors, with their metal cooking pans, the traditional cooking pot of the Iberian peninsula was earthenware, a material more suitable for slow-simmered stews than frying over a high heat.

The name of the region itself – Extremadura, land beyond the river Duero – indicates that this is a land apart, no-man's land, the sun-blistered, wind-blasted limits of the granite-strewn *meseta*, Spain's tip-tilted central plateau.

Geographically, the territory stretches along the border with Portugal from the banks of the river Duero in the north to the Sierra Morena in the south. Sparsely populated, emigration was the only choice in medieval times for those who couldn't scrape a living from the harsh terrain or were caught by the romance of the lands of the setting sun. The soldiers of Extremadura held the Christian line of defence against the caliphs of Al-Andaluz, and many of the *conquistadores* who took ship for the New World – Hernán Cortés and Francisco Pizarro among them – were sons of Extremadura.

Culturally, the region takes its lead from the great university city of Salamanca, halfway house between Seville, capital of the Spanish Main, and Santiago de Compostela, centre of Christian pilgrimage that ranks with Jerusalem and Rome.

Travelling in a camper van in the 1970s and '80s with my children between the ferry-port of Santander on the Bay of Biscay and across the plains of Extremadura to our home in a remote valley overlooking the Pillars of Hercules, we followed the *ruta de la plata*, the silver road, which runs from the pilgrim city of

Santiago de Compostela in the far north-west to the great harbour port of Seville in the south. We pitched camp along the way whenever darkness overtook us, and took our midday meal in one of the little *ventas*, rural restaurants, where the truckers parked up in the heat of the day for a plateful of whatever was simmering on the back of the stove, the day's ration of pulses – chickpeas or lentils or white beans – cooked in a single pot, an earthenware *olla*, flavoured with a chunk of ham-bone and enriched with olive oil.

At that time, our neighbours in the valley kept goats for milk and meat, a sty-pig to eat up the scraps, and ran herds of the old Iberico breed to forage for acorns in the cork-oak forest round about. While the valley's climate was too damp to cure the hams, these were sent on donkey-back to the mountains of Ronda or, if someone's cousin offered the service, to Jabugo in the Sierra Morena in the mountains above Seville, where Extremadura meets Andalusia.

The hams, all from the black-foot Iberico breed, packed in grey sea salt harvested from the salt flats of Cadiz, travelled up on the narrow mountain paths in paniers made of esparto-grass, prickly dwarf palms, used as cheese-drainers and mats. By the time the haunches arrived at their destination – a week or so on foot – they had already absorbed enough salt to prepare them for the next step in the curing process: wind-drying in the cold mountain air.

As a family we kept our own sty-pig to eat up the household scraps, and when the day came for slaughter – men's business, much to my relief – preparing the meat was women's business. I learned from my neighbours how to salt down the bacon, *tocino*, and melt down the fat for storage as lard, *manteca*, used as an enrichment in stews and to spread on bread. The main business of the day for the women was cleaning the intestines in the stream as the casings for blood sausage, *morcilla*, and chorizo –

hand-chopped pork pushed through a hand-turned mincer, spiced and flavoured with marjoram and garlic and hung on a pole to dry.

The final task was the preparing of the haunches for their journey into the mountains, the Christmas treat. A salt-cured, wind-dried ham, hung on a hook in a dry kitchen, will keep sweet and good right through the summer. The scraps and sawn-up bones were – and are – used in much the same way as a stock cube, to add depth and richness to sauces and bean-pots.

Later, when my children were grown and gone and I began to write about food and cooking, I set about rediscovering what had given me such pleasure in youth – my own and my children's. While we in the valley salted down the meat of the annual *matanza* for our own winter stores, the free-ranging herds of black-foots that roamed the cork-oak forest provided an additional source of income for the self-sufficient farming community of the valley. The forest also provided charcoal for heating and cooking, and a cash-crop from the sale of the cork itself – a thick layer of silvery bark stripped from the trunks every five or seven years, depending on the age of the tree.

But that was then, and things have changed in the post-Franco years – the old dictator finally left the planet in 1975 – evident not least in the depopulation of communities such as that of our valley. Meanwhile, the introduction of the more docile breeds of domesticated pig, particularly the Large White, turned the production of serrano ham into a commercial enterprise, supplying a mass market in Spain and elsewhere. Nevertheless, the preparation of *pata negra* with the hams of the Iberico pigs remains very much in the hands of artisan producers, among them the curing-houses of Salamanca.

The university city of Salamanca is one of the most beautiful in all of Spain. It is also something of a gastronomic place of pilgrimage for the gourmets of Madrid, a hundred miles to the east across the plain, owing to its reputation for the excellence of

the *pata negra* and a wealth of tapa bars and family-run restaurants in the city's main square, Plaza Mayor.

On a fine evening in autumn a stroll through the city centre, newly polished and pedestrianised, reveals one glorious golden building behind another. The architectural outlines are simple – perfect proportions and soaring height – but a closer look reveals intricate decorative carving in the silversmith style, *platero*. The carvings are the work of artisans from Seville, capital of the trade with the New World, where the galleons that sailed the Spanish Main unloaded the silver and gold that replenished the coffers of the Catholic kings after the struggle to unseat the caliphs of Al-Andaluz. With the spice route closed to the east, it was no accident that, in the same year that Granada fell, Columbus set sail into the west to search out a new spice route, returning with stories of fabulous wealth in what was named the New Indies.

History dictates the gastronomy of Spain as nowhere else in Europe. It is impossible to disentangle the legacy of the past from everyday life – even now – whether in architecture, art, literature or music, but above all in her culinary habit. Even today, the gastronomy of Spain – both traditional and the modernist cuisine of Catalonia's Ferran Adrià – owes as much to the cooks of the sybaritic Moors as it does to the wheat fields of La Mancha, the olive groves of Jaen, the fishing grounds of Galicia, the irrigated gardens of Granada, or the mountain-cured hams of Extremadura.

No one knows more about the excellence of Iberico pigs as the raw material of salt-cured, wind-dried *pata negra* ham than José Luis, owner and cellarer-in-chief of the city's most cele- brated ham-curing house. The enterprise exports all over the world under its trade name, Joselito, named five generations back for the founding father.

'The eldest son is always called José,' announces José Luis cheerfully as he orders a plateful of his own magnificent ham at a bar in the Plaza Mayor. 'This can be confusing, so I have to have two names so that when my mother scolded me, everyone knew it wasn't my father she was shouting at, even if it was his fault that I had stayed out late with him in the tapa bars.'

José Luis is a prosperous businessman in his middle years, charming, impeccably tailored in Savile Row suiting, if a little portly owing to his evident enjoyment of the good things of the table. He is as proud of Salamanca's status as the oldest university in Spain as he is of the hams which – and I am in no position to argue since I'm invited to sample his wares – have no rival in all the land.

Furthermore, he continues, there's no possibility I will be allowed to pay my own way, even though our tour of the Plaza Mayor's many eating places is scheduled to last all evening. There's a strong tradition of hospitality throughout the Iberian peninsula – Portugal as well as Spain – and while it's rare to be invited into someone's home for a meal, even as a fellow Span- iard, hospitality extends to public eating places, where picking up the bill as host is a matter of *orgullo* – personal pride – a rule that applies to all non-locals, men as well as women.

José Luis raises his glass in the Spanish equivalent of 'cheers' – '*salud, amor y pesetas*' – a toast to health, love and money, to which I reply with the courteous '*y tiempo para gastarlos*' – and may there be time to enjoy them. While the toast is delivered in well-rounded Madrileño, the precise speech of the educated Spaniard, my own slips easily into Andaluz, a distinctive accent that swallows the ends of the words, causing much merriment among the natives when delivered by a Spanish-speaking foreigner.

The Plaza Mayor, main square, is a handsome quadrangle of arcades, balustraded windows and perfectly proportioned eighteenth-century buildings, many of which are given over to the provision of good things to eat and drink.

Salamanca's university was founded in 1215 – Oxford dates from 1167 – and much of the city's reputation for culinary excellence comes from the need to satisfy the appetites not only of impoverished students but of pilgrims on their way to Santiago de Compostela.

Since Salamanca is herself a pilgrim destination, the tapa bars of the Plaza Mayor are kept busy all year round with the provision of the little mouthfuls which come free with a glass of wine. More substantial dishes are provided for those who can afford a *ración* – a paid-for dish for sharing between four. Citizens as well as visitors drop in at sundown for refreshment after the day's work, including a few slivers of *pata negra*. Even though it's wildly expensive, even in Spain, there's a fine appreciation of excellence in the pleasures of the table, and even the poorest will save up for a few slivers of the best at Christmas.

What distinguishes the hams of black-foot Iberico pigs, while no longer as free-range as they once were, is that the beasts are fed at least in part on *bellotas*, acorns. Serrano hams are prepared with the meat of domesticated breeds fed on grain, so the meat is softer and less dense in flavour and texture. The secret of the flavour lies in the frill of golden fat which must on no account be trimmed from the meat.

So how, I enquire of Don José Luis, do you tell if the ham on the hook in the market is really a *pata negra*, considering that my own experience tells me that not all Iberico pigs have ebony trotters.

At first sight, you can tell from the slenderness of the haunch, the narrowness of the ankle and the colour of the veil on the exterior fat, replies José Luis. And if you're in any doubt, the metal tag affixed to the trotter is the best guarantee of origin. Gone are the days, he adds, when it was possible to pass off one for the other.

As for the detail, the process by which the miracle is achieved, all will be revealed when I accompany him and his *compañeros* of the pig-curing fraternity on a tour of Joselito's ham-curing cellars the next day. This is an invitation of considerable generosity, since few non-professionals are allowed to witness the inner workings of a naturally secretive industry. How long the hams are left in salt, the length of time allotted before the hams are transferred to the maturing vaults, these are all a matter of skill, tradition and judgement.

Meanwhile, since the ham-curing industry guarantees a ready supply of variety meats to the tapa bars, our evening's entertainment is a guided tour of the delicious things that can be done with the interior workings of the pig.

José Luis knows everyone in town and our progress round the square is a riot of well-wishers anxious to recommend the speciality of the house to a foreign food writer with such an admirable grasp of the native tongue. This leads to rather too many glasses of the sharp red non-vintage wines of Rioja and an inability to remember what came with it. Nevertheless, my notes on what I can remember of the lengthy tasting menu lists the highlights, each taken in a different eatery, each no more than a mouthful. The stars of the tapa show of the Plaza Mayor, I note, are *chicharrones*, bubbly chunks of pork-skin fried crisp; trotters and tripe slow-cooked with chickpeas and chilli, *callos con garbanzos*; *morcilla* – black pudding – flavoured with cumin and topped with softly cooked rings of onion, *morcilla encebollada*;

frittered brains and sweetbreads – *tortillitas de sesos*; braised pork tongue, *lengua de cerdo estofada*; pigs' ears shredded and crisped in olive oil with garlic, *orejas de cerdo al ajillo*; tails and snouts slow-simmered with tomato and peppers, *chanfaina con tomate*.

Next day, nursing a mild Rioja hangover not entirely mitigated by the cure, a tiny cup of very strong coffee with a shot of anis, I arrive for instruction in the process of curing *pata negra* – a considerably more sophisticated version of what happened in our cork-oak forest. I keep quiet about previous experience of the artisan hams of the valley. My Andaluz accent is already a source of amusement since everyone in Spain knows that Andalusia drinks well and eats badly – *Andalucía bien bebida y mal comida*, as the saying goes.

José Luis, after a restorative nip of *pácharan*, a particularly lethal sloe gin from the Basque country, leads the way into a vast underground cavern with serried ranks of haunches in various stages of blossoming moulds.

First, explains José Luis, I should understand that the hams of Spain, both serrano and *pata negra*, are unlike all other raw-cured hams in that, once salted and wind-dried, they are cellared – aged in much the same way as wine – a process that allows a thick blanket of technicolour mould to develop on the exterior of the haunch, though this shrinks to a thin veil as soon as the ham is brought back to air and light.

Preliminary salting and wind-drying takes advantage of variations in climate from one ham-curing region to another. Salamanca is particularly well favoured in this respect since the breeze in the uplands in which the hams are cured is flame-hot by day and ice-cold at night. When the hams are hung in the attics after salting, the buttery fat melts by day and firms up again at night, massaging itself into the lean. The Ibericos that forage the *dehesa* of Extremadura, scrubby oak forest, have the advantage of plenty of exercise, delivering lean, muscular haunches well provided with exterior fat. When a ham is judged ready for cellaring – from nine to twenty months – it is transferred to the caverns to begin the maturing process, a slow procession from one room to another according to the judgement of the cellarman.

Certain moulds – crimson, snow-white, ultramarine and ochre – are available in one part of the cellars and not in another, but each is essential to the maturing process. The larger the ham, the longer it can be matured. A ham from a well-grown beast can be cellared for seven years, improving every year.

'We use the nose for testing,' explains José Luis, tapping a nostril. 'This is done by using a bone-needle, a sinew from the haunch.' He holds up a long, thin, ivory-coloured poking-stick and shoves it into a particularly well-blossomed haunch as far as the bone.

'Here.'

Obediently I sniff. The fragrance is sweet and delicate, a little caramelised, with a scent of hay meadow.

José Luis nods appreciatively. 'You're right. This is exactly the fragrance we look for. After a little practice – say twenty years – we could offer you a job.'

I agree that ham-testing would be the perfect occupation for a food writer, and in my case, could be combined with an appreciation, as a painter, for the magnificent technicolour bloomings on the haunches.

The tour is over. But fortunately for me – and the *compañeros* of the ham fraternity waiting in the tasting-room upstairs – a seven-year-old ham is ready for sampling. It is indeed a magnificent sight, settled in its wooden cradle in the middle of a long table round which the fraternity is already enjoying a preprandial glass of oloroso, a dry golden liquid which has already served seven years in the barrel. Sherry is matured from barrel to barrel on the *solera* system, picking up flavour and depth as it moves from the topmost and youngest barrel to the oldest, until

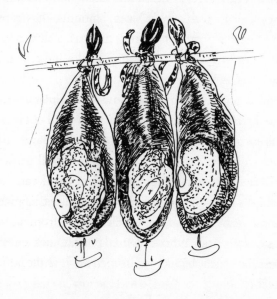

it's judged ready for bottling. Our oloroso, a gift from one of the fraternity, a winemaker from Jerez, is declared the perfect companion for a seven-year-old ham.

We are provided with an expert carver, José Luis himself. Ham-carving, he explains as he sharpens the slender blade of a long flexible knife, takes many years of experience. Twenty at least, he adds with a grin – as long as it takes to appreciate the fragrance.

There are rituals to be observed in which I need instruction. Before cutting after cellaring, two or three days must be allowed for the inside temperature of the ham to reach room temperature. After cutting, the ham must be kept as dry and warm as a newborn baby – any trace of humidity in the air can spoil even the most perfectly cured ham. Long thin hams weigh heavier than short plump hams – it's all to do with the ratio of bone to flesh. The more a ham weighs in proportion to its size, the better it will be.

The way to carve a ham, he continues, is to start at the shoulder. When carving, the little black trotter must be pointing upwards. Only the portion of the haunch to be carved should be trimmed of skin and a little of the outer fat – not too much, as it's the fat that carries the flavour.

José Luis wishes each stage to be appreciated in full, so I busy myself with my notebook.

Hand-cutting is much preferable to machine-cutting, when the ham needs to be de-boned, losing much of its natural character. Machine-cutting is better than no ham at all, but this is not what José Luis considers appropriate. When cutting, the first to arrive on the plate is the meat from the top cut, the *tapa* – the lid or covering – the best and sweetest and most buttery because of the process by which the fat is massaged into the meat. The *contra* – the other side of the ham, when the top has been carved and the haunch is turned over – is less fatty and the meat is darker and denser. Within these divisions, each section changes flavour and becomes less exquisitely buttery as the knife gets nearer to the bone. The hock, the last piece to be carved, is sinewy but very delicate in flavour, while the *culata*, the piece nearest the trotter, though well flavoured, is a little salty and suitable only to flavour the *olla*.

Iberico, as with all serrano or mountain hams, must be carved from the bone in short curls, *lonchas*. Strong men come to blows over the correct order of carving, but the cardinal rule is that carving should be with rather than against the grain. Parma ham, being softer and less dense, and therefore inferior – an opinion endorsed by the rest of the fraternity – is sliced against the grain. Once sufficient ham has been carved, the cut surface must be protected with a layer of carved-off fat and a cotton cloth, and hung in a dry current of air. If the ham is kept in the fridge, as some do who know no better, it will grow a furry green jacket in two shakes of a pig's tail.

So how do you tell, I enquire, if what's on the plate is the real thing?

This is easy. Iberico fat melts at blood temperature, which is about the same as a warm evening in a tapa bar such as those of the Plaza Mayor. To check that your *jamón ibérico* is as it should be even before you taste it, pick up your plateful and hold it sideways. If the ham sticks to the plate, it's Iberico. If the meat drops, you've been sold an imposter and you should demand the return of your money.

José Luis demonstrates the truth of his words. Sure enough, the carved curls of ham, neatly spread out in a single layer, remain firmly in place on the plate. With *pata negra*, he continues, look first for the little white crystals no bigger than a pinhead that confirm the beast has fattened on acorns. Now pick up a curl – advice eagerly followed by the rest of the fraternity – and let it gently feel the warmth of your fingertips while you admire the burgundy transparency when you hold it to the light.

Meanwhile the carving continues. Each *loncha*, a ruby curl fringed with pale golden fat, is tenderly placed among its fellows on a large china plate. *Pata negra*, while it's possible to appreciate it as a private pleasure, is best eaten in company, accompanied by wine and stories and the good fellowship engendered by the enjoyment of something supremely delicious.

Now it's time to appreciate texture and flavour. Here, too, instructions must be followed. Each morsel must be delicately placed on the tongue, allowing the fragrance to reach the sensors at the back of the throat. The first bite delivers the faint crunch of the crystals. Now for the flavour, which is sweet, clean and nutty. Next comes appreciation of the texture: a little chewy but velvety and dense. The final pleasure is a little catch just behind the molars and an aftertaste of dry grass hot from the sun.

The lesson is over and conversation round the table turns to accounts of other haunches similarly appreciated under circumstances which range from romantic to practical. Wind-dried ham is travellers' food – convenient for the pocket when slipped inside a couple of slices of sturdy country loaf with a thick brown crust from the high heat of a wood-fired oven. José Luis himself admits that he fell in love with his wife over her appreciation of a hand-carved feast of ham – *pata negra*, of course. Table talk is always romantic in Spain, given that there's enough food to fill the belly. Days of plenty are doubly appreciated in a region where hunger came not only with the failure of harvest but most painfully with war – civil and otherwise – when the soldiers emptied the store cupboards, fields were left fallow and the population starved.

Next day, I have a date with Joselito's herdsman, Juan Antonio, among the prickly holm oaks of the *dehesa* – the name given to the desolate lands of the west – where semi-wild herds of Ibericos, black-foot pigs, still survive in much the same way as they did in our cork-oak forest in Andalusia. Ibericos are well adapted for survival in regions where other breeds would fail, storing up fat in the good times to carry them through the lean.

The pigs of Extremadura are huge, humpbacked beasts – grey or reddish or black – stronger and heavier than our cork-forest foragers. Their feeding grounds are among stony pastures dotted with scrubby little trees with prickly leaves whose acorns, *bellotas*, are as fat and sweet as chestnuts. In the season on our way south, we would buy paper cones of the fresh nuts offered for sale by the roadside.

Anyone travelling through the *dehesa* at the beginning of autumn when the pigs are in their foraging grounds might not even notice the grey ghosts among the silvery rocks, cropping acorns and tubers, under the watchful eye of the herdsman keeping an eye out for pig rustlers and wild boar, *jabalí*, a love interest for the Iberico sows. Wild-boar piglets are stripy rather than plain, and any piglets born with stripes are likely to end up on the spit sooner rather than later.

There are forty million pigs in Spain, of which a million are Ibericos. Some, as I know well, forage the cork forests of the province of Cadiz, others crop the lower slopes of the mountains of Granada, and more fatten in the chestnut woods of the Sierra Morena, but the most magnificent are those that forage for *bellotas* and sweet roots among the prickly scrub oaks and rough red earth of Extremadura.

If the pig was philosophically important in re-Christianised Spain, it took on almost magical importance when times were hard, particularly in wartime. Even the carved-out ham-bone was handed – or rented – from one household to another when soldiers had slaughtered the livestock and emptied the store cupboard. The herdsman who cared for the pigs and followed them round their feeding grounds knew what they ate and where and when. What's good for pigs is also good for people, making the difference between life and death.

Juan Antonio, herdsman to the Joselito Ibericos, is tall, lean, fit, weather-burned – and taciturn. He spends his days – spring, summer, autumn and winter – in the company of his pigs. Actually, he says, he prefers pigs to people. You know just where you are with a pig. All their faces are different, each has its own personality, and his pigs, he has to admit, provide all the companionship he needs.

I decide to share my pig-keeping experiences in Andalusia. Recognising a fellow pig-enthusiast, Juan Antonio softens a little. He too remembers the days when the *matanza* was the most important event of the year for all the family. They did indeed keep a sty-pig of the Iberico breed when he was a child. Even though he knew that the *matanza* was inevitable, it was not a happy event for a child who had fed and nurtured a pig from babyhood. But he was happy enough to eat the hams his mother prepared for the Christmas treat. She salted the hams and hung them to take the wind in the attic. His grandmother and the aunts also prepared chorizos, but his mother never did, though she salted the shoulder meat as well as the haunches. Certain households did certain things and others didn't. It was a question of personality, just like the pigs.

We have established common ground. I take out my sketch-book and paints as Juan Antonio leans on his crook and watches his charges. At rest, he becomes almost invisible, immobile in the landscape with face and hat and cloak matched to the colour of earth and trees and the rocks. He begins to talk, perhaps because he feels I can be trusted not to ask silly questions or romanticise a way of life that has always been hard. In the old days, the pigs were left to roam the *dehesa* at will. Nowadays the terrain is roughly divided into fields by dry-stone walls topped with thorn branches, and the herds are moved season by season from one field to another, allowing the young oak saplings time to grow into mature trees. The foraging pigs in the fields are all castrated males. This, too, is different from the old days, when the herds were allowed to move in family groups. The females are all kept as breeding stock and safely corralled at home. A sow takes one hundred and fourteen days to gestate and, given opportunity with the boar, will be pregnant again on the next full moon after the piglets are weaned.

The scrub is cleaned bare beneath the trees where the Ibericos are feeding. Foraging is rotated, leaving a neighbouring field where oak seedlings are given time to gain hold. The Ibericos eat roots as well as acorns, turning over the earth and leaving it bare, but since nothing else will grow on the *dehesa*, the land has no other use. Acorns are available for just three of the winter months, from November to January, and the young pigs are allowed into the fields to forage when they're ready – between a year and a half and two years –

when their teeth have grown enough to allow them to crack the acorn shells.

Juan Antonio picks up a handful of *bellotas*, smaller and darker than the ones I remember from the cork oaks, cracks one between his teeth and shows me the nut-brown flesh. 'This is good.' He pops it back in his mouth and chews appreciatively.

'What's good for pigs is good for people. I like the *bellotas* but I don't like the *criadillas de tierra*.' *Criadillas* are truffles. Juan Antonio shudders. 'I'm told you can take them to market and they pay good money for them in France, but I don't like them at all, even though my grandmother said they were glad of them in wartime because they give the taste of meat when you have nothing else to flavour the pot.'

Criadillas de tierra – earth testicles – is the country people's name for one or other of the dark-fleshed truffles that look, at first sight, like lumps of coal. One, the more valuable of the two, second only to the Piedmont white, is the Périgord black, *Tuber melanosporum*. The other, *T. aestivum*, is the more widespread summer or Burgundy truffle. I know both of them well and have,

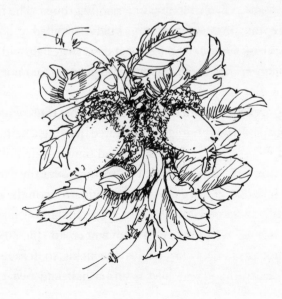

on occasion, given the right territory and time to explore, been able to gather my own. The summer truffle matures at the moment when it is of interest to both pigs and people – from May to December. The high-value black – *melano*, as it's known to those who pay high prices in the markets of the Périgord – doesn't come to maturity until late November, and has been in cultivation in Soria, not far to the south of us, since medieval times. Truffles are host-specific and symbiotic – they exchange nutrients with a suitable tree through a mycelium, a delicate web of thread-like roots. The presence of truffle mycelium on a host tree – oak, beech and hazel are all suitable for the black – is signalled by a circle of bare earth round the trunk and the unmistakable fragrance released when the subterranean tuber is ready to spread its spores.

If the truffle is close to the surface, it is possible to feel the outline through bare feet or even thin-soled shoes, while a keen nose will pick up the scent in a handful of soil. There is also a small red fly that lays its eggs on ripe truffles and jumps to safety when approached, but can be relied upon to return rapidly to its laying grounds.

The most reliable method of searching, however, is to find someone who knows the territory: Juan Antonio.

The chances of finding *melano* at this time of year are slim – truffles only release their scent when ripe – but there might well be *aestivum* in the fallow land where the holm-oak saplings are left to sprout and the pigs are not permitted to forage.

Perhaps, I enquire of Juan Antonio, he might have noticed the signs?

It's possible, he admits, that something might be found, as long as he's not required to smell it. The pigs certainly love the nasty little things and gobble them up whenever they find them.

He swings his legs over the rough wall that divides the foraging grounds from the fallow field and motions me to follow. Sure enough, around a sorry-looking scrub oak, the ring of bare earth is unmistakable. I can scarcely breathe for excitement. I drop to my knees and move slowly round the circle, rummaging beneath the carpet of leaves, feeling for the loosening of the earth and the slight change in temperature that might indicate the treasure beneath.

Juan Antonio watches me without comment, though I know well enough what he's thinking – why should this absurd foreigner who knows all about the *matanza* want to find, let alone eat, something fit only for pigs?

My fingertips feel the telltale bump and the warmth of the earth. I close my fist around a pocket of the red dust, bend my head and inhale the unmistakable scent – a fragrance of rare roast beef, heady and fresh, and – well – to put it daintily, the appeal of the mating sow to the boar.

And here it is in my hand, a little nugget no bigger than a walnut, coal-black and rough-surfaced under its coating of earth, the treasure itself.

I cup the truffle in my hand and inhale. A truffle just lifted from its bed is irresistible. A subterranean tuber dependent for ecological success on a spore-spreader must not only be found, eaten and passed through its predator's digestive system – pigs, people and (in my own observation) hedgehogs – but must imprint itself on the memory as well as the taste-buds. And the truffle is indeed endowed with a memory trigger. They've done the chemistry.

No one ever forgets the experience of where and when they tasted their first truffle, or with whom. Mine – I was a gastronomically adventurous child – was at the age of twelve at the Tour d'Argent in Paris, courtesy of my gambling grandfather, a bon viveur of the first rank, who made up for a run of bad luck at the tables with dinner at a place of his choosing with his granddaughter. The star of the show at the Tour d'Argent was pressed duck prepared at table, a performance my grandfather found much too much of a fuss. More modest in presentation was their famous *poulet en demi-deuil*, chicken in half-mourning, a poached bird entirely covered with fine slices of black truffle slipped between the meat and the skin. I was too young to appreciate the subliminal message, but I never forgot the fragrance.

The truffle, I decide, will make a delicious little supper this evening, when I drive south to keep an appointment in Seville.

If it were me, I tell Juan Antonio, I would eat my truffle with a *loncha* of your wonderful Iberico ham.

If it were him, says Juan Antonio, shepherding me back over the wall in case I find another, he would hand it over to his favourite pig. But if I want to know what his grandmother would have done, she would have put it into the *olla* with the beans.

And Juan Antonio would have to go hungry to bed?

Not at all. The *bellotas* he holds in his hand – and will take home to eat with a glass of wine while his wife prepares his supper – are as delicious as freshly roasted almonds, and just as nourishing.

I push my precious little nugget into my pocket. Later, I shall eat it all by myself with a sliver of *pata negra* – possibly, though not necessarily, since I fear another rough red hangover, in the company of José Luis and the *compañeros* of the tapa bars of the Plaza Mayor.

For now, I follow Juan Antonio's example and gather a handful of acorns.

It's been many years since I've tasted a fresh *bellota*. With the first bite of the crisp sweet flesh, memories of my days travelling back and forth from our home in the valley return in a rush.

Even in the 1970s, thirty years after the end of the Civil War that brought Franco to power, memories of the war were still sharp, and never sharper than at the time of the *matanza*. The feast of liver and lights that followed the day's work – the men of the valley went from household to household, each on its allotted day – triggered stories of the days of deprivation.

Pepito Moreno, chief slaughter man at the *matanzas* of the valley, and supplier of sty-pigs in spring when his own foraging pigs produced their litters, set his herds free to roam the forest as soon as the army – Republican or Nationalist – was reported on the move.

'We called the soldiers "*bisoños*" – people with needs. We couldn't deny them. They were our fathers or husbands or brothers – some on one side, some on the other.'

If the old saying in the countryside is that hunger is the best sauce, then the cooking of Extremadura reflects the simplicity and lack of pretension of a land in which famine was never far from the door.

Richard Ford, writing in the 1850s in *Gatherings from Spain*, defines the flavour of Spain's traditional *olla*, a one-pot meal of beans or chickpeas flavoured with garlic and enriched with olive oil, named for the implement in which it's cooked. The beans and the fat together thicken the sauce, but the flavour comes from the bone.

'The importance of the sauce,' explains Ford, 'is that it carries that rich burnt umber, raw sienna tint which Murillo imitated so well; and no wonder, since he made his particular brown, *negro de hueso*, bone-black, from baked *olla* bones, as is done to this day by those Spanish painters who indulge in meat.'

Buried among the beans for colour and sweetness, there must be dried peppers, *ñora* – the raw material of pimenton, Spanish paprika – and the cooking liquid is water, never stock or wine. The enrichment I prefer is olive oil stirred in at the end, when the beans are perfectly creamy and soft, but in our house in the valley it was often a spoonful of *manteca*, the lard from the *matanza*.

But the element that gives the dish its distinctive flavour and colour is mountain ham – serrano or *pata negra*, never mind the name – and it doesn't have to be much, just a few scraps from the knuckle and a sawn-up length of bone.

Pepito, the herdsman of the valley, was in no doubt of the importance of the bone. In wartime, he remembers, the ham-bone was used again and again – even the faintest hint of its presence was enough to give savour to the sauce.

Myself, I'll settle for Bartolomé Esteban Murillo's shimmering *negro de hueso* – I have admired it myself in the great collections of the Prado – source of that earthy fragrance that links the artists of Spain to my own and my children's childhood.

LENGUA DE CERDO ESTOFADA (BRAISED PORK TONGUE)

Tongue, most delicious of all the variety meats, is finished in a braising sauce of onion, cinnamon and wine. For a more substantial dish, serve with thick chips fried crisp in olive oil (chips served with stews is a very Spanish habit).

Serves 6–8 as a tapa
1 kg pork tongue
1 carrot, scrubbed and chopped
1 onion, peeled and quartered
1 celery stick, chopped
1 bay leaf
12 peppercorns
salt

For the braising sauce
2 large onions, peeled and finely sliced
4–5 tablespoons olive oil
1 small cinnamon stick
1 tablespoon pimenton (Spanish paprika)
1 glass oloroso sherry or dry cider
salt and pepper

Scrub the tongue under the tap and leave to soak in salted cold water for an hour or two. Drain and transfer to a saucepan with enough water to cover generously. Bring to the boil, skim and add the aromatics – carrot, onion, celery, bay leaf, peppercorns – and a little salt. Cover with a lid and leave to simmer for 40–50 minutes, until the tongue is still firm but cooked through. Reserve the broth and drain the tongue. As soon as the tongue is cool enough to handle, slip off the skin – it comes off quite easily – and remove any little bones and extra fat from the root end. Slice thickly and reserve.

Meanwhile, prepare the braising sauce. Set the onions to fry very gently in the olive oil in a frying pan, salting lightly and allowing 30 minutes for the onion to soften without browning. Add the cinnamon stick, pimenton, sherry or cider and bubble up to evaporate the alcohol. Transfer to a casserole with the tongue slices, and add enough of the reserved broth to submerge everything completely.

Bring to the boil, then turn down the heat, cover with a tight-fitting lid and leave to simmer gently for about an hour, until the juices are reduced to a thick sauce and the meat is perfectly tender (check and add more broth if it seems to be drying out). Taste and season.

CALLOS CON GARBANZOS (TRIPE WITH CHICKPEAS AND CHILLI)

Tripe, liver and lights – rejects from Salamanca's salt-cured Iberico trade – are the raw material of the little tapa which comes free with a glass of wine in the bars of Salamanca's Plaza Mayor.

Serves 4–6
350 g chickpeas, soaked for 8 hours or overnight
500 g ready-cooked tripe, cut into matchsticks
1 tablespoon serrano or *pata negra* scraps
2–3 garlic cloves, peeled and crushed
2 bay leaves
½ teaspoon crushed black peppercorns

For the sauce
4 tablespoons olive oil
1 large mild onion, peeled and finely chopped
1 red pepper, deseeded and chopped
500 g tomatoes, skinned and diced (or tinned)
1 or 2 dried chillies, de-seeded and torn
1 glass red wine
salt and pepper

Drain the chickpeas and put them in a large pot with the tripe, ham, garlic, bay leaves and peppercorns, and add enough water to cover everything generously. Bring to the boil, skim off any grey foam which rises, and leave to bubble gently for 1½ hours until the chickpeas are perfectly soft. Some chickpeas take much longer than others. If you need to add water, let it be boiling.

Meanwhile, warm the olive oil in a frying pan, then add the onion and red pepper. Fry gently until the vegetables soften. Add the tomatoes, chillies and wine. Boil the mixture to evaporate the alcohol, and season with salt and pepper.

Now reduce the heat and cook uncovered for 20–25 minutes, until you have a thick, spicy sauce. Stir the sauce into the chickpeas and tripe and cook everything together gently for 15 minutes to marry the flavours.

TORTILLITAS DE SESOS (SWEETBREAD FRITTERS)

Offal – brains, sweetbreads and all those bits and bobs known as 'variety meats' – is the food of the urban poor. Country people rarely had access to any fresh meat at all, unless at the annual pig-killing or *matanza*, when the tender and spoilable innards were cooked and eaten immediately.

Serves 6–8 as a tapa
250 g sweetbreads
250 g pig's brains
1 tablespoon sherry or white wine vinegar
1 bay leaf
salt and pepper

For the batter
4 tablespoons self-raising flour
½ teaspoon salt
6 tablespoons water
2 tablespoons olive oil, plus extra for frying
1 teaspoon pimenton (Spanish paprika)
1 tablespoon very finely chopped onion
1 tablespoon chopped parsley

Soak the sweetbreads and brains for an hour or two in cold water with the vinegar. Drain, rinse and bring to the boil in enough lightly salted water to cover, plus the bay leaf. When the meats are firm and cooked through – about 20 minutes – drain and leave to cool, weighted between two plates. Once cool, skin and dice.

(recipe continued overleaf)

Prepare the batter when you're ready to cook. Sieve the flour and salt into a bowl, and gradually blend in the water and oil until you have a thin batter. Stir in the paprika, onion and parsley. Fold in the diced sweetbreads and brains.

Heat 2 fingers' depth of oil in a frying pan. When the oil is lightly hazed with blue, drop in the batter by the tablespoonful – not too many at a time or the oil temperature will drop. Fry the fritters until golden and crisp, turning once. Serve piping hot straight from the pan, with a chilled glass of wine to cool your tongue.

MORCILLA ENCEBOLLADA (BLACK PUDDING WITH SLOW-COOKED ONIONS)

The secret to this simple combination of spicy Spanish black pudding and onion is the *soffritto* – thinly slivered mild Spanish onion gently fried without browning for at least half an hour until meltingly soft and golden. Spain likes its blood puddings flavoured with paprika, garlic, cloves, pepper, marjoram, coriander and cumin, with or without small cubes of pork fat. Rice is added as well. Simmering the loops of black pudding in a cauldron over a wood fire in the yard is the last chore of the traditional *matanza* (the annual pig-killing).

Serves 6–8 as a tapa
4–5 tablespoons lard or olive oil
500 g mild onions, peeled and finely sliced in half-moons
500g *morcilla* (Spanish black pudding), cut into short lengths
salt and pepper

Heat the lard or oil in a wide, heavy pan, add the onions and let them cook very slowly for at least half an hour, until they are perfectly soft and only lightly caramelised.

Remove and reserve the onion, reheat the pan with the drippings and fry the *morcilla* pieces on the cut sides until they crisp a little (*morcilla* is already cooked, so really only needs heating up). Serve with the onion.

ISLANDS

ISLANDS WERE SETTLED RELATIVELY LATE IN human history. The inhabitants of the last of the planet's habitable spaces to be colonised can be distinguished from mainlanders by philosophy rather than any of the physical or geographical characteristics by which one tribe separates itself from another.

As an islander-by-marriage myself – the maternal line of my husband's family came from Mull, innermost and most fertile of the silver sisters of the Hebrides – I have first-hand experience of what it means to live, even with modern comforts, storm-bound for half the year and at the mercy of wind and weather for the rest.

Colonisation of islands, however fertile, was a last resort for a mainland population obliged, for one reason or another, to abandon their homeland and find sanctuary across the waters that separate one landmass from another. With them came their domestic animals and the wherewithal to plant their crops. Together the newcomers set about converting a ready-made landscape to suit their needs.

As a result, those who live on islands, however geograph-ically divided, are as like to other islanders as Darwin's Galapagos finches are to their brother finches on other Galapagos islands, and for much the same reason. Once possessed of the right-shaped beak – a problem for finches – or having adapted their needs to suit their surroundings – a problem for humans – man and bird found little reason for change. Islanders – avian and human – are conservative by nature. Palaeontologists scraping around in prehistoric middens find domestic implements still in use on islands to this day.

My husband Nicholas knew and loved the Western Isles from childhood, and I too learned over the years to love their windswept beauty. When our children were grown and gone and there was reason to find a place where he could write without distraction, the island became our home. As far as our crofting neighbours were concerned, it was enough that the family kilt, a length of mud-brown homespun, had seen distinguished service in support of Bonnie Prince Charlie at the Battle of Culloden in 1746. The loss of independence that followed defeat by the English armies is nowhere felt more keenly than on the islands.

Thirty years ago, the islanders – a crofting community whose activities as farmers, shepherds and fishermen depended on the season – supplemented self-sufficiency with summer services to tourists. For the rest of the year, the island way of life was more or less as it always had been: hard-working, neighbourly and frugal. The original settlers were dark-haired Celts, short of stature and fierce of disposition, who intermarried, to put it politely, with the tall, blond, blue-eyed Vikings who dropped anchor in the sheltered coves to re-victual their long-ships by raiding the island's cattle. The cattle were not, as might be expected, the shaggy-haired, wide-horned, semi-feral brown highland cattle of the Scottish mainland, but small, black-coated, short-haired dairy herds introduced from Ireland by the monks who settled Mull's smaller sister, the sacred island of Iona.

To this day, the descendants of those hardy souls whose livelihood depended on the rocky outcrops littered throughout the world's oceans share far more than sets them apart. Those things that islanders share with other islanders – philosophical rather than physical – include long memories, traditions preserved through singing and storytelling, wariness of strangers, care for widows and orphans, an egalitarian way of life and a willingness to do whatever it takes to survive.

Island-dwellers have good reason to distrust strangers. Even if seemingly they come in peace, there's no guarantee that these same strangers won't run off with your wife, your cattle and the contents of your store cupboard. Some defend their own by retiring inland, some hold fast to their territory, some greet newcomers with open arms in the hope they'll do no harm. Whatever the choice, island existence is fragile, good reason to look after your own.

Crete

'I HOPE ALL THESE PEOPLE ARE LIKING SNAILS.'

The speaker, Ariadne, is a dark-haired Cretan beauty of the kind recorded on the vases unearthed in the ruins of the palace of Knossos. Her audience – a hundred of us food writers, nutritionists, chefs and academics, mostly American – are gathered together for breakfast in a vast hotel on the outskirts of Heraklion on the fourth day of our conference on the Seven Countries Study, whose half-century we are here to celebrate.

'Today, I am happy to tell you, those of you who wish to accompany me into the mountains will be able to gather and pre-pare this important foodstuff for yourselves.'

None of us has anticipated the need for liking snails, let alone gathering, preparing and – presumably – consuming the fruits of our labours. Some of us can't eat the slithery creatures for religious reasons; others don't want to have anything to do with something so slippery and slimy and, not to put too fine a point on it, primitive. A quartet of us – Nancy Jenkins, author of *The Mediterranean Diet*; Paula Wolfert, author of *The Food of the Eastern Mediterranean*; Aglaia Kremezi, author of *The Food of Greece*; and I – are anticipating snails with undisguised enthusiasm.

We are here to celebrate the fiftieth year of the migration of the Cretan Diet into the Mediterranean Diet and from thence to the Seven Countries Study, an assessment of the general health of those who live around the shores of the Mediterranean that continues to this day. The Cretan Diet that started the whole thing off was first identified as a blueprint for longevity and health by Ansel Keyes, a heart specialist from Minnesota seconded to Naples Hospital in 1945 to look after Italy's war-wounded.

The good doctor observed in the course of his ministra-tions that his patients from the islands – most of them members of the resistance movement on Crete – were unlike those of Minnesota in that they were never likely to be in need of his expertise since their hearts were beating like clockwork and their arteries were magnificently unfurred. A visit to the island itself confirmed that the secret was a diet of grains, greens and olive oil, wine in moderation, modest amounts of cheese and yoghurt, fish occasionally and meat only on feast days.

The omission of snails from the roll-call, continues Ariadne, is unjust. Snails were the reason the self-sufficient peasantry of the Cretan hills – not to mention those who took up arms and were obliged to live from the wild – survived the German Occu-pation in rude good health. The soldiers emptied everyone's store cupboards and slaughtered the sheep and goats, but they left the snails untouched.

Snails, Ariadne continues, warming to her theme, have not been accorded their proper place in the Cretan diet, even though in her own experience in her grandmother's village, the succulent molluscs are – or were, since most of the crop is now shipped off to France, Italy and Spain – eaten three or four times a week.

The proper accompaniment to a dish of Cretan snails is Cretan *paximadia*, twice-baked barley bread. *Paximadia*, fist-sized rock-hard rusks, are as much a statement of Cretan identity as – well – the Cretan diet of grains and greens. Once split and dampened with a little water, they are ready to mop up a sauce, or heap with ripe tomato and a sprinkle of oregano, or top with a sliver of salty *myzithra* cheese and a handful of young dandelion greens.

And finally there must be olive oil, as much as the crumb can hold of the thick green juice freshly pressed from ripe fruit no bigger than a fingernail, gathered from thousand-year-old olive trees descended from others the juice of whose fruits, many millennia ago, filled the tall earthenware jars stacked in close-crammed ranks in cellars preserved beneath the palace of Knossos.

Ariadne inspects her audience for evidence of enthusiasm.

'Those who wish to accompany me on our expedition into the mountains for this special event, please to raise your hands.'

A couple of dozen hands are tentatively raised while the rest remain firmly clenched round their coffee cups.

This field trip is of unparalleled interest, continues Ariadne encouragingly, to all of those who wish to discover the truth of the Cretan diet. Snails are one of the most venerable foodstuffs known to man. Snail debris has been found in the middens of Neolithic Jericho. There is evidence of snail feasts enjoyed

seventy thousand years ago in the fertile valleys of Mesopota-
mia. All snails – small, middle-sized and the monster molluscs
sold in African markets – are edible and good, but none are more
delicious than the vineyard-fattened snails of Crete.

Ansel Keyes' investigations on Crete, the moment of truth
for the Cretan diet, came to the attention of the Rockefeller
Foundation, who sent a group of scientists to verify his findings.
The scientists confirmed that the islanders enjoyed remarkably
good health, with many climbing hillsides like mountain goats
well into their nineties. Longevity and vigour could be ascribed,
they concluded, to a diet limited by what could be grown, harvested or husbanded in a region known for mildness of climate,
fertility of soil, ancient vineyards and olive groves of equal
antiquity.

The study inspired our host, Dun Gifford – Boston Brah-
min, friend of the Kennedys, veteran of the America's Cup – to

set up Oldways Preservation Trust, our hosts at the conference, an organisation dedicated to persuading the founders' fellow Americans to stop eating saturated fats, white bread, fizzy drinks and hamburgers in buns and start eating the diet of deprivation as experienced on Crete.

Three days into the conference, not a few of us would rather jump naked into one of the oil derricks overshadowing the hotel than experience another back-projected flow chart. As a result, Ariadne's offer of escape to the hills, with or without snails, is irresistible – at least to me and around a dozen others, including Nancy, Paula and Aglaia.

'Your attention, please, kind ladies and gentlemen! I have brought some examples of the most important foodstuff, also of great antiquity, which is eaten with our snails.'

Ariadne gets straight to the point by banging on the communal breakfast table with what looks like a fist-sized nut-brown billiard ball. The ball splits in two, revealing a pale-brown crumb.

'This,' says Ariadne, brandishing the two halves, 'is the *paximadia* which is eaten with the snails that my grandmother, Kiria Eleni, will be preparing for us today when some of us visit her in her village.'

Paximadia is the daily bread of Crete. When eaten, as anticipated, with snails under the shade of a thousand-year-old olive tree in the Cretan hills, it explains more about the longevity of Cretans than any amount of Seven Country studies and an army of scientists. Neither Paula, Nancy nor I have much confidence in the science of things, preferring direct experience to staring at diagrams and graphs. Ariadne's proposal, snails included, is a lot more appealing than listening to PowerPoint lectures in an air-conditioned conference hall.

Ariadne starts our education without delay. Dismissing the hotel's international breakfast buffet – a hybrid array of Florida orange juice, Swiss muesli, Israeli grapefruit, German sausage and French pastries – she distributes the Cretan version of the breakfast croissant.

A few of us bang the balls on the table, producing shards of crumbs. One or two of us split the ball with the hotel cutlery and proceed to butter and spread the crumb with jam.

'This is not the way to eat *paximadia*,' says Ariadne severely. 'How to eat *paximadia* is like so.'

She cracks one of the billiard balls into a bowl provided for cornflakes, dips her fingers daintily in a water glass and sprinkles the dry crumb with droplets. 'Not too much – just enough to soften. And now you may eat your *paximadia* as you wish at any time of day. Me? I like it right now with American coffee.'

She pours herself a bowl of the hotel's reheated coffee, adds a splash of the hot milk considered appropriate for tea-drinkers among those who don't drink tea, and tips in the softened *paximadia*.

'This is good,' she says, spooning up a mouthful.

I crack and soak. She's right. It is indeed good – nutty and toasty, like coffee-flavoured porridge.

'*Paximadia*,' our instructor continues, 'must stay a little firm, unless it is for babies or toothless old people, although this is not much experienced on Crete, where there is little work for the dentist. My grandmother, *ya-ya*, is nearly ninety years old and has all her own teeth. You will meet her today and see for yourself.'

Nearly-ninety-year-olds with teeth seems like an excellent recommendation for a diet – any diet – though I reflect that this might also have to do with an absence of sugary fizz among those who rarely find themselves in supermarkets.

Barley-meal formed into ashcakes, an early form of *paximadia*, has been found in prehistoric rubbish dumps along with snail debris, Ariadne continues, spooning up her coffee-flavoured porridge. There is evidence that leavened ashcakes or barley rusk – true *paximadia* – were carried in saddlebags by Alexander's soldiers, provisioned Viking longships and victualled Spanish galleons on the long Atlantic crossings. It can therefore be assumed that Cretan *paximadia*, being extraordinarily hard and resistant to invasion by weevils and other collateral damage, fuelled the discovery by Europeans of the Americas, a fact which will certainly be of interest to her audience.

Ariadne pauses, then resumes with renewed passion. Her audience will certainly find other forms of *paximadia* prepared on other islands – and indeed on the mainland – some of which are even made with inappropriate wheat flour and sweetened and spiced or rich with milk and egg.

'True *paximadia*,' adds Ariadne indignantly, 'must be made with Cretan barley flour kneaded with Cretan water and leavened by wild yeasts released by fermenting grape-must as it turns itself into Cretan wine. No salt. You may even find *paximadia* made in America,' she pauses, glaring dangerously, 'though these will certainly be covered in sugar and chocolate sprinkles which, as everyone knows, means ninety-year *ya-ya* will have no teeth.'

Paula, Nancy and I consider this warning with respect. All three of us are grandmothers ourselves, but have a good few years to go before we're ninety.

The bus leaves the coastal highway and turns inland on a newly finished road running through maize-fields and avocado plantations, crops introduced from the New World and planted, says Ariadne over the intercom, as a result of subsidies from Brussels.

The bus is not in the first flush of youth. The engine labours noisily as the road winds upwards. It is three hours to our destination but, Ariadne promises, this is reduced to two hours on the way back owing to rapidity of descent. Her grandmother, by way of showing us the beauty of the snail, has agreed to prepare *bouboutie*, a dish that takes its name from the bubbling noise the snails make when cooking. The dish will, of course, be eaten with *paximadia* and a salad of wild greens that flourish in the olive groves and vineyards, thus delivering all the essential elements of the Cretan diet.

Ya-ya, Ariadne finishes triumphantly, is the only woman left in the village who gathers her own snails and bakes her own *paximadia* and prepares her own *trahana*. Snails can be eaten with *trahana*, the ancient preparation of dried dough not unlike a primitive form of pasta found in the *pitoi* of Knossos as well as, incidentally, in every supermarket and corner-store in Greece and on the islands, even in Heraklion.

Snails can be eaten with anything you like. There are as many recipes for snails as there are for any other meat – though if you are in a hurry, you can just push them on the fire and eat them with a little vinegar.

'I am told they only eat them in France with garlic and butter,' adds Ariadne disapprovingly. 'This, I think, would not be good.'

Nancy and I enter into an enthusiastic bout of recipe-swapping with Aglaia Kremezi, the only Greek food writer among us. Aglaia's favourite is *sagliara me piperes*, snails cooked in olive oil with green peppers and potatoes. Nancy, our Italian expert, makes a case for *lumache alla romana*, snails cooked as they like them in Rome, in a fresh tomato sauce with anchovies, pepperoncini (fiery little dried peppers) and mint leaves. I, on the other hand, love the little summer snails no bigger than a fingernail that my children and I gathered by the bucketful from dried-out thistle stems when we lived in Andalusia. We cooked them as everyone else did in the valley, in a big pot in a broth flavoured with pennyroyal, black pepper, coriander seed and chilli. Reheated daily, the potful would last us for a month. If you'd cooked them carefully by gently raising the temperature of the broth so the snails didn't disappear back into their shells with fright, you could nip the little molluscs from their brown-speckled shells with your teeth. Big brown snails similar to those found in Crete are gathered from the rice paddies of Valencia for the traditional *paella con caracoles* – a dish of such venerable pedigree that it takes its name from the implement in which it's cooked, a double-handled iron pan of Roman design.

Ariadne is unimpressed.

'The snails of Crete are mentioned in Homer.'

I stop talking as we lurch towards a hairpin bend, reversing to make the turn. On the non-driver's side the drop is vertical all the way down to a dried-out riverbed.

'This place is *very* good for snails,' says Ariadne, waving her hand at the lush valley below.

The bus grinds upwards as the vegetation thins. This is goat territory, threaded with paths which stop and start without warning among grey rock patched with lichen and the many-branched flower stems of *asphodel*, a tall lily with white flowers streaked with crimson and known as the food of the dead, perhaps because it grows enthusiastically on ancient battlefields.

I once lost my way in such a place on another island, Ulysses' island of Ithaca. I had been wandering in the hills among tall stands of flowering lilies, not long before sunset, following a goat track that stopped without warning at the edge of a precipice sheer to the sea. The sun was already low on the horizon. There was nothing to be gained from retracing my steps, and no way forward. So I stayed where I was, in the lee of a rock among the lilies, fearful of shadows, hoping to pass the hours of darkness in a place of safety. I heard the goat-bells first, and then the herd and herdsman. The path to the village was close at hand and I fol-lowed my rescuers, four-footed and two, feeling foolish to have been so fearful. Later I discovered the place was indeed a battleground. There were lilies everywhere and they never lie.

_&&_

Adriane has been visiting her grandmother's village every summer since she was a child. After the war was over, few of the survivors returned to the villages and the farming households lost their menfolk.

And this, she continues sadly, means that grapes are left to rot on the vine, olive trees which have borne fruit for more than a thousand years go uncropped, and the snails that grow fat in untended vineyards and olive groves are gathered by workers from Algeria and Morocco, brought in by dealers who export the crop mostly to France, Italy and Spain, but also the gourmet restaurants of New York and Hong Kong and all the other places where the food of the poor becomes a luxury for the rich.

Ariadne has reservations about the conclusions drawn by the Rockefeller scientists whose discoveries we are here to commemorate. It's only common sense that the Cretan diet was – is – far more than a list of ingredients which, when combined in certain ways, can be measured, quantified and reproduced under laboratory conditions. Even more absurd is the notion that an entire way of life can be packaged up and delivered to supermarket shelves as a ready-meal.

In 1947, the year the Rockefeller scientists came to visit, those who remained, her grandmother among them, were mostly women, children and old folk. The scientists wanted neat and tidy answers, so they asked neat and tidy questions. What they didn't ask was what really matters: how far you had to walk to fetch water from the well, what you ate or collected along the way when you walked from one village to the other, what happened when the soldiers emptied the store cupboard. Because the questions were all the same, the answers were all the same, which didn't allow for elaboration or storytelling, as is usual among Greeks, who are natural tellers of tales and very much appreciate the talent in others.

'Whenever we Cretans throw a party,' adds Ariadne, 'there's always someone with a good joke or story who wants to make themselves more or even less important than they really are, and that's when you know where the truth is. But the scientists didn't want to write anything that wasn't scientific. They wanted facts, and facts don't fit into stories. You will know what I mean as some of you, I think, are storytellers yourselves.'

'Absolutely right,' says Nancy.

Ariadne nods. 'So what was written down is that the Cretans ate barley bread and olive oil and a little wine and maybe some yoghurt and curds and cheese and perhaps some eggs from the chickens who ate up the scraps.'

No one spoke about the snails, she continues, because all the questions were to do with the foods the scientists understood: pulses, grain foods, vegetables, goat meat, pork, cheese, chicken. Snails were not mentioned, even though they were plentiful enough for people to eat every day and were the only food the German soldiers didn't steal. Even though what the scientists wrote down about the Cretan diet was by no means the whole story, they went home and prepared charts and discussed how these could be used to prevent clogged arteries and blocked heart-valves.

They didn't take note, however, of the inconvenient truth that the Cretans were poor and the Americans rich, and that the good health enjoyed under conditions of near-starvation was the diet of necessity. Necessity dictated that the islanders ate only when they were hungry and walked everywhere they went.

If we were to experience the real Cretan diet, we would not be sitting in an air-conditioned bus making a day-trip into the mountains for a gastronomic entertainment specially laid on by the tourist authority. This is something to be borne in mind when considering Ariadne's grandmother's delicious dish of snails.

Ariadne clicks off the microphone.

This is quite a speech. Our guide has pulled no punches and her chastened audience falls silent.

'Bravo,' says Nancy quietly.

By now we are deep in the mountains. On either side are steep slopes blanketed with pink-blossomed rock roses, little yellow-faced bee orchids, wild hyacinths of a singing blue. The carpet of wild flowers gives way to steep terracing with untended olive trees and abandoned vineyards. The only sign of human habitation is a few rough stone shelters dotted among the terraces.

Before we reach our destination, Ariadne decides we should learn a little of her grandmother's life and times. The name by which she is known is Kiria Elena. Kiria and Kirios are courtesy titles accorded by children to their elders, and to teachers and doctors and anyone else who merits respect.

'Now I will tell you a little story about my grandmother, Kiria Elena.'

In the old days, she continues, her grandmother told her that life was very strict and there was little time or opportunity for courting, but there were dances at Christmas and festivals at midsummer when young people could walk together to the sanctuary of the Virgin on the headland and eat honey cake and throw flowers into the sea. The flowers were a tradition on the islands, a way that the living could remember the dead and call on their blessing when needed. The outing was an opportunity for courting, and if it should so happen that Whitsun was celebrated before Easter – a baby on the way before the wedding – the Virgin took care that no one carried the blame.

On an island such as this, Ariadne continues, there is much to remember and stories to remember them by. As a young girl, Kiria Elena loved dancing, so she went barefoot all through the winter to save her shoes for the dance. Her young man was a wonderful dancer, the best, as well as handsome and kind and all things a young girl looks for in the man of her dreams. The two fell in love and were married and had a short time for happiness and just enough time for a little daughter to be born, Ariadne's mother and Kiria Elena's only child. And then came the war and the young father, Ariadne's grandfather, was killed in the fighting in the hills.

His companions brought the husband's boots back to the village so his wife would know for certain she was widowed. The boots – calf-high and made of polished black leather cut from a single piece – were stitched to order by the cobbler for every boy when he became a man, with the wearer's initials woven into the pattern so everyone would know they were his. And after they brought back the boots and Kiria Elena knew she was a widow, she never wanted to marry again even though she was still pretty and young.

When her daughter, Ariadne's mother, left the village as soon as she was old enough to take work on the coast, she found herself a husband, Ariadne's father. And because she herself had grown up in the village, she sent Ariadne and her sister to stay with their grandmother in the holidays all through the summer.

Then one year, when it was the end of summer, just before Ariadne was off to Athens to study at university, her grandmother brought out the very same boots from the locked chest where she kept her treasures, and they fitted her granddaughter as perfectly as Cinderella's slippers, even though they were made for a man and moulded exactly to the shape of his foot.

Inviting admiration, Ariadne stretches out a booted foot shod in soft black leather, stitched and moulded to the calf close as a glove.

'See? I'm wearing them now, as I always do whenever I visit Kiria Elena. *Ya-ya* is a strong woman who had to work and look after her family without a man, and so am I. She's proud that I earn my own living and make my own choices. Had she been born in another time, my grandmother would have thought it not right that only sons were given boots, and she would have demanded that the cobbler make her boots of her own. So now, whenever I come to visit, I wear the boots.'

She pauses thoughtfully. 'Although *ya-ya* pretends she doesn't notice, I know she's pleased. She knows that, even though I never met him, my grandfather who is no longer with us is not forgotten.'

The coach slows and turns down a dirt track that runs along the side of a river until it opens out into a wide valley. Overlooking the valley, tucked beneath a steep cliff, is a cluster of stone-built houses rising to a blue-domed basilica. Some look abandoned and the streets are deserted in the midday sun.

We come to a halt in a flurry of dust and a scattering of chickens beside a gate set in a dry-stone wall topped by a prickly cactus hedge. Beyond the gate are a yard and a vine-covered terrace shading a neat single-storey dwelling with a tiled roof. Rusty olive-oil tins planted with scarlet geraniums line the terrace, and preparations for the midday meal are evident from a pile of brushwood and a trestle table covered with a white cloth set ready in the shade.

At the gate waiting to greet us is Ariadne's grandmother, Kiria Elena. She has the same large eyes and aquiline nose as her granddaughter, but her dark hair, though thick and lustrous, is streaked with silver and plaited around her head. Her face, at a distance, seems extraordinarily unlined and her eyes are bright blue rather than dark, as is sometimes the way on the islands.

Ariadne is first to descend from the bus, running up the steps and into her grandmother's open arms. As soon as we are all assembled from the bus, Ariadne's face is bright with happiness as she introduces her guests to her grandmother one by one.

'Kiria Elena wishes me to tell you please to forgive her lack of English. She bids you *kalimera*, you are welcome. As you will notice, there are friends and neighbours come to join the party. We Cretans can never resist a party.'

Behind, comfortably ensconced at the table in confirmation of her words, is a trio of even more elderly folks who, judging from the lined and weathered faces turned to inspect us, might well be the centenarians we have been discussing at the conference.

Ariadne greets each of the onlookers by name with an enthusiastic embrace.

'As you can see, we are all family. I think I was a little spoilt when I was a girl as I always wanted my own way. If *ya-ya* wouldn't let me milk the goat in case she kicked over the bucket, or climb the ladder to collect the olives for fear I might fall, all I had to do was run away to Kirios Nikos or Kiria Lydia or Kirios Alexis and they'd let me do whatever I wanted.'

As she speaks, her eyes light up with happiness.

'I can tell you that Kirios Nikos showed me how to milk the goat without squeezing too hard on the teat so she didn't kick over the bucket, and Kiria Lydia taught me how to tell which herbs were good for medicine, and Kirios Alexis carried me on his shoulders to help with the olive harvest. Now, whenever I return, there's always a gathering and I'm still the little girl who wants her own way.'

There is much laughter at the translation, and Kirios Nikos asks a question.

'Kirios Nikos wants to know if I remember to drink a spoonful of olive oil every day and always add a little ouzo to the water in my glass to make it safe, just as he taught me.'

'And do you?' asks Nancy.

'Of course. I always do what Kirios Nikos tells me.'

This statement, when translated for the audience, is greeted with gales of affectionate laughter.

Ariadne's attention now turns to a couple of firmly lidded plastic buckets set in the shade beside the water pump. When one of the lids is lifted, a mass of enquiring eyes on stalks attached to greeny-yellow bodies protruding from glistening brown shells surge towards the light.

The lid is swiftly replaced at a word from Kiria Elena.

Her grandmother is the authority here, and she is not yet ready to embark on snail preparation. First we are to follow our hostess to the gathering grounds in the vineyards to see what we can find.

Paula and Nancy are already on their feet and eager for the chase, even though Ariadne warns us that we are late in the day for gathering and the molluscs will be hard to find. Snails are most easily picked early in the morning, just before sunrise, when they come out of their hiding places and climb to the topmost tip of the vines to drink the dew.

I wait behind for Aglaia to finish a conversation with Kirios Nikolai on the edible greens to be found in the olive groves in this particular part of the island. Gatherers need to know the lie of the land before setting off on the hunt, as I knew from my time with my young family in Andalusia, where the children learned from their school friends how to gather edible leaves and shoots along the roadside.

In our valley, field mushrooms were found in autumn in the burnt patches left by flash-fires, leaving room for the tender green shoots of asparagus that appeared in spring. In damp corners under the cork oaks that surrounded our house, drifts of snowy-blossomed wild garlic were the first sign that summer was on its way. And in the dry pastures by the sea, we would gather the young rosettes of tall yellow thistles to add to the winter pot, and look for pennyroyal to dry for a medicinal tea, the cure for a summer cold.

Nevertheless, I know from experience on other islands – and in the markets in Athens and Thessaloniki on the mainland – that the Greeks are the plant experts of the Mediterranean littoral. City-dwellers as well as country people head for the hills at weekends in spring and after the first rains of autumn with their knives and gathering baskets.

Aglaia inspects the carpet of wild flowers beneath the olive trees with professional expertise. *Horta*, wild greens, are seasonal and local. Rarest and most prized are the juicy buds of the wild artichoke and the tulip-like bulbs of the tassel hyacinth, *volvi*. Commonest of all – and here in quantity, though too well grown to be worth the gathering – are sow thistle, field poppy, wild fennel and dandelion.

'Greeks all love their *horta* almost as much as they love to tell stories. There are many references to wild foods in the writings of our poets and playwrights. We even use the same names for medicinal plants as our ancestors did.'

She stoops to pluck a hank of feathery green stuff from a tangle of leaves. 'Smell this.' I crush the sprig in my fingers and lift it to my nose.

'Dill?'

'Yes. We call it *anito*. It's what we use for salads and in our *dolmades*, stuffed vine leaves. It's stronger than fennel, *maratho*, which is what we use to flavour the brine for the olives.'

Dried fennel stalks are also used in Spain, I add, to pickle unripened green olives, though I'm aware that Greek olives are only pickled when ripe.

Aglaia nods, then bends down to pluck a slender plant with a little seed-head and leaves all the way up the stalk. 'This is *vlita* – what botanists call amaranth. We like them cooked a little – not too much – and dressed with *ladolemono*, oil and lemon. Sometimes this is all I want to eat in the middle of the day in summer, with maybe a piece of fresh cheese and some good bread from a wood-fired oven and perhaps a slice of ripe tomato with oregano. Or as *hortapita*, a pie we bake for Easter, or in a stuffing for little fried pastries. *Vlita* is very important on the islands, where they keep the old traditions alive. On the mainland, in the villages where snow falls in winter and the ground is still frozen in spring and there are no *horta* for the Easter pies, they dry bunches of *vlita* and hang them in the cellar and soak them when they need them, so they can have fresh greens all year round.'

The difference between Greek and Turkish cooking, Aglaia continues, is very simple. Turkish cooks use spices to flavour their food and Greeks use herbs. And not just any herbs – you won't find pre-blended herbes de Provence sold in Greek supermarkets as you do in France or Britain or America – you must choose the right one for the dish. Except for oregano, which grows wild on Greek hillsides and is used as a flavouring for almost everything. Mint is the herb to use in a crisp vegetable fritter made with eggs, thyme is the essential flavouring for lamb, while the herb most compatible with Cretan snails is rosemary.

Aglaia and I are slow to reach the gathering grounds, and when we do, we find Nancy and Paula sitting together on a rock in the shade of an olive tree, discussing the relative merits of Greek and Italian olive oil. Olive oil is an emotionally charged subject and the discussion is getting heated.

The others – those who have accepted the invitation to take a stroll – are already straggling back home behind Kyria Elena. Our own vineyard pickings are thin. The snails are hiding from the midday sun beneath the thick canopy of vine leaves, or taking shelter in crevasses among the twisted roots. When Aglaia and I show Ariadne the few brown-speckled shells we have managed to winkle from the hiding places, our meagre offerings are greeted with a smile.

'I think we would all go hungry if *ya-ya* hadn't already gathered more than enough to feed us all. And if this was all we had to offer, *ya-ya* would certainly scold us and send us back for more.'

🌿

On our return, there is work to be done rinsing and scrubbing the bucketfuls of delicately patterned brown and cream shells with their slippery little occupants.

Nancy and I are allotted snail-scrubbing, a task made easier since the snails have already cleaned themselves after a week of starvation rations and are speckled with little black scraps, a sign that they've already evacuated their diminutive digestions. Rejected debris, the scraps that litter the shells, are stored at the end of the body, deep inside the shell.

Snails are voracious feeders, capable of working their way through almost anything green and juicy, toxic or not, leaving bite-marks on fungi and heaving up a bucket lid if not firmly weighted down with stones, as I know well from my own experience of snail-gathering, though I'm keeping this to myself.

As we all work together, Ariadne talks quietly of life in the village with her grandmother when she and her sister came every summer for as long as she can remember. As the eldest, it was Ariadne who helped her grandmother with the younger girl and negotiated the transition from the easy living of the coast to the realities of life without plumbing or running water or the convenience of a modern kitchen or even access to a supermarket – an apprenticeship that forged a strong bond between the two, not least because Ariadne was always eager to learn.

'I was a curious child and asked questions all the time, though *ya-ya* didn't seem to mind. All Greeks are curious as cats. In ordinary life, everyone wants to know everything about everyone so they can make it into a story. It doesn't matter what it is – who's courting who, or just something like what people ate for dinner. *Ya-ya* learned as I did, from watching and learning. She didn't need a book to tell her how to cook snails or prepare *trahana* or bake *paximadia* or know when the olives are ready for gathering.'

The snails are nearly ready for the pot. Ariadne pushes her hand into the bucket, disturbing the forest of semi-transparent bodies and pinhead eyes, allowing the shells to trickle between her fingers like worry beads. Then she fills the bucket with water from the well, and the little black scraps float to the surface.

'See this? This is what must be rinsed away in fresh water every day till there's no more left. I always loved to do this when I was a child.'

The snails are ready for salting, the final stage before they're judged ready for the pot.

The shining brown shells froth white under showers of salt. Ariadne rinses off the foam in a bucket set under the pump, hands working to free the sticky covering. Half a dozen more saltings and sluicings are required before the snails are declared ready for cooking.

Meanwhile a fire has been lit with the brushwood and a boiling pot set to simmer.

'I hope everyone is hungry. *Ya-ya* thanks you for your patience. She knows Americans like fast food and our snails are very slow. But I tell her you are special Americans who are happy to wait.'

This statement, when translated for those who speak only Greek, is greeted with shouts of laughter.

Kiria Elena inspects the buckets, gives the shells a final scrub under the pump and tips the snails into the boiling pot with a loud whoosh and a clatter.

Ariadne translates her grandmother's instructions.

'Kiria Elena says to tell you that when the pot boils, the froth must be skimmed with a branch of rosemary. This must be done three times until there's no more froth. And then the snails are clean and ready for the *bouboutie*, which, as I think you will remember, is the noise the shells make when you stir them into the sauce. Kiria Elena makes the best *bouboutie* in sauce you will ever taste.'

The ingredients for the sauce – big greenish-red tomatoes chopped into juicy chunks, fat purple onions sliced and sprinkled with salt – are left to simmer gently with olive oil and wine in a shallow raw-iron pan, much like that used for a Spanish paella, set over the coals in place of the snail-pot.

Under the fig tree, the trestle table is set ready with bowls and glasses, wine in jugs, and water fetched from the stream in a *pithoi*, the tall, pointy-based earthenware jar which is also used to store oil or wine, which has been left to cool in the shade. There is, too, a basket of the barley bread, *paximadia*, without which a meal cannot be complete, a bowl of *trahana me tiri*, tiny scraps of the pasta-like dough cooked in soured milk and finished with a handful of crumbled white cheese, and an earthenware serving dish piled with a steaming heap of Aglaia's favourite salad, *vlita ladolemono*.

By now the snails have been stirred into their sauce and are clicking merrily against the sides of the pot. Ariadne lifts the lid and inhales the fragrance, releasing puffs of scented steam. Picking up one of the shells between thumb and forefinger, she loosens its occupant with a quick twist of a cactus thorn, pops it into her mouth and chews appreciatively.

The snails are ready and Kiria Elena takes over, providing each bowl with a handful of crushed barley-rusk and topping it with a ladleful of the shiny brown shells slicked with olive oil and scarlet juice.

We all take our places at the table to receive our bowls and thorns, some of us more cautiously than others. The occupants of the slippery shells, once prised loose, are juicy and chewy and taste deliciously of their rich red sauce. Talk continues as the bowls are slowly emptied – no one can eat snails in a hurry – as Kiria Elena presides over the feast and Ariadne refills glasses with water and wine.

Once the debris has been cleared from the table – bowls scooped out with a spoonful of *trahana* – there are ripe green figs, the first of the season plucked straight from the tree, a creamy fresh cheese to eat with walnuts and honey, and little cups of sweet black Greek coffee brewed over the fire.

Conversation and laughter flow around the excellence of the food, the delights of home-pressed wine, the pleasure of the day, the beauty of the countryside, happiness to be found in good fellowship and a final round of toasts drunk in little glasses of ouzo.

Farewells completed, sleepy and replete with good food and wine, we scarcely notice the rapidity of descent on the homeward journey – a blessing in disguise, considering that our driver is in a hurry to return to his family before nightfall and deliver us to our beds.

The following day, free to wander on the last day of the conference with my sketchbook among the ruins of Knossos, I notice the tasselled heads of wild barley among the grasses that have found a foothold in the tumbled stones. There is, too, among the silvery tufts of wild olive and the twisted roots of a grapevine, a scattering of snail shells.

Retreating to the cool of the marble-floored museum among plaster copies of artefacts too valuable to be left unguarded and glass cases containing four-thousand-year-old domestic implements considered of no commercial value, I join a group of schoolchildren, excited and curious, bubbling like yeast among the tourists.

To the island's children, the utensils on display are the stuff of everyday living, their uses known and understood. No need of labels to explain that the stack of earthenware jars with pointed bases and narrow mouths, *pithoi*, are used for storing olive oil and wine, or that the glazed pottery bowls restored from fragments can be warmed on a charcoal fire when rennetting milk for cheese, or are convenient for kneading flour with water before setting dough to rise, or salting snails as Kiria Elena prepared them for the pot.

I settle down to paint in the shade of a bay tree, a soothing patch of green. Midday is hotter than Hades among these barren stones, and my paint dries on the paper as soon as I lift the brush. From these same stones rose sun-struck Icarus, borne upwards on eagle feathers until Apollo took offence and singed his wings.

Legends such as this are ten a penny among the islanders, one story clipped to the other like links on a chain. The mountain people of Crete, Ariadne's ancestors, are an ancient race, older even than the palace-builders of Knossos. They were here long before the mainland Greeks made the maze where Theseus fought the Minotaur. They were still here when the marble halls were swallowed up by the sea.

Nature was generous to the wanderers who first set foot on her shores. Nomads from the steppes of Asia who crossed an unknown sea in fragile leather coracles with their flocks and herds found themselves in paradise. There were nuts and fruits free for the gathering – wild almond and pear trees, grapevines fertilised by wild bees, olive trees with bitter little fruits that could be pressed for oil. Among the grasses on which they pastured their flocks were emmer wheat and barley. Over the centuries they learned to cultivate the grain and plant vineyards and olive groves on man-made terraces carved from the hillsides.

The changes that came were rapid and final, a story told in abandoned terracings, untended vineyards and uncropped pastures, sucking the life from mountain villages where only the old remain, their usefulness outgrown, their knowledge of no more value than a slick of olive juice scraped from a *pithoi* dragged from the depths of the seabed.

The schoolchildren wandering round the museum's exhibits

have no appetite for a diet of barley bread and snails, and even less desire to gather cash-crops in the olive groves. Not even Ariadne would want to live as her grandmother lives, still less those of us who eat our fill of whatever we like whenever we want and sleep and eat in warmth and comfort in centrally heated homes, work in air-conditioned offices and travel everywhere in cars. Nor, for that matter, would the chemists and nutritionists gathered together in a conference hotel to evaluate the findings of the Seven Countries Study after fifty years of taking notes and making charts. As for the food writers among us – I speak for myself but have no doubt the same is true of Paula, Nancy and Aglaia – there's only so much talk of monounsaturates and anti-oxidants a person can take.

Yesterday, on our journey back down the hill from the village, I began to wonder what Ariadne herself had learned from our expedition into the mountains, whether she thought her little group of volunteers had come to a better understanding of the famous Cretan Diet they were assembled to discuss.

Her answer is simple and direct. 'I live in the city. Of course I read the magazines and newspapers that tell us to eat so much of this and not so much of that because the chemists have done the science. But I have always known that *ya-ya* cooks good food for the happiness it brings and the pride she takes in what she does.'

Kiria Elena's only regret, her granddaughter continues, is that there are no young people left in the villages to learn from the old folks to take pleasure in what's set on the table, be respectful of what comes from the earth and use it in its proper season.

'*Ya-ya* never went to school, but she's wiser than a whole library full of books. Perhaps your experts don't understand this important truth. Perhaps they don't want to see what's right under their noses.'

BOUBOUTIE (SNAILS BUBBLED IN BROTH)

The name of this venerable preparation is onomatopoeic and derived, some say, from the tap-tap of the shells as they bubble about in the pot. Others maintain it derives from the foam the molluscs produce when scrubbed with salt. Whatever the truth, once the little fellows have undergone their preliminary bubbling, you are free to finish them, shelled or unshelled, in whatever way you would cook any other meat. Here they're finished in their shells with tomato and chilli flavoured with sage.

Serves 4–6
1 kg large live snails (all land-snails are edible)
sea or kosher or dishwasher salt (plenty)

For the sauce
4–5 tablespoons olive oil
1 medium onion, peeled and diced
3–4 garlic cloves, peeled and crushed
1 sprig sage
2–3 bay leaves
1 generous glass red wine
1 tablespoon ouzo or raki
1 kg ripe tomatoes, skinned and chopped, or tinned
2–3 dried chillies, crushed
salt

To prepare live snails, you may either buy them ready starved, or keep them in a large lidded bucket (with breathing holes) for 3–4 days to a week, rinsing off the gunge every day. The less they eat, the less gunge they produce. There are those who feed them with aromatic herbs or lettuce leaves, and others who sprinkle them with bran as a final meal. I do none of these things.

Once starved and rinsed, scrub the snails under running water with rough salt, rinsing off the baba – the white gloop they exude when subjected to such unkindness. Continue with the salting and rinsing until there's no more gloop.

Transfer the clean snails to a large pot with enough plain water to cover, then bring gradually to the boil so that the snails don't get scared and shrink right back into their shells but think it's just a shower of summer rain. Once the water boils, skim off the foam that rises, turn down the heat, and simmer for 10–20 minutes depending on the size of the snails, then drain.

The snails are now ready for their sauce. You may if you wish remove them from their shells and nip off the little black cloaca at the end. Or you can omit this step and have the pleasure of sucking the sauce off the shells and winkling the molluscs from their shelter with a sharp instrument – a small bendable fork with the middle tine bent inwards, a toothpick, or a cactus prickle.

To prepare the sauce, warm the oil gently in a shallow pan and add the onion and garlic. Fry for a moment. Add the sage sprig, bay leaves, wine and ouzo or raki, and bring to the boil to evaporate the alcohol. Stir in the tomatoes and chilli and leave to bubble uncovered for 20–30 minutes until you have a rich thick sauce. Allow to cool a little before you stir in the snails, adding enough water to dilute the sauce to a depth at which all the shells are covered. Bring to the boil again, turn down the heat, cover loosely with a lid and simmer for 15–20 minutes until the snails are well flavoured and the sauce reduced to its previous thickness. Taste and add salt.

This dish will keep hot without spoiling. Ladle on to crumbled *paximadia* or bread rolls dried and browned in the oven.

TRAHANA ME MELITZANES (PASTA SHREDS WITH AUBERGINES AND ONION)

Scraps of *trahana*, a primitive little hand-made pasta, were found in the storage jars at the palace of Knossos. Travellers never leave their island without it: *trahana*, it's fair to suppose, provisioned Agamemnon's ships as they sailed to Troy to recapture runaway Helen. The pasta can be made with any milled or crushed grain, which is formed into a dough using any liquid from milk and water to eggs to yoghurt – it's simply a way of combining a grain food with a protein source for storage. The alternative grain to *trahana* is bulgar wheat, which works with the same accompaniments and can be eaten savoury or sweet.

Serves 4–6
500 g strong bread flour (unbleached stoneground is perfect)
1 teaspoon salt
2 large eggs, beaten
100 g plain yoghurt

For the sauce
2 large firm aubergines, sliced into thick chips
100 ml olive oil
2 large onions, peeled and sliced vertically
2 garlic cloves, peeled and chopped
1 tablespoon tomato purée
500 ml stock or water
salt and pepper

Prepare the *trahana* first. In a large bowl, mix the flour with the salt, then slowly work in the eggs and yoghurt with your hand until you have a few pieces of very stiff dough. If you need more liquid, add a little water. If the mixture is too soft, add more flour. Leave the dough, covered with a cloth, to rest and dry out a little – overnight in a warm kitchen or in summer sunshine on a dry day.

Soak the aubergine chips in salted water for half an hour, drain thoroughly and squeeze dry (this is only necessary if the aubergines are a little elderly).

Heat the olive oil in a large frying pan and fry the onions and garlic gently, sprinkled with a little salt, until soft and golden – allow 10 minutes. Push the onion and garlic aside, add the aubergine and continue to fry gently, turning the pieces in the hot oil until golden and soft. Add the tomato purée mixed with the stock or water, bring to the boil and cook for another 5 minutes to blend into a thickish sauce. Taste and season.

Grate the *trahana* straight into the hot sauce and simmer, stirring to avoid sticking, for 5 minutes or so until the little shreds are cooked and nearly all the liquid has been absorbed. Ladle into bowls and serve without delay.

Notes: To dry *trahana* for storage, leave out the salt when preparing. Grate the dough on to a clean cloth over a roomy tray, allowing the gratings to fall loosely in a single layer like grains of wheat or barley. Leave to dry out on the cloth for 2–3 days in a warm dry kitchen, tossing them lightly every now and then to keep the pieces separate and evenly dehydrated until they're as hard as catapult pellets. Thereafter they can be stored in an airtight jar more or less for ever.

To prepare as a breakfast dish, treat as rolled or porridge oats: bring equal amounts of milk and water to the boil and stir in a handful of *trahana* per half-litre of liquid. Simmer for 3 minutes or so, until all the liquid has been absorbed. Eat with honey and yoghurt, or with grated cheese for supper.

To prepare as a pilau or risotto, treat as you would round rice: fry in a little olive oil with your chosen flavourings, then add the cooking liquid and simmer until soft (10 minutes, no more).

VLITA LADOLEMONO (SPRING SHOOTS WITH OIL AND LEMON)

Amaranth – a member of the spinach family that grows wild on Mediterranean hillsides – has been brought into cultivation for the sake of its leaves, seeds and tender young shoots since classical times. Among other wild or semi-cultivated shoots prepared as cooked salads are wild asparagus (bitter *Asparagus acutifolius* as well as the milder-flavoured cultivar, *A. officinalis*), thistle rosettes, young dandelion, chicory, black bryony (shoots only – the berries are toxic), malva, wild spinach and hop shoots.

Serves 4
1 kg amaranth shoots or thin green asparagus

For the ladolemono dressing
150 ml olive oil
juice of 1 lemon

Trim the shoots – some of them are both woody and sandy – and rinse thoroughly. Steam or cook in boiling salted water until just tender – 3–4 minutes, just as you would cultivated asparagus – and drain immediately in a colander under a splash of cold water to stop the cooking process. Transfer to a serving dish.

Prepare the oil and lemon dressing. Mix the olive oil in a jug with enough lemon juice to please your palate – it all depends on the sweetness of the oil and the bitterness of the greens. Dress the salad or hand the jug round separately, as you wish. Salt or pepper is not necessary.

MELOPITTA (CRETAN HONEY CAKE)

Honey cakes are baked to give comfort in sorrow at funerals, and for joy and happiness at weddings, Easter and Christmas.

Serves at least 12
350 g plain flour
2 teaspoons baking powder
1 teaspoon ground cinnamon
350 g ground almonds
6 eggs, separated
350 g light olive oil
175 g honey
juice and grated zest of 3 oranges
1 tablespoon flaked almonds

To finish
175 g honey
4 tablespoons water
1 tablespoon orange-flower water (optional)
1–2 curls finely pared orange peel
1 small cinnamon stick

(recipe continued overleaf)

Preheat the oven to 180°C/Gas 4 and oil a 20 cm square baking tin or similar.

Sift the flour with the baking powder and cinnamon and mix in the ground almonds. Whisk the egg yolks with the oil and honey until light and fluffy. Fold the egg-yolk mixture into the flour, alternating with the orange juice – the mixture should be soft but not too runny. Stir in the orange zest. Whisk the egg whites until stiff and fold them in.

Pour the mixture into the prepared tin and sprinkle the almonds over the top. Bake for about an hour, until the cake is well browned, shrunk from the sides of the tin and the top is firm to the touch. Check after 40 minutes and cover the cake with foil if the top looks like burning.

Meanwhile, make the syrup. In a small pan, simmer the honey, water, orange-flower water (if using), orange peel and cinnamon for 3–4 minutes. Strain and pour over the cake when it comes out of the oven.

To serve, cut into neat little squares and serve with more honey and Greek yoghurt drained overnight until thick enough to hold the shape of a spoon.

You may, if you wish, wrap the squares up neatly as little parcels in greaseproof paper for your guests to carry away as sweet memories when they leave. This is traditional and serves much the same purpose as the goodie-bags handed out to children at the end of a party.

Maui

MAUI, MOST FERTILE OF THE ISLANDS OF HAWAII, is the place to go for a second honeymoon. The first can be anywhere. When two people are in love, who cares if it rains or shines? My own first honeymoon was something of a disaster since the groom, proprietor at the time of *Private Eye*, was recalled to deal with a little problem of libel raised by Winston Churchill's son Randolph. Not so little, as it happened, since the libellee was Winston Churchill himself and his son was in no mood to let a scurrilous satirical magazine off the hook. In the event, negotiations were successful and the magazine was saved, but Nicholas's ownership came to an end.

We never managed that second honeymoon, not least because four children born in quick succession put paid to any thoughts of romantic holidays for some twenty years until the children were grown and could fend for themselves. Practicalities got in the way of any honeymoon re-run and with my companion in life, the father of my children, off somewhere else on other business – a common experience for two writers under the same roof – I am here on Maui alone. But if we had had the opportunity for a second honeymoon – and if Nicholas's career as Soho's king of satire in the sixties had been a less expensive business – the island would have been about as perfect as anyone could wish.

For the visitor on Maui, anything is possible if you have the wallet for it. Unless, that is, you go native and never leave – riding the wave by day and slinging a hammock under the stars by night, free as the nectar-sipping hummingbirds that poke their sharp little beaks into the hibiscus flowers that close up by night and unfold scarlet petals every morning in the sunshine. Myths are easy to spin in lotus-land, paradise on earth – and many of them are true.

Residents of the fiftieth State of the Union – at least in the closing years of the twentieth century, the time of my visit – are a mix-and-match of incomers, some new, some old, and a few who can claim line of descent from the original inhabitants, Polynesian ocean-wanderers who settled the islands around fifteen hundred years ago.

First to drop anchor in one of her sheltered bays, Captain James Cook kept a ship's journal that took note not only of latitude and longitude, but of the wonders observed along the way. The entry for what he named the Sandwich Islands for his benefactor – the gambling earl who gave his name to what became his compatriots' favourite snack – describes a race of tall, well-built, well-fed, handsome people, living peacefully from fishing and farming in small communities by the shore. The gallant captain – blue-eyed and yellow-haired and suitably regal in his naval uniform – was greeted by the islanders as the long-awaited incarnation of Loni, their all-powerful harvest-god come to claim his dues at the end of summer, the right time of year. When the captain demanded that the galleys of his two ships be replenished from the islanders' well-stocked store cupboards, they were happy to oblige with breadfruit, dried fish and coconuts. Second time around, when the ships returned at the end of winter from a failed attempt to batter their way through the ice of the Northwest Passage, things didn't go so well and the captain, caught in an onshore skirmish after a misunderstanding over ownership of a skiff, was returned to his shipmates as a bag of well-scrubbed bones.

Things don't always go as planned. It's in the nature of the job that travel journalists are destined to find themselves, like Captain Cook, in the right place at the wrong time: checked into the Arctic in an ice-hotel in high summer, camel-riding in the desert in the month when it rains. Or indeed, as now, in the most luxurious resort on an island paradise in the low season.

The Hawaiian archipelago, a necklace of some hundred and thirty volcanic peaks flung across eighteen hundred miles of the blue Pacific, is something of a geological Johnny-come-lately. Fiery magma flows along the ocean floor beneath, cooling the earth's white-hot heart, constantly throwing up new volcanic peaks and reclaiming old. Most of these peaks are no more than perches for seabirds, but a few are habitable.

Polynesian ocean-wanderers settled the islands sometime between the second and sixth century, beaching their canoes, unloading their pigs and chickens, planting coconuts for food and shelter, and settling down to cultivate their crops and live the good life undisturbed for more than a thousand years.

As seafarers, the Polynesians caught fish and ate it as nature delivered – in the raw.

Eaten without delay, fish flesh is firm and sweet and silky on the tongue and has none of the fishiness familiar to those who live on land. Fishermen know this – perhaps not the casual weekend fly-fisherman, but those who earn their livelihood from the sea.

Tired of the uncertainties of trawling an unpredictable ocean for food, the newcomers dug fishponds by the shore. And once a year, when the tuna shoals migrated from their deep-sea feeding grounds to breed in shallower waters, the inhabitants of the islands remembered who they were: sea-wolves, hungry for prey. The feast of fish flesh that followed the hunt was – and still is – a reminder of restless wanderings relived in song and dance and the sweet-salt taste of the sea.

There are other, more casual ways to appreciate the delicacy of fish flesh eaten raw. It's the fisherman's fast food, free for the taking, the oceanic equivalent of a handful of berries plucked from a hedgerow. Take a walk along a quayside wherever the day-boats land their catch, and you will, likely as not, pass a fisherman pausing for a moment to peel a prawn or fillet a fish or flip open a mussel-shell and pop the morsel in his mouth.

As a market snack, raw fish is convenient and easy – and with any luck will come with a squeeze of lemon, as might happen in an oyster bar in London or New York or anywhere else where a dozen succulent bivalves find a market. And as it does, though in less sophisticated surroundings, in the port of Bari in Puglia where raw cuttlefish is the traditional Friday fast-day food. And in the fish market where I did my weekly shop in Andalusia, my favourite stallholder would absent-mindedly fillet a silvery anchovy with a flick of the thumb and chew it reflectively, while his customers – me too – tested the freshness of the catch by tasting its salinity with a finger poked in the brine – the longer the boat has been at sea before landing the catch, the saltier the juices.

While other raw-fish preparations of the Pacific Rim – sushi, sashimi and ceviche – are appreciated well outside their lands of origin, Hawaii's secret is poke. Poke or pokee or poki – opinions differ on how to spell it – is a preparation of raw tuna, *mahi*, with a preference for yellow-fin, second only to the mighty blue-fin in size and strength. A full grown yellow-fin measures six foot nose to tail, weighs twice as much as a sumo wrestler – a sport popular on the islands – and requires at least four canoe-loads of muscular Polynesian seafarers working together to bring it home for lunch. Poke, as a result, was a ceremonial dish that could only be prepared as a result of co-operation between tribes, and only when the tuna shoals were on migration from their deep-water feeding grounds to the shallow waters where they spawn. Young fish need nursery slopes, just as young children need safe places to play.

Although yellow-fin, blue-fin and their lesser brethren – skipjack, frigate mackerel, bonito – are still caught in quantity by the big commercial trawlers in the waters around the archipelago, as a high-value fish saleable throughout the world they rarely come to market on Hawaii.

Poke, as far as I can ascertain in my research before departure, disappeared from the traditional menu when Hawaii's indigenous fishermen relinquished their fishing grounds to Japanese

trawlermen. With the raw material no longer available – at least for free – there was no reason to launch the great seagoing canoes and work together to gather the harvest. And no reason either to prepare a ceremonial dish that tells the story of a nation's beginnings.

Nevertheless, long after the reason has been forgotten, the memory remains. Dishes that tell us who we are and where we come from, I have learned over the years, are far more than a list of ingredients and method. They might disappear for a generation or two – discarded as evidence of the deprivations of war, or dismissed as unacceptably primitive – but sooner or later, they reappear.

While I am on the islands to experience what is billed as the new cuisine of Hawaii, a sophisticated take on traditional regional cooking, I have hopes of a beach shack somewhere along the coast that serves bite-sized chunks of raw tuna dressed with sesame and salt, even if only as a by-blow in a sushi bar.

Hawaiian Regional is an offshoot of Pacific Rim, which came from California Style, which took its lead from Alice Waters at Chez Panisse in San Francisco. Alice's Mediterranean-style home-cooking inspired a new wave of innovative young chefs whose cooking is edgier and sharper than Alice's laid-back no-choice menu, a style better suited to Los Angeles, where Wolfgang Puck at Spago serves *pizza in bianco* topped with caviar to Hollywood royalty.

A second wave of even edgier, more innovative chefs, trained in Japanese knife-work and influenced by Mexican fast food, developed Pacific Rim, a style that adds Latino, Southeast Asia and Hawaiian to the original mix. The new cuisine of Hawaii, as interpreted in the luxurious watering-holes of the archipelago by chefs trained on the mainland, takes whatever it wants from anywhere it likes.

My presence in the islands on behalf of the readership of

House & Garden is partly to appreciate the joys of Hawaiian Regional food and partly to report – on behalf of a readership that can afford long-distance travel to sunny places in winter – on the facilities for rest and relaxation in Maui's newly refurbished Ritz Carlton.

The second duty of the conscientious travel writer – as I see it – is to report on the story behind the story. As a food writer, I look for whatever it is – ingredient, dish, way of preparing or gathering or cooking a foodstuff – that says this place is unlike any other.

Sometimes I know what I'm looking for before I arrive, sometimes it's just waiting to be found, sometimes it's vanished for good. I'm hoping that poke – as one of a number of raw-fish preparations reincarnated in Pacific Rim cuisine – has survived in its original island form as a beach snack as well as in new and sophisticated Hawaiian Regional form.

Regionality is relative. Hawaii, as the only provisioning stop on the trans-Pacific route, has long been in the business of changing her culinary habits in order to give her tourists what they want. Once the archipelago had been mapped and identified as conveniently positioned between the shores of America, Asia and Australia, the inhabited islands – mostly Oahu and the Big Island, Hawaii itself – became a recreational and re-provisioning opportunity for ships on the trans-Pacific passage. First to take advantage of the stopping point were merchant ships and whalers, mostly Portuguese and New Englanders. In exchange for island hospitality, the visitors delivered syphilis, measles, mumps and hard liquor, all of which proved fatal to those who lacked natural immunity. As a result, a century after first contact, three in every four of the original inhabitants had vanished.

Those islanders who survived the first onslaught retreated from contact with the incomers and showed no desire to take employment in the sugar plantations established by European entrepreneurs. As a result, the plantation owners brought in labour from elsewhere – mostly the Caribbean and the Philippines. Meanwhile the fisheries were sold on to Japanese trawlermen and a variety of commercially valuable crops – pineapples, macadamia – were planted on land previously under subsistence cultivation; the fishponds by the shore were left unstocked; the coconut plantations were cropped for copra – dried coconut flesh – rather than as a source of food, refreshment and material for building and furnishings; and even the tuna fisheries, most valuable of the deep-sea harvest, were no longer available for free but were turned into a source of profit for pelagic factory-ships.

The island of Maui, as observed from the air, is a matching pair of emerald-green volcanic peaks joined together by a narrow bridge of land, surrounded by black rock, white sand and a turquoise sea.

My destination, the Ritz Carlton, while undeniably magnificent and well provided with marble halls and exquisite plantings, stands empty of visitors and silent.

Management explains the problem with an apologetic spread of the hands and a smile. What can you do? It's the down-season. Her name is Lisa, and she has a very sweet smile. The trouble in the down-season is that the therapists are re-training, the golf course is undergoing a facelift, the health spa is closed for a make-over and the kitchen, while able to provide an excellent breakfast by the pool, is unfortunately unable to offer service in the dining room.

This, I assure Lisa, poses no problem, as it will allow me, with her invaluable assistance, to undertake an in-depth exploration of island gastronomy both traditional and new in its most innocent form, as experienced by the natives themselves.

'Perfect,' says Lisa, adding that she's sorry I will not be able to experience the delights of the high season at first hand. However, a tour of the facilities will be a way of assessing the pleasures awaiting high-season visitors, though we can agree it is not quite the same as the full makeover in the beauty parlour and a round of golf with the hotel's professional. I keep it to myself that I've never yet had a makeover that didn't leave me looking like Joan Collins on a bad-face day. Or that my most recent experience of the royal game was when I was seven years old and obliged to carry the putter for my mother when she won the Coca-Cola Cup at Punta del Este in Uruguay. Coca-Cola, nanny told me, was popular at my mother's diplomatic cocktail parties since the ladies took it with whisky so their husbands didn't know what they were drinking. These thoughts occupy me while we take a tour of inspection, starting on the orchid-draped terrace where breakfast is served and ending with my balconied accommodation at the non-business end of the hotel, well away from all the refurbishing.

Before she leaves me to shower and unpack, Lisa wants to know if there's anything particular I have in mind for tomorrow.

I explain about the poke and my hopes of discovering the preparation in its original form. There is no doubt, I can see from my advance copy of the book, of the popularity of raw fish among the chefs who have contributed their recipes to *The New Cuisine of Hawaii*.

Lisa promises enquiries. In the interim, an air-conditioned vehicle with guide and driver – his name is Sean and, in spite of the Irishness of the name, he is island-born – will be at my disposal first thing in the morning. If there's anything that comes to mind between now and then, Sean will be able and willing to deliver the goods. Meanwhile, in the absence of any certainty concerning poke – I detect a note of disbelief in Lisa's voice – perhaps my readers might appreciate a visit to an orchid farm under the guidance of the owner, one of the island's characters?

Taking the course of least resistance – who knows what might happen along the way? – I agree that orchids seem suitably luxurious for the readers of my magazine, who are sure to be interested in a character – though with the proviso that characters, in my experience, are either an invaluable source of information or taciturn to the point of non-communication.

Lisa cannot offer an opinion from first-hand experience, but she does know that the orchid character is of Portuguese origin, from the Azores, and his orchids are sent out all over the world, including to hotels of the Ritz Carlton group in London and Paris.

As for the rest, Lisa considers that poke may not necessarily be available in its original form since ordinary Hawaiians buy their tuna in tins from the supermarket, along with tinned salmon and tinned sardines, which are cheap and nourishing and don't go off in the heat. And while sushi, the sophisticated Japanese version of Hawaii's poke, is certainly a popular fast food on Waikiki Beach, the most sought-after kind is the vegetarian option, the avocado-stuffed California roll.

I wake early next morning to the rattle of palm trees and crashing of surf. The previous night's supper was calorie-controlled consommé with a salad of lily buds and hibiscus blossoms. Both are edible and interesting but insubstantial, and I'm hungry enough to do justice to the full Hawaiian.

The full Hawaiian – mango muffins with bacon, syrup and cream – is available on the breakfast loggia, a shady terrace under a jacaranda tree beside the inkiest of ink-black ornamental pools fed by the splashiest of waterfalls that bounces over lava rocks through stands of yellow canna lilies, purple tree-orchids and white-flowered jasmine. Among the greenery flits an assortment of rainbow-coloured butterflies and nectar-sipping hummingbirds. Even in the down-season – especially in the down-season – a tropical island is about as close to paradise as a person avoiding a calorie-counted diet can get.

Finding me lost in reverie of taking up permanent residence on the island – how could a person not be wonderfully productive in a writing-shed under the palm trees? – Lisa arrives to inform me that vehicle and driver await.

The Cadillac has smoked windows, white upholstery, air-conditioning – and Sean.

'Pleased to meet you, ma'am.' Sean has bright-blue eyes, sandy hair and greets me with a wide smile and a firm handshake. I reciprocate with equal enthusiasm. We are to be together for the next two days. And Sean, source of information on all things Hawaiian not available from guidebooks, is my best hope for a glimpse of the inside story. Quite apart from my responsibilities to report on haute cuisine and high luxury to the readership, I am as curious about the incomers, second-wave settlers, as I am about the original inhabitants.

It seems to me, from my travels as a food writer, that islands attract other islanders. And islanders are naturally suspicious of incomers, particularly mainlanders. I am beginning to hope that my own credentials as an islander – albeit from the other side of the world – might serve me well on this particular island, where at least we share a language. There will, I hope, be plenty of opportunity to find what I'm looking for over the next few days, even if Sean and Lisa are by no means convinced of its existence, even as an important element of New Hawaiian Cuisine.

And what, Sean enquires, as the electronic gates close behind us, is his passenger's special field of interest? I explain about the food-writing as it relates to my interest in Hawaiian gastronomy, with particular reference to poke.

Sean laughs. As an Irishman, albeit Hawaiian-born, he wouldn't eat his fish raw if it was the last food on earth. Or any fish at all, for that matter, cooked or raw. This admission is followed by a repeat of the poke joke, and we both laugh. Since we are to be in each other's company for the next two days, laughter is good.

I press a button to lower the window and the heat pours in. Sean reverses the window and I don't argue. The outside world is wet and hot and full of creatures that sting. Mosquitoes the size of coffee-saucers splatter the windscreen. I suspect it's hotter than Hades out there – or will be at midday, which is the time when everyone who's not soft in the head, in Sean's opinion, slings the hammock on the lanai and goes to sleep all afternoon.

I am not so soft in the head that I don't catch Sean's drift.

Today, Sean informs me, there will be no time for traditional hammock-slinging – or indeed much chance of poke – since his orders are to take his important guest to see the sights and meet the local characters. In any case, we have a date at the orchid farm and that, as one of the island's main attractions, is not to be missed.

Tomorrow is another day. Tomorrow perhaps there will be poke. The Cadillac is quiet and the highway smooth. I ask Sean about his family. His parents were immigrants from the Emerald Isle, the old country, who took US citizenship when Hawaii joined the Union in 1959, which, in Sean's opinion, is the best thing they ever did. Nevertheless he wears a shamrock on St Patrick's Day and is married to a good woman with whom he has two kids who are encouraged to remember their paternal roots.

The children's grandparents, continues Sean, have recently retired to Honolulu to be near the medics, depriving his good lady of useful babysitting. Sean has no wish to move his own family to the big city even when he and his wife need the medics.

'Maui is a good place for kids and old folk. Not like Honolulu.'

And no, Sean has never paid a visit to the Old Country, even though his roots are certainly there, and has no desire to do so.

His mother's stories of nine brothers and sisters in a single room —
or no room at all — as the family was landless and often roofless,
cured him of any sentimentality about his ancestral homeland.
His mother was sent as an orphan by Carmelite nuns to care for
the sick in the hospital in Honolulu. The nuns went home but
their orphaned novice stayed behind to marry his father, a sea-
man from Cork, hospitalised on the island for a broken leg.

'The kids like to hear the stories, and maybe sometime
they'll go back and take a look. But we're all Hawaiians now,
and that's how it should be.'

Sean, so far, is proving an excellent source of non-Hawaiian
information, leaving Joe Bento, supplier of orchids to the stars,
my best hope of usable copy.

Fortunately I am not, on this trip, confined to matters of the
kitchen. Excursions into matters of interest of a non-culinary
nature are permitted. Such, I hope, as orchids. We are to meet at
the only gas station on the north side of the island, where Joe
collects his orders and delivers his orchids to be couriered to the
mainland.

Joe, whatever the colourfulness of his character, is in no
hurry to greet his visitor. The reverse. He appears to be asleep
on his feet, propped against the cattle-catcher of a battered four-
wheeler stuffed with spidery greenery, with a bushwhacker hat
tipped over his face.

Sean gives him a quick burst of the horn and the hat tips
back, revealing a weather-beaten face and eyes whose colour is
impossible to detect behind the aviator shades.

His greeting is short and to the point.

'So you're the scribbler. Get in.'

I do as I'm told and the engine roars into life.

'Mind you bring her back safe,' shouts Sean over the din,
whacking the rear of Joe's vehicle as if it were a horse.

Joe grunts. He is short, wiry, has seen at least seventy

summers, and doesn't do idle chitchat. I rather like him for his ability to communicate only when necessary, even though I fear his character might be the non-communicating kind of colourful. And anyway, even if he did care to share his thoughts with his passenger, the engine and road preclude oral communication, necessary or otherwise.

We rattle up a side road and then turn on to a track through a green avenue of what looks like very tall grasses, coming to a halt at a gap in the vegetation. The grasses reach right down to the edge of the ocean, swathes of the greenery patched with blackened stumps.

'Sugarcane,' Joe announces as he cuts the engine and points. 'See the burn? Lazy bastards. Makes the canes easier to cut. There's a law against it. Makes no difference.'

The engine splutters back into life and the vehicle buckets upwards through dense forest until a broad rim of felled wildwood opens up into new plantings.

'Macadamia,' shouts Joe over the rattle of the engine. The noise stops abruptly as we come to a halt among neat lines of young trees with narrow leaves and clusters of green seedpods.

'Good money. Third after beef and pineapples if you can handle a ten-year wait. Same as my orchids.'

Joe turns to inspect his passenger through narrowed eyes. 'Know anything about orchids?'

I hesitate. My only experience is in the jungles of Mexico, where clumps of orchids are common enough, although it was rare to find them in flower. The vanilla orchid, a particularly modest variety with insignificant blossoms, was doubly hard to spot.

'You write about food?'

Indeed I do.

'Know anything about *prosçiut*?'

Of course. *Prosçiut* is Portugal's serrano, mountain ham,

salt-cured and wind-dried, prepared with the haunches of the black-foot pigs of the old Iberico breed that forage the frontier forests between Spain and Portugal. Serrano hams, I continue, provisioned the fragile wooden ships that sailed towards the sunset with Cristóbal Colón. Had the sailor from Genoa managed to persuade the king of Portugal to unlock his coffers in 1492, there would have been no need to offer his services to the Spanish queen, and Portugal would have been lord of the Spanish Main.

Joe laughs. 'Guess you'll pass.'

He unwraps a package. Slices of what looks like salt-cured air-dried ham have been sandwiched between thick slabs of dense-crumbed yellowish bread speckled with little scraps of bran.

'Here. Eat.'

I do as I am bid.

The bread is cut from a loaf I recognise as *broa*, Portugal's rural staple, a yeasted cornmeal bread baked round for portability – square-edged tin-breads are strictly for townies. When stale and dried-out, bread kneaded and baked in the old way stays sweet and clean without mould and is the raw material of Portugal's national dish, *açorda*, a breadcrumb risotto prepared and cooked in much the same way as the Spanish paella.

'Portuguese,' says Joe. 'Good stuff. Not like that rubbish in a packet.'

Indeed it is and isn't, I agree.

Joe finishes eating, removes a cheroot from behind his ear, lights it with a match, spits on the tip and replaces the match in the box.

'Can't be too careful. Plenty of folks would like to blame other folks for the fires in the cane fields.'

He takes a deep drag, clamps the cheroot between his teeth, removes the shades and inspects his visitor with what seems to be dispassionate interest. It is, he feels, time for explanations.

What do I want and why am I here?

I explain the likely appeal of orchids grown in such a beautiful place to a sophisticated readership such as that of the magazine for which I write. Some of the readers may even already be customers, since Hawaiian orchids are seen everywhere in all the best places.

Joe snorts.

He is the only professional orchid-grower on the island of Maui. The orchids are his babies. He's never wanted to raise a family or do anything else but look after his orchids, although had he wished to find himself a wife, there are plenty of Portuguese on the island who work hard and make money, mostly in macadamia.

The owner of the macadamia plantation is himself of Portuguese descent. Macadamias, he continues, suddenly warming to his subject, are undoubtedly the future. The trees were introduced from Australia in the 1970s as a new crop on the island, labour-intensive, high-value and well-paid because of the export trade.

The view of the ocean across the cane fields, the blue sky overhead are soothing to the spirit, and Joe is willing to talk a little of his life.

One of four brothers, he was born on the Azores, where the only money came from ship-victualling or leaving the island to work on the merchantmen or the whalers. All the brothers wanted to leave the island, and all took work on the whalers. All four skipped ship and settled in Boston behind the harbour until they made their fortunes. They bought cheap and sold whatever people wanted to buy – walking sticks, sacks of coal, ladies' underwear, trucks. The margin was 5 per cent. If you were greedy, the word went out and no one would buy. When Joe had made his pile, he just kept right on going west until he came to the islands and found a place that was right for his orchids.

After that he never went home. At first the orchids were a hobby before they became a business. The casualty level's too high for anyone to make even a modest fortune, but Joe has no regrets.

'It's something about them,' he adds thoughtfully. 'The way they live on air and don't bother to flower till they're good and ready. Takes patience. Nobody has patience any more – 'cept me and the macadamia guy. And maybe my friend Rosa.'

Joe slams the vehicle into gear.

The message is clear. Enough of the talking, it's time to move on or we'll never get home before sundown.

The track narrows into a rutted green tunnel tangled with vines, and the vehicle coughs and splutters alarmingly before the ruts open out into a wide plateau shaded with tall trees.

'This is it,' says Joe, surveying his kingdom approvingly. 'Never saw the need for anything fancy.'

There is indeed nothing fancy about Joe's orchid sheds. What looks like at least half an acre of plastic sheeting has been hammered into wooden frames to form a roof over long lines of Formica tables laden with wooden boxes.

In the boxes, neatly organised in rows, are spidery clumps of foliage spiked with flower sprays – pink, purple, green, yellow, ivory, white with russet freckles – all with silky curled-back petals and pouting lips.

'Waiting for their pollinators,' says Joe with a touch of melancholy. 'Last chance for love. Comes to us all.'

I take out my sketchbook and paints.

The orchids are extraordinarily beautiful and a little carnivorous, like pampered beauties at a cocktail party scanning the room for conquests. Joe talks gently to his plants, inspecting the leaves for aphids and brushing invisible flecks of dust from the petals. I work in silence, happy to have the opportunity to paint something so perfect in a setting like this.

The orchidaceae, quite apart from their beauty, have a curiously intelligent method of spreading their seed. They mimic their insect pollinators – bees or flies or wasps – to attract them to the blooms. European ground-orchids store their nutrients in tubers, which are higher in protein than fillet steak. These, when prepared as *salep* – dried and ground to a powder – are used in Turkey to thicken ice cream. In Britain, the same preparation – known as *saloop* – makes an appearance in Charles Lamb's *Essays of Elia* and continued in popularity in both rural and urban areas as a restorative milky drink as late as the 1930s.

'Never heard of it,' says Joe, glancing down at my sketch of one of the orchid clumps. 'Looks good. Come back any time.'

On the way back down to rejoin the road, Joe slows the vehicle as we pass a clearing that looks like a graveyard for motorised rust-buckets.

A brick oven stands to one side with a pile of firewood.

'Rosa's place,' says Joe, sliding to a halt. 'She's Portuguese, like me. Rosa bakes bread and I help her when it's time for the *matança*, the pig-killing.'

So the bread and ham we ate this morning was Rosa's?

Joe nods. 'She won't take payment. I make sure she has enough firewood for the baking, and give her a lift into town when she needs it. She came here in much the same way as me, working her way from Lisbon to Boston to San Francisco, saving all the time, same as me. And then she came to the island and bought shares in a bus company and worked in the ticket office. The company went bust, so she took the buses instead of what was owed, parked them up here and moved in.'

A window opens and a wrinkled brown face pokes out. 'Eh, Joe! What story you telling your *novia*, *cabrón*?'

Cabrón, to put it delicately, means cuckold. Joe shouts something equally indelicate back in Portuguese.

Rosa cackles with laughter and the window bangs shut.

Joe laughs. 'You know what they mean by fishwife? That's Rosa – a little bit of home, just like the *matança*. And when it's all done and the meat's cut up and ready just the way Rosa likes it, she salts down the back fat and dries out the hams and makes enough chorizo to keep me and her going right through the winter. And maybe someone digs a pit for a hog roast and someone else brings a gallon of rum and everyone sits around and talks over the bad old days and why none of us would ever go home.'

I know the feeling.

Sean meets us back at the gas station, looking refreshed and a little drowsy.

He has, he says, been working on the poke problem. Tomorrow is another day. Tomorrow there will be poke. Maybe. Given that nothing can be guaranteed and nothing is sure in this world or the next.

Death and taxes excepted.

For a laid-back islander, Sean seems unusually cheerful the following morning. We greet each other in the lobby like long-lost friends – which, by now, we are.

'Beginner's luck,' he grins. 'I have a buddy, name of Patrice. Runs a fancy restaurant on the hotel compound. Buys his fish down the coast when the boats come in. If it's fish you're after, raw or cooked, Patrice is your man.'

The man himself, lanky frame folded along the back seat of the Cadillac, is snoring gently, mouth ajar.

We are on our way to Mauiea, a little fishing port where Patrice intercepts the inshore boats and does his deals for the restaurant.

'Don't mind him,' Sean says. 'Late night. Rum cocktails.'

Me too, I say, and Sean laughs.

Leaving the cane fields behind, the road sweeps onwards round the coast, passing through small groups of single-storey dwellings shaded by giraffe-necked coconut palms, tall as skyscrapers.

Sean keeps up a running commentary on the sights passed along the way. The palms, he says, were a source of income, the first commercial crop on the island. Gathered when ripe, the coconut flesh was pressed and dried for sale to the copra trade. Sent to the mainland for processing into oil for cooking and industrial lubricants, the benefit to the harvesters was nothing like the profits made by the processors. The circle was completed when the residue, copra cake, was sent right back to the islands to fatten up the beef cattle for the sugar barons.

Did the sugar barons, I ask, take over the cattle trade?

Sean shrugs. 'They're middlemen. They saw the profit. The rich get rich and the poor get poorer. You don't need high school to work it out.'

Sean slows the vehicle as the coconut palms give way to rolling fields of sugarcane. 'See that?' He waves at the cane fields. 'That's progress. All you could see when I was a boy was taro. There might be an acre or two of yam, but mostly it was taro. Schoolkids were let out to help with the harvest, whole families working together, us kids picking up for the diggers and bundling leaves for the cutters. Nobody wanted to work the cane fields, whatever the pay. So they brought in labour from elsewhere – Latinos, West Indians, Filipinos.'

So what happened then?

Sean shrugs. 'They paid them a little more than anyone could get at home, they saw life on the islands was good and never went home. Like me.'

The vehicle moves smoothly onwards through the avenue of cane, mile upon mile of green wall ready for harvesting.

After an hour or two – my headache is improving but I'm

sensible enough to close my eyes – the vehicle slows and Sean switches the radio to a hula station.

Patrice wakes up with a start.

'*Eh, les mecs – qu'est on s' foute?*'

Patrice's default language is colloquial waterfront French. What he needs to know, roughly translated, is what the hell's going on.

Sean laughs and rolls his eyes.

We've arrived.

In spite of the loss of the deep-sea fisheries, fish-landing and fish-processing are fifth in commercial importance on Hawaii. Most of these activities take place in Mauiea.

We turn towards the harbour through lines of neat modern bungalows fronted by clipped lawns with well-tended flower-beds. Visible through gaps in the bungalows is the wide sweep of a sheltered bay with white-painted sailing yachts bobbing at anchor.

The real business of the town is being unloaded from a line of battered clinker-built fishing boats tied alongside a wooden jetty. Those unloading, men and women, are all in a variation of the island uniform – tattered cut-off jeans and faded floral shirts, well patched.

Mauiea – though off the beaten track, at least for tourists – is a working port equipped with a battery of modern holding tanks, storage facilities and a hangar where fish auctions are held. The wholesale price for tuna is the same in Mauiea as it is in Sydney or Tokyo or London or New York, and trades are on commission. The money is paid off-island. The smart money goes where it pays least tax.

As soon as the vehicle rolls to a halt, Patrice uncurls, yawns noisily and opens the door, introducing a blast of fish-laden air.

Without a word or a backwards glance, he lopes off down the quayside.

'Skipped breakfast,' says Sean. 'You know how it is with chefs.'

Patrice walks alongside the fishing boats, pushes his way through a little crowd of spectators surrounding the holding tanks and disappears from view.

Sean and I follow. Two of the tanks are filled with a heaving carpet of bright-red crayfish.

Spiny lobster, says Sean. Pacific variety. No claws.

I am suddenly overwhelmed with happiness to be here, in this crazy bustle of noise and people, with Sean and Patrice, the scent of the ocean and the shimmering crates unloaded on to the quay-side. This is as good as it gets. I might almost give up my quest for – let's not even discuss it. For now, it's enough that we're here, and the future might, just might, hold good things to come.

I take out my sketchbook and paints. This, as usual, is a sign for Sean to let me work without interruption for the time it takes to make a sketch.

Within my line of sight are the contents of the second holding tank, a writhing mass of sausage-shaped yellowy-brown sea-monsters.

These, Sean explains as I apply yellowy-brown paint to paper, are sea-slugs that live in shallow waters close to shore and are dried for soup. The Chinese pay good money for them – which tells you a Chinaman will eat anything. Right now, I am overwhelmed with gratitude that it's the down-season, and that Sean has rescued me from the full twenty-four-hour makeover and eighteen holes of golf, which would have otherwise been my lot in the up-season.

The first sketch completed, I move along the row of tanks until I reach the last in the line. This, the only one to attract an enthusiastic audience, is packed with gaping orange-fleshed bivalves as big as dinner plates, each equipped with what looks like a baby elephant's trunk.

Sean leans over the tank.

'We call them squish-squish. Largest clam in the world. Makes a great chowder and you only need one. The Japanese eat them raw – can't get enough of them.'

The trunks wave around like opium-smokers in a silent movie, emitting little puffs of sandy water. The audience pokes and prods, encouraging more puffing.

'Watch this.'

One of the spectators, a matron of impressive bulk even among the generously proportioned matrons of Hawaii, reaches into the water, grabs one of the bivalves and whacks the protruding trunk on the side of the tank.

'See! That's what I do when I'm mad at my husband.'

Everyone watches as the trunk springs into tubular erection, triggering gales of laughter. The joke may not be new but it's enjoyable and there's always the possibility the trunk may not perform.

As soon as the crowd disperses – there's only so much entertainment to be had from a clam, however priapic – Patrice comes into view in earnest conversation with a couple of bearded fishermen in blue overalls. They disappear into a glass-fronted office where negotiations, visible through the window, are clearly becoming heated.

The perennial problem for a restaurateur such as Patrice, says Sean, is tailoring supply to meet demand. The fishermen need certainty; a restaurateur needs flexibility. A deal will be struck and Patrice will get what he wants, but only as a favour and maybe in return for dinner at the restaurant to celebrate something special – a wedding anniversary, an important birthday. The community sticks together and not everything is about the money.

We leave Patrice to his negotiations and head for the general store on the harbour front.

At the back of the store, a couple of white-coated young men are exchanging gossip in Spanish. Filipinos, says Sean, watching as they fillet multicoloured fish in seconds and flip them on to the grill. Sean doesn't eat fish and there's no point in ordering anything without Patrice. So we collect mugs of milky coffee at the counter – island-grown beans, says Sean proudly – and settle down on a bench outside in the morning sunshine.

Patrice is happy when he reappears. Even though the price of tuna – particularly belly, the richest and most sought-after cut – has gone through the roof, he's secured the supplies he will need for the restaurant when the season opens again.

'*Pour les prix, on est foutu* . . .' Patrice's use of the 'f' word to describe the prices carries emphasis rather than despair. '*Les Japonais, les Californians* – they all want it,' he says, waving his hands. 'What can one do?'

Patrice has arrived with a lidded bucket, now placed protectively between his boots, from which wafts a faint scent of the sea.

Sean catches my attention, nods at the bucket, taps his nose with his finger, and winks.

My spirits lift. Just the same, I don't mention the poke word.

Meanwhile, I tell myself that, as a journalist employed to write about food and travel, it's my duty to the readership to report on what's on offer at the counter in the form of a top-of-the-range, high-quality breakfast.

I share this thought with my companions.

Patrice rises to the occasion with two dozen oysters on the half-shell with lime wedges – he's very particular about the limes – one for me and the other for himself. As an afterthought, he adds six doughnuts hot from the fryer for Sean. After some discussion with the fish-flipping fellow chefs, he adds a double portion of breadcrumbed prawns with ketchup, a couple of spider crabs just cooled from the steamer and a side order of sweet-potato chips wrapped in a banana leaf.

'That should do it,' says Patrice with a grin. This is the first time I have seen him smile.

Patrice and I eat our fish messily and greedily. For a lean lanky Frenchman – or rather, Provençal – he can put away an astonishing amount of fish.

'How can you eat that stuff?' says Sean, biting into his third doughnut.

Patrice shows me how to eat the spider crabs by levering up the carapace with the thumb, discarding the feathery brown gills, snapping off the mouthpiece and chopping the body into lollipop sections with the white meat attached to each leg. The result is artistic and demands a sketch. This takes time and Sean is impatient.

That's it, says Sean, wiping the sugar from his chin. Paints or no paints, it's time to head down the coast to Lahaina, an old whaling town, a tourist attraction which anyone writing about the island must certainly visit.

I agree, though only if he can guarantee the presence of a golf course and fully staffed health spa. Sean laughs. He appreciates the irony. He knows where my enthusiasms lie and, if his views on profitability and sugar barons are any indication of his politics, he's on my side.

Patrice has a plan and it doesn't include Lahaina. Our final destination, the reason for the bucket, is a little fishing village popular with surfers where Patrice's ex-sous chef runs a beach shack.

Patrice stretches out on the back seat, props himself against the door and decides to talk. It is, he says, pleasant to encounter someone whose French is not only fluent – although my accent is a little too *Parisienne* for a man from Marseilles – but who can discuss such important matters as the correct preparation of a bouillabaisse and whether or not it should be served with an aioli. And if there must be aioli, then the question is whether or not this traditional preparation of garlic and oil should be made like a mayonnaise, with egg yolks, or simply rely on the perfect emulsion of the newest, just-formed garlic cloves and the thickest, fresh-from-the-presses olive oil.

I plump for the latter, a decision which makes us friends for life. Friends should understand each other, and the journey will pass pleasantly and productively if we share our stories. Mine – well, marriage, children and home-cooking – the usual.

Patrice, on the other hand, was born into the catering trade. His parents ran a little bistro, nothing grand, on the Marseilles waterfront opposite where the fishing boats land the catch. His father did the cooking and his mother kept front-of-house, and Patrice waited on tables in the evenings after school. At weekends he went to stay with his grandfather on the other side of the city by the deep-water harbour, where the ocean liners and merchant ships came and went.

'*Grand-papa* worked on the whalers. He knew all the flags and where all the boats were going and where they came from. The whalers put in to all the islands in all the oceans and he said the islands of Hawaii were the most beautiful of all, and the people too. Before he died, he told me some day I would go there and he would go with me in my heart.'

It is some time before Patrice resumes his story, and I have no wish to interrupt his thoughts.

When he resumes, the Provençal accent is even more pronounced.

'The bouillabaisse is my signature dish – I am from Marseilles, how could it be any other way? It started when *grand-père* was no longer there to take me to the harbour and watch the ships. I was sad, so I went on to the rocks in the early morning to think about him and look out over the ocean. But I was young and I soon forgot the sadness, but I still went out on the rocks to catch the *rascasse*, which is the spiny rockfish you need for bouillabaisse. At first I sold them for a few *sous* in the street. Then I learned to make a broth with the *rascasse* and the soup-fish the fishermen could sell, and soon people began to tell each other about the boy who made good soup and how fresh it was and cheap. I promised my grandfather in my heart that I would use the money I had made from the soup to come to the islands. So as soon as I could I took ship for San Francisco, a place where a French chef, trained or not, could earn good money.'

After ten years working on the mainland, Patrice saved enough to come to the islands and open his own restaurant.

'I did what had to be done and kept my promise. I'd had enough of Caesar salad and blackened bluefish – where's the skill in that? But a classic bouillabaisse is worth the trouble. So I made my reputation with what I call my island bouillabaisse, the bouillabaisse of Hawaii.'

He pauses, then resumes.

'This is how I do it. I start as my mother did, in the usual way, with the onion and carrot and celery cooked very gently in olive oil, but I add a little paste of ginger and lemongrass. And I'm not particular about the fish. It's not true that you cannot make a bouillabaisse except in Marseilles. I make it with what-ever is fresh off the boats. We have spiny lobster, shrimp, clams like you have seen this morning, scorpion fish, goat fish, *kula*, *merpachi*, *mahi-mahi*. If I make it in Hawaii with ginger and lemongrass, it's the bouillabaisse of Hawaii. And if I make it somewhere in India, maybe I add a little cumin and cardamom and put in turmeric instead of the saffron – *et voilà, bouillabaisse à l'indienne.*'

Patrice smiles, his face turned to the horizon.

'So this is how I keep my promise to my grandfather. And when I can feel his presence very strongly, I make the bouilla-baisse just the way he liked it and take it out to the lanai and eat it from a bowl and watch the sunset over the ocean.'

The fishing village is scarcely a village at all but a single strip of wooden huts set back from a narrow strip of white sand up which some half-dozen dugout canoes have been dragged above the waterline. The huts are painted in soft sun-bleached colours with silvery lanai, against which are propped brightly painted surfboards.

Patrice picks up the fish bucket from the boot and disappears into a tin-roofed shack just beyond the boats, reappearing after a few minutes with a triumphant grin and a wave.

At last there will be poke. It will be ready in two hours but not before, as the fish needs to marinate for exactly the time it will take us to walk along the beach from one headland to the other.

We set off in single file along the edge of the sea. There are turtle-prints on the sand and a rim of driftwood and ocean debris along the tideline. Among the hanks of weed are more interesting plunder – the upper half of a turtle shell rubbed smooth by the seabed, the bleached-out jawbone of a shark with a few of the curved teeth still loosely embedded in the rim. Both are

valuable commodities unlikely to have gone ungathered in the days when beachcombing was a source of raw materials for necklaces, bracelets and weapons of war.

We follow the curve of the bay along a heavily wooded shoreline fringed with coconut palms and tall stands of banana grass.

Patrice hacks down a fruiting stem with a penknife, shoving the blade into a papery stalk as thick as a telegraph pole, sending a crowd of brightly coloured beetles scurrying for sanctuary. The fall releases a long stem clustered with bright hands of yellow fruit, at the end of which is a fat green flower-bud streaked with red.

'Taste. Eat.'

I do as I'm told. The banana flesh is almost as crisp as an apple and sweet as honey, with thick, sticky, vanilla-flavoured juice.

'*C'est délicieux,*' I say.

'*Bien sûr.* Of course.' Patrice nods and smiles. 'Everything that grows here is good – aubergines, courgettes, tomatoes, peppers for my Provençal dishes. Ten years ago, *rien*, nothing. Now I can have everything I want, even the beautiful *ail rose*, the garlic of Provence, for the aioli for the bouillabaisse. Then I take *un petit café*, a little cup of very strong, very black coffee as they make in Marseilles. So why would anyone live anywhere else?'

Patrice's coffee beans come from the plantations at Kona on the western slopes of the Big Island, where coffee has been grown for more than a century, when small-berried trees suitable for island conditions were imported from Java. Although most of the production goes for export – as with so much else – Patrice buys his raw beans direct from the growers, dries them himself in the sun, then roasts them like popcorn in a pan until nearly burnt, which is what is needed, he explains with a grin, for the good stuff you have to take with plenty of sugar and swallow in a single gulp.

A drum roll in the distance summons us back to the shack.

As soon as we reappear, a figure with a faded kanga wrapped round his waist and the muscular brown torso of a surfer ambles through from the lean-to kitchen. Balanced on one hand is a carved wooden bowl.

'Meet Henri,' says Patrice, hanging an arm round his friend's shoulders. 'Best sous chef I ever had . . . and then he met this beautiful girl . . .' Patrice describes a shape with his hands. '*Et phutt . . . c'est tout fini.*'

Henri sets the bowl on the table and laughs – his teeth are very white and his eyes are Mediterranean blue, and I can see why a beautiful girl, any girl, would fall in love with him.

'*Allez, les gosses – mangez.*' Come, children, and eat, seems like the right kind of invitation.

'*Pour la digestion*,' says Patrice, dropping ice into glasses and adding water and a few drops of Pernod. The alcohol turns the water cloudy and the fragrance of aniseed joins the scent of the sea.

'*Bon appétit*,' says Sean, opening his bag of doughnuts.

In the bowl are little packages wrapped in banana leaves, each with a flap secured by a thorn. Inside the packages are translucent pink cubes of fish flesh shiny with oil and ginger juice, and dusted with toasted sesame seeds and tiny specks of green chilli.

Poke is all about texture, the smoothness of sesame oil and roughness of toasted seeds, perhaps a little chilli and a few shreds of sea lettuce – nothing to sharpen the taste-buds, just a slick of sweetness and the taste of the sea.

'The recipe is very simple,' says Henri. 'All you have to do is carve it and cut it and dress it as you like with a little sesame oil and maybe a little bit of sugar, but nothing sour. Then you must wait for the fish to take the flavourings. *Et voilà*. Some like it with chopped onion, others like to include sea lettuce, *limu kohu*, and if you don't have enough fish you add some avocado.'

'Worth the wait?' asks Sean cheerfully, licking jam and sugar off his fingertips.

Indeed it is. The little cubes of silky flesh are firm and tender, the dressing buttery and smooth. I take my time, savouring the grassy kick of the chilli, the sea flavour of the juices and the crunchiness of the seeds. I lick my fingers clean and walk down to the edge of the ocean, needing to dip my toes in the water and feel the movement of the tide in the coming and going of the waves.

Whatever this may have meant to the wandering seafarers who first made landfall on these shores, the story's still here. And perhaps, it seems to me as we make our farewells, that's where it should stay. Some things are best left hidden – discovered by chance and a kindly nod in the right direction from the gods.

·℮·℮·℮·

POKE WITH SEAWEED AND SESAME

You'll need sashimi-grade tuna for this sophisticated version of Hawaii's traditional way with freshly caught big-eye or yellow-fin tuna (organically farmed salmon is the alternative). You can replace the sea lettuce, *limu kohu*, with a handful of rocket or any other mustardy leaves and a pinch of toasted Japanese nori flakes.

Serves 6–8
1 kg sashimi-grade tuna
1 mild red onion, peeled and finely chopped
generous handful of sea lettuce, shredded
2 red chillies, de-seeded and finely chopped
4 tablespoons toasted sesame oil
2 tablespoons macadamia nuts or walnuts, toasted and chopped
1 teaspoon sea-salt flakes (Hawaiian red salt, if you can get it)

To finish
3–4 tablespoons sesame seeds
3 tablespoons cane sugar
2 tablespoons light soy sauce
2 tablespoons toasted sesame oil

Dice the fish into bite-sized pieces. Toss with the rest of the ingredients except those used to finish, cover and leave to stand for an hour at room temperature.

To finish, toast the sesame seeds in a dry pan over a medium heat

148

(have a lid handy – they jump). Add the sesame seeds and the rest of the finishing ingredients to the fish, mix well, and serve in emptied-out coconut shells or small bowls. For a light lunch, serve heaped in halved, pitted avocadoes.

HAWAIIAN BOUILLABAISSE

This classic fish soup is a dish that speaks to the heart as well as the stomach. All and any non-oily fish will do – avoid salmon and all members of the sardine family, including mackerel and herring. The only essential is an element of glueyness, found in spiny rock-dwellers such as *rascasse*. On Hawaii, the nearest is rock cod, *nohu*.

Serves 6–8
3 kg fresh fish (*rascasse* or rock cod, grouper, snapper, eel, gurnard)
2 litres fish stock or water
1 glass dry white wine
3–4 shallots or leeks, trimmed and diced
2 large tomatoes, scalded, skinned, de-seeded and diced
12 saffron threads
1 stalk lemongrass, peeled and diced
1 cm slice of fresh ginger, peeled and finely chopped
½ teaspoon black peppercorns, crushed
3–4 yellow-fleshed potatoes, peeled and sliced
salt

For the rouille
4 garlic cloves, peeled
½ teaspoon salt
1 stalk lemongrass, peeled and diced
1 cm slice of fresh ginger, peeled and finely chopped
2 red chillies, de-seeded and chopped
2 red peppers, whole (or ready prepared)
1 thick slice of stale bread

(recipe continued overleaf)

To finish
6 tablespoons olive oil
6–8 thick slices of stale bread
1 garlic clove

Bone, skin and fillet your fish as appropriate (save the trimmings), cut into bite-sized pieces, transfer to a plate, salt lightly, cover with another plate and set in a cool place to firm.

If using water rather than ready-made stock, simmer the fish trimmings with aromatics – green celery, parsley stalks, leek tops, a bay leaf – in 2 litres of water for 20 minutes, then strain.

Bring the stock to the boil in a large pan with the wine, leek or shallot, tomatoes, saffron, lemongrass, ginger and crushed peppercorns. Turn down the heat and simmer for 20–30 minutes. Add the potatoes, bring back to the boil, reduce the heat and leave to simmer for 10–15 minutes until the potatoes are nearly soft.

Meanwhile, make the rouille. Crush the garlic with the salt, lemongrass, ginger and chillies. Roast the peppers over a direct flame until the skin is charred, pop them in a plastic bag to soften for 20 minutes, then scrape the flesh from the skin. Soak the bread in a little water and squeeze it dry. Pound all the ingredients together into a smooth paste in a food processor or with a pestle and mortar. Set aside while you finish the soup.

Bring the broth back to the boil before you slip in the fish fillets. Add the olive oil, cover the pan, bring everything swiftly back to the boil and remove from the heat immediately.

Stir a ladleful of the hot fish broth into the rouille and mix. Rub each slice of dried bread with a cut clove of garlic, spread with a little of the rouille and place a slice in each soup plate. Divide the fish between the plates and ladle in enough broth to submerge everything. Hand the rouille round separately and provide water bowls for rinsing fishy fingers.

CALIFORNIA ROLLS

California rolls – sushi rice rolled round a finger of avocado – were first popularised by Japanese immigrants on the West Coast, then re-exported to Japan. The easiest way to make them is using a bamboo rolling-mat, though greaseproof paper will do.

Serves 4
225 g round-grain or Japanese sushi rice
350 ml cold water
1 packet sushi nori
1 small avocado

For the dressing
2 tablespoons rice vinegar
2 teaspoons caster sugar
½ teaspoon salt

Rinse the rice thoroughly in a sieve under the tap until the water runs clear. Measure the cold water into the pan, tip in the rice, and leave it to soak for half an hour. Bring rapidly to the boil, turn down the heat a little, cover with a tight-fitting lid and steam for 5 minutes, until all the water has been absorbed. Turn the heat right down, and let the rice dry out, still covered, for another 15 minutes. Turn the heat off and leave for another 10 minutes to allow the grains to swell.

Mix the dressing ingredients together and spread the rice on a china dish to cool it down rapidly. As the rice cools, sprinkle it with the dressing – it's ready when cooled to room temperature.

To assemble the rolls, lay a sheet of nori – prepared seaweed wrapper – shiny side down on a bamboo rolling-mat. Have ready a bowl of warm water with a drop of vinegar.

Moisten your hand in the water, take up a palmful of rice and spread it all over the nori, leaving a thumb width's edge at the top.

(recipe continued overleaf)

Remove the avocado from its skin using a dessertspoon, then cut the flesh into long fingers. Arrange the fingers of avocado in the middle, parallel to the short edge, and roll up the bamboo mat to make a long cylinder of rice – the flap of nori will stick to the far side of the roll. Using a sharp knife dipped in the warm water, cut the roll into 8 sections (press, don't saw). Repeat with the remaining ingredients.

MANGO MUFFINS

You can make these puffy little fresh-fruit muffins with papaya, peaches or apricots if mangoes are not in season, and the orange juice can be replaced with apple or grapefruit. For a dessert, serve straight from the oven with a slurp of egg custard or runny cream.

Makes 12
1 small ripe mango, peeled and pitted
150 ml orange juice
1 large egg
250 g plain flour
1 teaspoon baking powder
½ teaspoon salt
100 g brown sugar
75 g unsalted butter, melted and cooled

Preheat the oven to 190°C/Gas 5 and butter a 12-hole non-stick muffin tin.

Blitz the mango, orange juice and egg to a smooth purée.

Sift the flour with the baking powder and salt in a large bowl and stir in the sugar. Make a well in the middle and tip in the mango mixture. Combine the two together (don't overwork) and then fold in the melted butter. Spoon into the muffin tin.

Bake for 15–20 minutes until well risen and puffy. Serve warm, perhaps with maple syrup and crisp bacon.

Sardinia

'PLEASE TO TASTE OUR BOTTARGA, *SIGNORA*.'

The Armani-clad saleswoman in the elegant produce boutique where I have taken shelter moves from behind her chrome and glass counter with a welcoming smile.

Proffered with smiling courtesy on the blade of a cut-throat knife is a translucent sliver of the island's most famous export, salted and sun-dried mullet-roe, fresh and sweet and scented with sea spray.

The emporium, appropriately, is named for Circe, island enchantress who bewitched storm-tossed Odysseus on his return from the siege of Troy. While I am not alone in taking refuge from the rain in what looks like the only tourist-friendly food emporium open at midday on a windswept Monday, it seems I am the only one who appreciates what's on offer.

'Please to taste. You will find this – how do you say it? – incomparable. We have just received our first delivery of the bottarga of Sardinia, which is prepared on the island of Carloforte. You may already know of it, and if you do, you will also know that the bottarga of Carloforto is the caviar of kings.'

I congratulate Circe's handmaiden on her perfect command of English. It is, I admit, as I accept the little sliver of the caviar of kings, far superior to my Italian, which is strong in the kitchen but a little ragged elsewhere. The Sardinian dialect, on the other hand, sounds familiar to my ear as there are strong similarities to Andaluz, the dialect of southern Spain in which I feel at home.

The sliver of exquisite fishiness on the end of the knife is no more than will cover the tip of the tongue, but the taste is explosive – salty and sweet, like sea foam coated with caramel. The texture is silky, buttery, satisfyingly chewy.

The raw material of bottarga is the twin-lobed egg sac of the grey mullet, a middle-sized, torpedo-shaped, blunt-nosed, small-mouthed, seaweed-eating, opportunist bottom-feeder that clusters around the hulls of sailing boats in yacht basins and ferry terminals throughout the Mediterranean.

The rest of the fish is also good eating – I like it raw, sliced thinly with lemon juice – but the prize is the roe. Egg sacs are only available in the breeding season in spring, when the fish come into the shallows to spawn. Once the roe is harvested, without breaking the membrane or separating the lobes, the sac is salted, pressed, dried in the sun and given a translucent jacket of beeswax. Lesser-quality bottarga is packaged in plastic for increased shelf life, a form in which it will last for years.

The boutique specialises in prettily packaged bottles of olive oil and fragranced vinegar, beribboned jars of bergamot conserve and walnuts in honey, cellophane packages of chocolate-coated citrus peel. Nothing to set my pulse raising, although a couple of other would-be purchasers, tourists like me, are clearly tempted by the ribbons and pretty packaging.

Bottarga, packaged neatly in nothing more than its covering of wax, is another matter.

'Once you have tasted our bottarga,' says the saleslady, 'nothing else will do.' She's right. Until this moment I have no intention of spending my money anywhere but in the market-place and certainly not on a luxury such as this. But one sliver and I'm hooked. I don't even need to enquire about the price. This is high luxury, better suited to those who eat their caviar from silver spoons and expect to pay for the best.

Nevertheless, a couple of locals with shopping bags indicate that tourists are not the only customers the shop attracts. Sardinians know what's good and will buy for pleasure as well as necessity. There a price to be paid for the happiness something so delicious brings. And when I sneak another little taste, I know she knows I'm hooked.

It is, my informant continues, my good fortune that the new season's supplies arrived early this year, before word gets out and the dealers flock in from the mainland. Competition for stocks is fierce, bribery not unknown, ridiculous prices paid even at wholesale, and by Christmas it will all be gone.

Sardinian is the best, she continues, but bottarga is certainly prepared elsewhere. It can be found on Sicily, Corsica, mainland Italy, France, Greece, Turkey, even Tunisia. But once a person has tasted the real thing, nothing else will do. And the bottarga of Sardinia, these perfect little twin-lobed beauties in their shiny beeswax jackets, will never disappoint.

'I'll take it,' I say. There are certain foodstuffs which cannot be ignored. Their appeal is as much about provenance – where and when – as what. Lobster live from the creel on a Hebridean quayside is more seductive than the same crustacean ready-cooked on the slab in a city supermarket. A truffle buried in a rice jar in a New York deli is not a patch on the subterranean fungi freshly dug from the red earth of a Siennese hillside.

The same is also true of bottarga tasted from the blade of a knife.

Truth to tell, it took no more than that introductory taste to convince myself that, as guest lecturer on an island-hopping pleasure boat, I would regret it for ever if I left it behind on the shelf. Storage is never a problem with salt-cured air-dried foodstuffs, which are designed to keep fresh and sweet from one year to the next when stored in a current of air in a warm kitchen – central heating, the northerner's equivalent of a Mediterranean climate, does the trick. No need for a sell-by date. Salt-cured foodstuffs are prepared for longevity, food for the pocket, shoved in the traveller's satchel to add flavour (and salt) to foods which might otherwise be bland.

The deal is done. The price is shocking, as is only to be expected. When I check my credit-card receipt – this is not a cash purchase – the figure is about the same as could be expected for a table-for-one at, say, Ferran Adrià's El Bulli before it closed its doors, or Heston Blumenthal's Fat Duck or Thomas Keller's French Laundry.

My purchase is already wrapped in smooth white wax paper when it comes with a final word of advice.

Should I find myself lacking the possibility of midday refreshment, as is likely in Cagliari on early-closing Monday, I should provide myself with a small flask of olive oil and a sheet of *carta di musica* – twice-cooked Sardinian flatbread. If I combine the two with the merest sliver of my purchase, I will not go hungry. This, after all, is traveller's food, and as a traveller I will find myself content.

Cagliari, Sardinia's harbour capital, is in the south of the island, well away from the luxury tourist enclaves of the island's northern shores. When approached from the sea, one's first sight is of a fortified harbour defended by a citadel, narrow streets that reach towards a handsome basilica, and a palm-fringed seafront backed by handsome eighteenth-century mansions.

There are fishing boats bobbing at anchor, a ferry terminal and the grey outlines of warships of the Italian navy. Above, flying in formation from west to east, a little party of flamingoes, scarlet and black, hooked bills held horizontally on long straight necks, vanish over the headland to their winter quarters in the wetlands beyond.

All of Sardinia – inland as well as on the coast – was heavily malarial in the old days. Even Cagliari itself, before the marshes in its immediate vicinity were drained. Malaria and pirates were the twin scourges of the coastal-dwellers, a reason for the population to retreat to the hills, leaving the defence of the island to the garrisons of the capital.

The produce boutique in which I have procured my prize is halfway up Via Cavour, Cagliari's impossibly steep main street. On a rainy October day I had been on my way to what I'm told is the best marketplace in all Sardinia – possibly the only marketplace, since most of the resident population not employed in the tourist business live from shepherding and farming and bring their goods to market in the capital.

On my way out of the shop, I decide to take the saleslady's advice and provide myself with a picnic. Just next door to Circe's magical cave is a busy little supermarket where I add a sheet of *carta di musica* and a small bottle of olive oil to my supplies before making my way up the steep cobbles of Via Cavour to the battlements at the top of the town.

The clouds have lifted to reveal a sky of cobalt blue and the waters of the bay below sparkle in the sunshine. Below, dwarfed by the warships, is my temporary home, a small cruise-ship converted from an oligarch's yacht, where my duties as lecturer are light – a couple of talks on the food of the islands illustrated from my sketchbooks – and rendered lighter still by a trio of professional opera-singers who entertain us in the evenings.

Early in the tour – we started in Athens and are due to finish in Seville – I discover, somewhat to my disappointment since I love company at table, that my fellow passengers, British to the core, are gastronomically unadventurous, preferring the certainties of the fully inclusive on-board catering to the uncertainties and possible extra cost of the local hostelries. In my own view – although I am here as a lecturer rather than a paying guest – this is a shame, since it removes so many possibilities of contact with the locals, even just a brief exchange over the menu in one of the little restaurants that serve fish from day-boats, or the pleasure of negotiating some particularly local speciality such as my bottarga.

Perhaps the lack of company is just as well, I reflect as I award myself another greedy little sliver of perfect fishiness to eat with the last scrap of the crisp, pale, black-blistered *carta di musica* that tastes a little sweet with the saltiness. I wrap up the leftovers to avoid temptation. Bottarga is too good for sharing with the gastronomically unadventurous. And in any event, Circe's saleslady has given me all I need to know about what to do with my salty little treasure when I get home.

'How do I like to eat it myself? First of all like this, from the blade of a knife, perhaps with a little glass of *vin santo*, sweet wine, when I come home from work in time to watch the sunset over the sea. Or with bread toasted over the fire and just a little olive oil, or grated over a plain *risotto in bianco* if the fishermen come home with empty nets.'

As a general rule, she continued, treat your bottarga just like pecorino or Parmesan and grate or slice it over spaghetti or Sardinian maccheroni or fregola, which is the couscous of Sardinia and is only made in the south of the island, where the North Africans came in to trade. Sardinian couscous is much more delicious than North African couscous because the grains are a little toasted, uneven in size and larger, making them better able to absorb the flavours of a dressing and more interesting when eaten on their own. With the North Africans you were never sure if they were traders or pirates or both.

'When you get your bottarga home – which is not so likely since you will not be able to resist – don't put it in the fridge but keep it on a shelf in the kitchen where it's warm and dry and it'll stay good right through the winter. The proper season to eat bottarga is the cold months, which is when there is no fresh fish in the market because the fishing boats don't leave harbour because of the storms. Some people like to eat it as a winter salad with slices of our juicy Sardinian oranges, or you can grate it into a sauce prepared with dried figs and nuts to toss with the pasta. And if there is any bottarga left after the winter, grate it and store it in a jar and keep it for when you want to make something taste truly delicious or because you have run out of something to make the pasta taste good. Or you can soak it with a little hot water and make it into a dipping sauce with olive oil to eat with bread – but it must be good Sardinian bread from the baker in the market which lasts for many days and never goes mouldy like supermarket bread.'

These thoughts remind me that the market shuts early today, as does everything else in the harbour capital – reflecting that seafaring is the traditional business of the townsfolk. Two o'clock, Circe's saleslady has already warned me, is the latest I can expect to find the stallholders open for business on a Monday, the shortest of the week's workdays as the fishermen don't leave harbour on a Sunday.

Sardinians have a natural distrust of authority, whoever the overlord – and there have been many who have attempted to impose their will on the islanders over the centuries. Italy's national hero, Count Cavour – the man for whom the piazza that provides me with a vantage point for my picnic is named – is a man who above all embodies the Sardinian temperament. Egalitarian, defender of the common man, Camillo Benso di Cavour was the architect of Italy's Risorgimento – resurgence – a term used to describe the process of welding an unruly bunch of warring states into a semi-unified nation. It was from their Sardinian strongholds that Garibaldi's red-shirts completed the task, defeating the combined might of the Papal States and the Austro-Hungarian Empire to found a new nation. The confederation remains loose – nowhere looser than on the islands, and none looser than the island of the *sari*, the name Sardinians prefer for themselves, who are proud of their reputation for a willingness to flout authority, if necessary down the barrel of a gun.

This – a well-documented dislike of interference from elsewhere – drew the author of *Lady Chatterley's Lover* to the island on honeymoon shortly after the end of World War I.

Settled on my bench in the winter sunshine, I open my copy of D. H. Lawrence's *Sea and Sardinia*.

The journey from Sicily to Sardinia did not begin auspiciously. The crossing was lengthy and the ferryboat battered and ill-provisioned. Lawrence's bride, referred to somewhat inauspiciously as Queen Bee (the marriage didn't last), had resisted her husband's desire to exchange the lemon groves and comforts of Palermo, Sicily's sophisticated capital, for a destination well known for brigands and thieves.

Lawrence's first sight of the island's harbour capital was, he tells his readers, strange but wonderful.

'And suddenly there Cagliari is,' he writes. 'A naked town rising steep, steep, golden-looking, piled naked to the sky from the plain at the head of the formless hollow bay . . . treeless, as in some old illumination, yet withal rather jewel-like: like a sudden rose-cut amber jewel naked at the depth of a vast indenture.'

Once ashore and the Queen Bee restored to good humour by an excellent meal at a harbourside café, the honeymooners set off, as did I nearly a century later, drawn towards the cathedral above the town, following what was then, as now, a narrow street twisting upwards like a corkscrew, until they reached the windy battlements of the Piazza Cavour.

The sky, he records, was blue, but the wind, as today, was like a blade of ice.

The pair paused, as has every tourist before and since, to admire the view from the bastions of the Piazza Cavour, the vantage point from which – then as now – can be observed the comings and goings in the harbour and a view of the box-like dwellings of Arab design set among palm trees beyond which stretched a low, malarial-looking plain.

The plain is no longer malarial, but the box-dwellings, palm trees and Arab-built houses remain. Nearly a century after Lawrence's visit, little has changed, although the goods on sale in the market are surely less plentiful and the atmosphere not quite as exuberant – which is only to be expected since the citizens of Cagliari are not immune to the convenience of supermarkets as well as elegant food emporiums presided over by Armani-clad saleswomen.

I follow my literary guide to the marketplace, a short stroll from the locked and barred cathedral closed for renovations. Above, the sky is still as blue and the wind as icy and at the covered market, while the buyers and sellers lack the brightly embroidered costumes of Lawrence's day, all is bustle and trade even though the stallholders are about to pack up for the day. Just the same, Lawrence's own vivid description of the marketplace a century ago more than makes up for any disappointment I feel at missing most of the fun.

'It was Friday,' he writes. 'We follow Madame going marketing followed by a small boy supporting one of these huge grass-woven baskets on his head, piled with bread, eggs, vegetables, a chicken and so forth, and find ourselves in the vast market house, and it fairly glows with eggs: eggs in these great round dish-baskets of golden grass: but eggs in piles, in mounds, in heaps, a Sierra Nevada of eggs, glowing warm white.'

In the bread and cheese market, he finds further delights. 'There are stalls of new, various-shaped bread, brown and bright: there are tiny stalls of marvellous native cakes, which I want to taste, there is a great deal of meat and kid: and there are stalls of cheese, all cheeses, all shapes, all whitenesses, all the cream-colours, on into daffodil yellow.'

Among all these good things, there are chickens, ducks and wild fowl, heaps of multicoloured vegetables of all shapes and sizes, huge bowls of black and green olives.

But the main pleasure of the marketplace, observes the future author of *Women in Love*, are the feisty buyers and sellers, women who consider themselves the equal of their men. 'Here is none of the grovelling Madonna-worship but women who know how to look out for themselves, keep their own backbone stiff and their knuckles hard.'

Never mind that it's a Monday and the market may not be as lively and overflowing with good things as it was in Lawrence's day; it is still, compared to other Mediterranean markets, a magnificent sight.

The produce on the stalls is irresistible even at closing time on a quiet day: huge white and purple cauliflowers, enormous fennels, baskets as big as a cartwheel of new potatoes, red and yellow carrots, scaly kohlrabi, feathery salads, sticky clusters of dates, boxes of dried figs, pomegranates, medlars, walnuts the size of tennis balls, almonds, oranges and *mandarini*, most exquisitely fragrant of all the fruits the island has to offer.

The traditional way of life on the island is shepherding and subsistence farming – limiting traditional cooking, as is

often the way with islanders, to what can be grown or harvested in its own season. The coast is sparsely populated. Those who lived by the sea moved inland in the lawless days when the Mediterranean was both highway and battleground, preferring wolves to pirates and windswept uplands to malarial lowlands.

Store-cupboard goods – cheese, cured pork-meats and salted wind-dried fish – supplement the daily diet of pulses and vegetables. Hard-grain wheat (now imported from Canada) is kneaded with water and dried as *pasta asciutta* rolled or pressed in traditional shapes: spaghetti, maccheroni, fregola. Wild leaves are gathered in spring, and in summer there are tomatoes, peppers, garlic, aubergines and the nuts and fruits that ripen to perfect sweetness in Mediterranean sunshine. In winter, there are oranges and dried fruits – figs and raisins – to make up for the lack of anything fresh.

There's no fresh fish in the market today, just as Circe's handmaiden warned me, but the freezers are packed and attracting customers. The inshore fleet lands fresh fish on the Cagliari quayside, but most, in the old days when freezers were not available, was preserved as salt-cured fish products for export, or sold to the inland islanders in return for the meat of young animals surplus to the needs of the shepherds.

The innards, being vulnerable to spoilage, provided the raw material of the traditional feast-day dish of the Sardinian uplands, *furria-furria* – turn-and-turn-again – a campfire dish for which the entrails – well scrubbed and dusted with oregano and thyme – are wrapped round a spit and turned over the fire until brown and crisp. The preparation is still popular: the citizens of Cagliari have not forgotten their roots and every one of the butcher's stalls is selling the unmistakable raw material ready-wrapped on skewers for the backyard barbecue.

Wandering around the marketplace, I find a few leftover coins in my pocket for a handful of fiery little peppers stuffed with goat's cheese, and consider – but wisely do not complete, since on-board facilities do not include access to the galley – a deal on big brown vineyard-fattened snails which, the rest of the queue informs me, can be prepared in a tomato and garlic sauce.

In need of refreshment and a vantage point for my sketchbook, I take a vacant stool at a café counter for a mouthful of strong black coffee poured over lump sugar in a tiny plastic cup and set to work on a sketch of the marketplace.

My activities attract a curious audience of small children too young to be in school. I work fast and with pleasure, encouraged by my young audience and the delight they take in the magic of paint as it flows from brush to paper, and the joy that greets the gradual emergence of a recognisable image of the marketplace and its customers and stallholders.

Thereafter, with the market about to close, I join the queue at a vegetable stall and hand over my last coins in exchange for half a kilo of fresh purple-blushed olives – I can't resist the purchase, even though there's no chance I'll be able to prepare them for the table. Sardinians, it seems, gather their eating-olives ripe and dark, as in France and Greece, rather than hard and green as in Andalusia, where my olive-pickling days were spent.

Communication is easy since the vegetable-sellers, a pair of dark-haired brothers alike as twins, are exchanging jokes in Spanish, dropping the ends of their words and using the familiar softened 's' of the Andaluz dialect.

The brothers are not themselves Andaluz, they reply. They learned to speak the language when working a thousand miles across the ocean in the banana plantations in Santo Domingo, where Spanish is spoken and the pay is in dollars.

'We follow the work to feed our families, *señorita*, because we are poor. Andaluz or Sardinian, we are all as poor as each other. We go where the money is.'

A pause and a smile.

Señorita, the affectionate diminutive of the matronly *señora*, is a courtesy I'm happy to accept. In the markets of Andalusia, mothers with children – even grandmothers – are addressed as if they are still young and unmarried, smoothing the relationship between seller and buyer. Another good reason to shop in a Mediterranean marketplace, as I was well aware from my own and my children's childhood, is that mothers with children, however unruly, are treated with kindness among the Latins. Infants in pushchairs are presented with a ripe strawberry to suck, schoolchildren are sent on their way with a sliver of cheese – and never mind if this is just to encourage their parents to buy; in the lands of the south there's a warmth and tolerance of childhood not always the way in the north.

'And you, *señorita*, how will you prepare your olives?'

I happily share my recipe. For those, such as I, of a curious turn of mind who don't mind displaying ignorance, there is much to be gleaned from joining the queue at the cheese or meat or vegetable stall, where the stallholders and their customers are ready and willing to deliver culinary advice and expect the same in return.

Given that nothing in the marketplace is more contentious than the preparation of the eating-olive, which, all in the queue are agreed, is the essential accompaniment to a glass of robust Sardinian red wine, I contribute my own experience of olive-pickling. Spanish olives, I explain, are picked green and unripe, cracked and washed in many changes of water until the taste is no longer bitter, then stored in a bath of brine flavoured with fennel and garlic, with or without the addition of dried chillies and chunks of lemon.

In Sardinia, I am told with enthusiastic waving of the hands, eating-olives are picked ripe, when the skin has turned purple but the flesh is still firm, and the salting comes before the washing. After a day and a night in salt to allow the juices to run, the fruit is rinsed with fresh water, salted again, juiced again, then salted and rinsed again until the water tastes sweet and clean. Nothing more. No seasonings or flavourings, since olives, when ripe rather than green, must be allowed to taste of themselves.

I purchase a kilo of freshly picked and not-yet-dried haricot beans – red, cream, brown and speckled – some podded and others, cheaper, sold in the pod. There are, too, pumpkins chunked and sold by the piece for a winter soup, the queue informs me enthusiastically. Advice is also offered on how to cook my kilo of multicoloured beans with at least two full heads of purple-skinned garlic – sold woven together and bunched with string for portability – in a dish of *fagioli alla gallurese* to be finished with *lardo*, salted white pork fat, and sauce made with the greeny-gold tomatoes, some as big as melons. Tomatoes stuffed with sardines and aubergines cooked in olive oil, a party dish, are topped with breadcrumbs and maybe a few luxurious scraps of butter and slipped under the grill to bubble and brown.

A Sardinian market is not for the squeamish. The neighbouring butcher's stall has an exuberant display of partridges in feather and rabbits still wearing their furry jackets, or ready-skinned with little white scuts and furry paws. Boiling fowl – elderly barnyard hens past their laying days – are split open to display a line of unborn eggs, golden globes of diminishing size, to be added, explains a neighbour in the queue, to a broth for a little additional protein, or scrambled with wild mushrooms from the woods, or, if you have keen eyes, *tartuffi di sabia*, sand-truffles found along the shore. There are, too, diminutive joints of milk-fed lamb best cooked with the little bulbs of wild fennel as *agnello alla finocchietti*, while the rabbits, says my neighbour, are good prepared as *coniglio alla montagnina*, with red wine, mountain herbs and olives.

Bread is sold by weight, quartered or halved or whole, some horseshoe-shaped with a dense white crumb and thick brown crust, or a darker-crumbed sourdough with a blackened exterior. Piled high on the bakery counter are crisp sheets of twice-baked flatbreads – *carta di musica* among them – which, says the baker, can be kept for years but after a time will need soaking to soften. Anything left for the morrow is sliced or crumbled and slipped in the cooling oven to crisp and brown.

I am tempted by fist-sized calzone stuffed with olives and artichokes. Or maybe a square of *coccois*, Sardinian focaccia, topped with mint and curd cheese.

I hesitate over a tray of *suspirus*, little macaroon balls dipped in lemon icing, wondering how I could bring something so delicate home for my grandchildren.

The baker is watching me with a smile.

'How many children, *signora*?'

'Seven grandchildren,' I say. 'And you?'

The baker nods and holds up four fingers.

'We are blessed,' I say.

Just before he pulls down the shutters, he reaches down behind the counter for a thick slice of spice-scented gingerbread loosely swaddled in wax paper.

'*Per i tuoi bambini a natale*,' he says, handing over the package. 'For your children at Christmas.' Then, reaching into a pocket, he finds a shiny new coin and pushes it firmly deep in the crumb.

'*Buona fortuna*,' he says, and won't accept my money.

INSALATA DI ARANCE E BOTTARGA (SLICED ORANGE AND BOTTARGA SALAD)

Serve this elegant little sweet-salt winter salad dressed with olive oil and finished with fine shavings of bottarga before a seafood risotto or pasta.

Serves 4

4 juicy oranges
1 mild red or white onion, peeled and finely sliced into half-moons
3–4 tablespoons olive oil
1 tablespoon black olives, pitted and sliced
2–3 tablespoons grated or shaved bottarga

Carefully pare the skin and pith from the oranges and cut out the segments. Toss with the onion, dress with olive oil and olives, and finish with a generous topping of bottarga.

FREGOLA CON SOFFRITTO E BOTTARGA (SARDINIAN COUSCOUS WITH ONIONS AND BOTTARGA)

Sardinia's unevenly shaped, lightly toasted, large-grain couscous, fregola, is traditional in the southern region around Cagliari (you won't find it in the north) and is eaten with juicy stews, much like Moroccan couscous. Here the dressing is an onion-only *soffritto*, which underlines the caramelised flavour of the grains and complements the saltiness of the fish roe.

Serves 4
1 large mild onion, peeled and finely chopped
2–3 garlic cloves, peeled and chopped
4–5 tablespoons olive oil
350 g fregola or any tiny pasta shapes
salt and pepper

To finish
75 g (1 wing) bottarga
handful of chopped parsley
squeeze of lemon juice

Cook the onion and garlic very gently in the oil until they soften – take your time and don't let the mixture brown (this is the *soffritto*).

Meanwhile, cook the fregola in plenty of boiling salted water until tender – 10–12 minutes – then drain, dress with a little of the onion-oil from the pan and fork it up to separate the grains. Toss lightly with the *soffritto* and top with fine gratings or shavings of bottarga. Finish with chopped parsley and a few drops of lemon juice.

SPAGHETTI CON PISTACCHI E BOTTARGA
(SPAGHETTI WITH PISTACHIOS AND BOTTARGA)

The Sardinian dressing for pasta – pistachios and parsley rather than pine kernels and basil – is finished either with grated bottarga or mature pecorino, Sardinia's Parmesan. The two – salty cheese and salty fish – are used interchangeably to add savour and a little extra protein to grain foods. Last year's dried-out bottarga is best grated and sealed in a jar, where it keeps pretty much indefinitely. When it becomes a little gritty, soften the gratings in the hot dressing before you toss it with the pasta.

Serves 4
100 ml olive oil
1 garlic clove, peeled
2 tablespoons shelled pistachios, roughly chopped
2 tablespoons fresh breadcrumbs
2 tablespoons chopped parsley
1 tablespoon grated lemon zest
350 g spaghetti

To finish
bottarga, for grating

Heat half the oil in a small frying pan and fry the garlic until it softens, takes a little colour and perfumes the oil. Remove and discard the garlic, or leave it in and mash it into the oil, as you please.

(recipe continued overleaf)

Reheat the garlic oil, add the chopped pistachios and stir over a gentle heat until the nuts are lightly toasted. Remove and reserve. Add the rest of the oil, heat and stir in the breadcrumbs. As soon as the breadcrumbs have taken on a little colour, stir in the parsley and lemon zest and remove from the heat.

Meanwhile, cook the spaghetti in plenty of boiling, salted water according to the instructions on the packet, until just tender (you need at least 3 times the volume of water to pasta so that the water returns quickly to the boil). Drain (not too thoroughly) and transfer to a warm serving bowl into which you have trickled a little olive oil. Toss the pasta with the pistachio dressing and finish with grated bottarga.

COCCOIS (SARDINIAN FOCACCIA WITH CURD CHEESE AND MINT)

Sardinian yeast-raised flatbreads topped with curd cheese and mint – a very Sardinian herb – are a cheap, cooked-to-order mid-morning break for office-workers or hungry schoolchildren on the way home.

Serves 2 (4 if sharing)
750 g strong bread flour (Italian 00 for preference)
1 teaspoon salt
1 tablespoon easy-bake yeast (or 25 g fresh yeast)
100 ml olive oil, plus extra for drizzling
100 g fresh ricotta or curd cheese
semolina, for dusting
handful of mint leaves, shredded
sea salt

Mix the flour with the salt and yeast (if fresh, just rub it in as for shortcrust pastry). Add the olive oil and about 300 ml warm water and mix to a soft dough. The texture should be quite sticky and as wet as you can manage comfortably – the softer the dough, the lighter the bread, the crisper the crumb. Or work it by hand, drawing the liquid into the flour gradually, fingers bent to make a hook. Form into a smooth ball and drop it back into the bowl.

Cover the top of the bowl loosely with cling film or a plastic bag and set in a warm place for an hour or so until the dough is light and spongy and doubled in volume.

Meanwhile, set the ricotta to drain in a sieve over a bowl. Brush a couple of baking sheets with oil and sprinkle lightly with semolina, tipping off the excess. On a semolina-dusted board, knead the dough to distribute the air bubbles and work in half the drained ricotta and half the mint leaves. Cut the dough in half and work each piece into a ball, transfer to the baking sheets and pat out to the thickness of your little finger. Dust with a little more semolina, cover loosely with a cloth and leave to rise again for 30–40 minutes, until puffy.

Preheat the oven to 220°C / Gas 7.

Prod the surface of the dough with stiff fingers to make dimples, drizzle a little oil into the dips, scatter with sea salt and sprinkle with the rest of the curd cheese and mint. Finish with a shower of warm water from your fingertips.

Bake for 20–25 minutes until well risen and browned. As soon as you take the focaccia out of the oven, drizzle the surface with a little more oil. *Coccois* is best eaten fresh from the oven, but is also pretty good reheated.

SUSPIRUS DI MANDORLE E LIMONE (ALMOND AND LEMON MACAROONS)

These little almond cookies flavoured with lemon zest and glazed with lemon icing are a Christmas treat for Sardinian children. If you want to cook ahead, omit the final glazing and they will keep well in an airtight tin.

(recipe continued overleaf)

Makes about 30–40
1 kg unskinned almonds
750 g caster sugar
zest and juice of 2 unwaxed lemons
4 large eggs
3–4 tablespoons icing sugar

To finish
250 g icing sugar
zest and juice of 2 unwaxed lemons

Grind the almonds to a powder and mix with the sugar and lemon zest in a large bowl.

Beat the eggs together and tip them into a hole in the middle of the ground almonds. Work the wet ingredients into the dry with your hands until the mixture forms a smooth soft paste (you may need a little icing sugar or warm water to achieve the result).

Preheat the oven to 180°C/Gas 4.

Spread 2–3 tablespoons of icing sugar on a pastry board. Dust your hands with icing sugar, break off walnut-sized pieces of the paste and roll into small balls. Roll the balls in the icing sugar and arrange them on a baking tray rinsed with cold water. Flatten each ball with a finger dusted in icing sugar so that the cookies bake evenly. Bake for 20–25 minutes, until lightly browned top and bottom, and transfer to a wire rack to cool.

To prepare the icing when you're ready to serve, sift the icing sugar into a bowl, mix in the lemon zest and, using a wooden spoon, beat in enough lemon juice to make a runny icing which holds its shape on the back of the spoon. Use this to ice the cookies when perfectly cool, and return them to a very low (or just turned-off) oven for 3–4 minutes to set the surface.

Tasmania

TASMANIANS, MANY OF THEM PROUD DESCENDANTS
of the rougher end of the convict trade, are accustomed to taking
life more or less as it comes with tolerance and without com-
plaint. As inhabitants of an island a few degrees north of the
Antarctic, on the receiving end of the Roaring Forties, this policy
is sound.

There is, however, the problem of the great abalone rob-
bery. Abalone is a giant limpet of considerable commercial
importance when sold into the right market. The right market is
not Tassie.

'Bastards don't even pay tax,' mutters the man in front of me
in the queue for a cab to Launceston, Tasmania's second township
and site of the island's only airport. 'It's a bloody disgrace.'

If tolerance is one thing, tax-free limpet-thieving is quite another.

'Citizens of Tassie! Let's get real about the great abalone rip-off!' bellows the *Hobart Examiner* on a ten-foot-high billboard strategically placed opposite the exit to the airport. 'What can we do to stop the thieving crims?' Tasmania's state newspaper is rightfully outraged by the criminals depriving Tassie of one of her most profitable exports.

Abalone is an unusually large and succulent single-shell mollusc that attaches itself to rocks by a long rubbery foot, the edible part, in the deep waters off the coast of Tassie. The meat, fresh or dried or canned, is much prized in Japan and China, where it fetches as high a price as shark's fin and the gluey little swifts' nests used to make bird's nest soup.

The islanders don't want to eat it or even gather it, since abalone is extremely tenacious when fixed to a rock. But there are unscrupulous traders prepared to pay others to do so, and a rip-off is a rip-off. To add insult to injury, the catch is never landed on Tassie's shores, enabling the crims to operate scot-free.

Tasmania is a holiday destination for the citizens of south-eastern Australia, Melbourne, Adelaide and Sydney. The draw is partly her history – pride is taken in her convict ancestry, and Tassie was home to a particularly brutal penal colony that

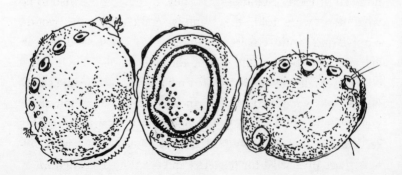

provided labour for sawmills to build ships for her colonial masters. And partly a wild and beautiful landscape with untamed wilderness, virgin rainforest and a climate in which fruit and vegetables ripen to perfection.

The Dutch were first to make landfall, but didn't settle. First to till the soil were the British, arriving initially as farmers and shepherds and later as convicts and jailers. The first penal colony was established in 1802 through orders from Sydney on instruction from London. Instruction from London explains many things on the dark side of the history of Tasmania.

Darkest of all is the loss of an indigenous race of sweet-natured lotus-eaters, small of stature and golden of skin, the original inhabitants of the island.

Early settlers describe a mysterious people who ran naked in the woods, somewhat more African than their mainland cousins in appearance, amiable and tolerant, who had long since forgotten – or never needed to know – how to make fire or cure animal skins or fish in the sea. Having no need of material goods of any kind, they lived contentedly by the shore, eating shellfish and sea vegetables.

The colonisers found them unfit for any useful purpose, indifferent to the demands of their self-appointed masters and lacking in any work ethic that might be of use for logging and ship-building, the main responsibility of the colonisers. Having no need of food or clothes or money, if they didn't wish to do what they were told, they simply melted into the woods, reappearing with equal suddenness in unexpected places, alarming the children and scaring the dogs.

The result, inevitably for the time, was that Tasmania's First Nation was wiped from the earth without regret. Their skulls were collected by Victorian anthropologists. Their solemn faces recorded in life – blunt-nosed, dark-skinned, etched with sadness – are preserved for posterity in engravings labelled *Male*,

Female, Infant. They left behind no carvings or artefacts or words or even thoughts, although there's evidence that they appreciated beauty in their surroundings in a few shell-middens observed by walkers along the western cliffs at exactly the points where the view of the sunset is at its most magnificent.

The contents of these depositories, in the absence of any living witness, tell of a diet of clams, mussels, oysters, razor-shells and seaweeds. All sea creatures and sea vegetables are edible, though some make better eating than others and a good number of the seaweeds are too tough to chew. And since the original inhabitants didn't swim, it's probable that the *Hobart Examiner*'s contentious abalone escaped their attention unless washed ashore on the beach.

Those of the settlers who were sensible enough to enquire what the natives gathered from the woods learned that certain leaves, roots and seeds were used for food or medicine or both. Most widespread of these and the only one whose edibility was guaranteed by the settlers is pigweed, *Portulaca oleracea*, a sprawling mat of greenery with fat juicy leaves and pretty little purple flowers which develop into tiny, black, highly nutritious seeds.

The colonies had to be profitable enough to warrant support from their investors in London. Colonial governors, responsible to British politicians, had to ensure their territories earned their keep through the provision of raw materials and labour. In the absence of an indigenous workforce on Tassie, convicts were brought in to work in the shipyards that provided Sydney with ships for the ocean crossings. Supplies of timber for the yards were floated downriver from ancient pine forests logged by convict labour.

The convicts, unlike the natives, did at least speak the same language as their overseers, wore clothes rather than running around naked, feared the forest worse than the whips wielded by their masters, and if they did manage to escape, were considered unlikely to survive. The few who did were given safe haven in the settlements, accepted into households where every strong arm was a godsend, and the authorities in Sydney were none the wiser.

High summer comes to Tassie when it's winter in the northern hemisphere. I am on the island with a brief from a country magazine whose adventurous urban readership might be encouraged to follow the tourist trail from the town of Launceston to Hobart, the capital. It's my first visit and I'm curious to explore.

Tassie's tourist trade has been stimulated by newly established wineries and innovative young chefs trained in Sydney and Melbourne opening restaurants within them. The clientele, on the whole, are weekenders from the mainland, where the craze is for bush-foods gathered from the wild. The locals are not convinced. Tassie may be well endowed with wilderness but those who knew how to live on forest gleanings are gone, and the incomers who replaced them are suspicious of unfamiliar eatables wrapped in paper-bark and flavoured with bush-pepper.

Launceston is Australia's third oldest town and sits four-square in the middle of the farmland of the north. While Hobart has a reputation for prosperity and attracts investment, the same is not true of Launceston.

Once out of the airport and through the suburbs, it's evident that Launceston's residential centre, two-storey balconied houses forming elegant town squares, is unaltered since the days of the Prince Regent, when the extravagant architecture of the Brighton Pavilion was all the rage. Iron fretwork canopies supported on dilapidated pillars provide shade for those who take their leisure after work, catching the last of the summer sunshine and watching the world go by.

My bed-and-breakfast is in a Victorian quarter built for immigrant workers, pretty little cottages with roses round the door. Some of the cottages, says my landlady, are holiday rentals or retreats for retirees from the mainland. Front yards are bright embroideries of English cottage-garden flowers. Wooden benches provided for rest and recreation are set against billowing hedges of blue-flowered plumbago, with jasmine and honeysuckle to scent the air. Reminders of high summer are everywhere: plump cushions of marguerites, tall stands of Madonna lilies, bottlebrush bushes awash with butterflies.

People eat early in Launceston. You're not too early at six, and later than seven-thirty is unthinkable. Tassie's culinary habit is basically English with a touch of Scots and Welsh. Workers and schoolchildren pick up pies and pasties from the bakeries at midday, but the evening's culinary entertainment belongs to the Mediterranean immigrants, mostly Italians and Greeks.

Shortly after seven on a quiet Monday, Launceston's fine-dining destination, the Gazebo, is heaving with families eating pasta with seafood from the blackboard menu.

I choose a seared seafood salad.

'Good choice,' says the cheerful Italian waitress.

The seafood – a pyramid of tiny scallops, monster prawns, infant squid and lemony salad leaves – is as bright and sparkling as a rock-pool just filled by the tide. Whatever else happens in the watering-holes of Launceston – and I have heard dire tales of English stodge – this is high-class Mediterranean, the kind of cooking you might find at a beachside restaurant in Portofino but without the yachts and the prices.

As the blue-beaked crow flies, a mere fifty miles separates the capital, Hobart, from Launceston, and I am on my way south on a tour bus promising the gastronomic experience of a lifetime, taking in overnight stops and wineries. I am not much of a wine-buff – my interest lies in how the wine tastes with food. And I find that very good wine – which I can certainly recognise (and I have an excellent nose for anything corked) – is for those who drink wine on its own, which cuts the enjoyment by half. The only exception, as far as I'm concerned, is what Australian winemakers call the 'stickies' – dessert wines, particularly the sweet wines of Valencia or Monbazillac, nothing grand, which taste of summer in winter.

The island grows most of its everyday food – meat, fish, vegetables and fruit – with market gardens concentrated in the warm north and orchards in the south, while the dairy herds of King Island, a few miles off the western tip, provide milk that tastes of hay meadow as well as delicious butter, cheese and cream.

The road follows the river at first, a broad, slow-moving ribbon that makes its way through Launceston and continues on its way through fertile farmland with orchards, wheat fields and pastureland. Black and white cows and brown-fleeced sheep alternate with enclosures of emu and ostrich.

Margie, our tour guide, is also incensed by the abalone scandal highlighted in the *Hobart Examiner*. It is, she says, disgraceful that such a high-value export is of no benefit to the islanders, and there must be corruption in the capital. There is always corruption, in Margie's opinion, wherever politicians are in the pockets of big business.

This is fighting talk. Margie is a staunch admirer of her namesake, Margaret Thatcher, and holds equally robust opinions. The abalone problem, she says, is no more than the tip of the iceberg in terms of loss to community coffers. The criminals – familiarly known as 'crims' – have stolen around seventy million Australian dollars, almost as much as the seventy-five million billed by the lawyers to the State to uphold the law. And the State, in the *Examiner*'s own words, has done bugger all about the thieving bastards.

The rest of the tour bus – about thirty locals in holiday mood exploring the culinary delights of their own island – agree with Margie, but with reservations. Tasmanians admire toughness and cunning and a willingness to ignore the law, as did those who survived the penal colonies. A view widely held among the islanders is that disobeying the law requires much the same skills as upholding it. And besides, says the man in the seat over the aisle, in the old days, when the island was awash with Sydney's overflow of hardened criminals from Britain – the ones who'd committed crimes a bit more serious than stealing a loaf of bread – the real villains were the bankers of London keen to ship out an expendable, unpaid labour-force to protect their investment in the colonies.

I pull my sunhat over my ears and bury my nose in my guidebook. As the only Pom on board, and a Londoner at that, I've no desire to put myself in the firing line in defence of my ancestors.

Gastronomic excitements anticipated on the way south – which is really north to a Pom like me – include the catering facilities newly opened in the wineries. Tassie's vineyards are clustered together in the warm north rather than the cold lands of the south, last port of call before the ice floes.

At midday, right on schedule, we turn in through electronically operated gates and proceed by way of an avenue of mulberry trees. Round each tree is a carpet of claret-coloured fruit gently turning alcoholic, attracting the attention of a flock of wine-sipping butterflies. Insects are as susceptible as any barfly to the mood-altering qualities of strong drink, and capable, in my observation in the cider orchards of my homeland, of behaving just as badly towards their fellow insects. There are serious amateur wine-buffs amongst our number, and I keep these thoughts to myself.

The winery is a long low steel and glass building dwarfed by huge steel storage tanks. Stretching out on either side are neatly tended vines heavy with ripening fruit. Lunch is a help-yourself buffet and will be followed, Margie assures us, by a tasting of the vineyard's finest wines and an opportunity to buy.

Mindful of having missed my chance to lose a pound or two at Launceston's Roman baths, I head straight for the salad buffet but am diverted by a basket of freshly baked muffins with olives and sun-dried tomatoes, both, Margie assures us, grown on the island.

The muffins are very good. I slip round to the kitchen to congratulate the chef and beg him to talk me through the recipe. The chef has 'Surfers Do It Standing Up' emblazoned on his T-shirt and 'Sheilas Rule' tattooed on one muscular biceps. Cheffing, surfing and women go hand in hand in Oz.

'Muffins? Nothing to it,' he says with a grin. 'Take your standard muffin batter, mix it up with whatever you want, tip it in your usual muffin tray, chuck 'em in the oven and take 'em out when they're done.'

This is more than I usually get when begging a recipe. Chefs are canny fellows and don't usually hand it out step by step. On the other hand, I've been in the kitchen for a good few years myself and can usually pick up the threads.

The really useful stuff, however, is not the recipe itself but what the chef has noticed while he cooks.

'Any advice,' I enquire cautiously, 'for Poms who reckon a muffin is a crumpet without the holes?'

Another grin is followed by just the advice I'm looking for: 'Mix the wet and dry stuff separately, leave the mix lumpy, heat the tin before you tip in the batter, fill the dips just short of the top and bake 'em really high.'

'Gotta go,' he adds cheerfully. 'Surf's up and sheilas wait for no man.'

The wine-tasting is judged a success by our amateur wine-buffs, which is pretty much the whole busload apart from me. I sip and suck and spit discreetly, as I always do at wine-tastings. The wines are workmanlike and unassuming – to use professional wine-talk – rough enough to taste good with shepherd's pie or cut the richness of an oxtail stew. English cooking is the norm in Tassie, and there's no doubt that the wines, more a touch of the claret than Burgundy, suit the style.

Back in the bus, notes are compared and views exchanged, some quite heatedly. The vineyard grows Pinot Noir and Riesling, the grapes that – in considered opinions – make the only respectable drinking wine produced in the vineyards of Tassie. Tassie's vintages, there's general agreement, are not yet anything serious but well able to hold up their heads with similarly priced wines on the mainland.

Holding up heads with the mainland is important in Tassie. Tasmanians, in the view of the mainland – how to put it delicately? – are born with more than one head as a result of being overly affectionate with their sisters. Or, in the absence of female relatives, their sheep.

The islanders retaliate with good humour and equal indelicacy. You won't find any Pommie-type whinging in Tassie. The first settlers, being Poms, built bread ovens and baked cakes. As a result, Tasmania's bakeries, mostly family enterprises which have opened shops along the old drovers' roads, bake better bread, cakes and scones than you'll find anywhere on the mainland and – come to think of it – anywhere else where Englishwomen set up house.

If the main difficulty on the island is obtaining fresh fish – apart, apparently, from the Gazebo in Launceston – oysters are no problem and nor is farmed salmon, but ocean fish goes straight to the markets of Melbourne and Sydney and the fishermen won't divide the catch for small-time customers. Even in Hobart, which is a fishing port in its own right, ordinary folk have to buy from the smaller boats, which means the supply is not reliable.

Island sensibilities are fine-tuned to suggestions of lack of excellence. What's more, no one on the tour bus is in any doubt that the best butter and cream in the world comes from King Island, just off the north coast of Tassie, and the islanders prepare excellent preserves since the climate is perfectly suited to orchard fruits and ripens berries to perfection.

Bread, butter and jam – and cakes, naturally – are undoubtedly what Tassie does best. Pit-stops along the road are timed to allow passengers to sample the skill of a local bakery, always well signposted and offering takeaway hot pies and conveniently sized cookies and cakes in the form of fist-sized iced fancies, muffins, fruit slices and Anzac biscuits.

Anzac biscuits, famously baked by Australian women for their men at the front in both world wars, are another reminder of bad behaviour by the Poms. After the movie *Gallipoli* arrived on Antipodean screens, Poms travelling anywhere down under are well advised to avoid discussion of lions led by donkeys.

Stone-fruit orchards and berry farms are a development of the kitchen gardens of the settlers, with no need to bring plants or expertise from outside. One such is Kate's Berry Farm, our destination for the afternoon. The bus slows and turns uphill into a side road at the hand-painted sign.

Kate herself awaits her visitors, hands on hip, outside of a pretty, white-painted farmhouse with roses round the door. Kate herself is auburn-haired – evidence on the island of Scottish descent – sturdy, dungareed, muscular and of the breed of island women who not only keep the home fires burning but chop the wood which heats the oven which bakes the bread and keeps the household fed.

Kate digs, plants and manages a hundred acres of blackberries, raspberries, strawberries and loganberries, with a side interest in a new orchard of stone fruits. Today's visitors are in luck as Kate's sister, her partner in the enterprise, has just picked the first crop of cherries.

'It's women like us who've always done the work on the farm,' says Kate, surveying her domain with pride. Stretching into the distance are neatly hoed strawberry beds and rows of raspberry canes, all laden with ripening fruit.

The men, she continues, take paid work somewhere else whenever they can find it to bring in the money. On a labour-intensive farm such as this all the women – daughters, wives, sisters – work. Most of the crop is sent fresh to market, but in times of glut, what cannot be sold is frozen for the time of year when the plants are dormant and there's time to prepare preserves. In the old days this had to be done straight away or the fruit would rot. Freezers are a godsend – an enterprise like this wouldn't work without them.

All business takes place in the farmhouse's front parlour, where guests can take a cup of tea with a home-made scone or a

slice of cake. In the cold months, when there's time to do other things, Kate's mother makes the jam, and her sister makes the ice cream to sell to visitors in the summer. Kate's Berry Farm ice cream is famous all over the island, exported to the smart restaurants of Hobart and Launceston, including the Gazebo.

The latest addition to Kate's botanical mix are apple-tree clones.

If we don't mind a short walk, Kate will take us on a tour of the glasshouse.

Our hostess is as proud of the lines of identical young shoots cosseted in the greenhouse as a mother with her newborn baby. Their living space is tightly controlled and growth restricted until they've grown into tiny trees and look like bonsai. The clones don't like being handled. There's no need to repot or replant until they're strong enough to take the stress.

Stress is the new buzzword among Tassie's producers. Word has spread from the growers of the Mediterranean that fruits and vegetables subject to stressful conditions are sweeter, denser-fleshed and more fragrant than those grown in greenhouses under perfect conditions. In Sicily, for instance, tomatoes produced under extreme conditions – minimal watering, poor soil and constant battering from wind and sea – can be sun-dried in half the time it takes elsewhere.

The little apple trees have a bright future, Kate continues. Bug-resistant and capable of producing perfect fruit throughout the growing season, there are opportunities for export world-wide. China has just discovered apples and can't get enough of them. No question but cloning is the future. Cherries will be next, and maybe even peaches.

'Time for chow!' shouts Margie, poking her head through the door and interrupting Kate's reverie.

Chow is what we are here for. We follow Kate into the new tearoom, a large airy addition to the front of the family's home.

Today there is a choice of home-baked scones to spread with thick yellow King Island cream and Kate's mother's award-winning raspberry jam. There are also apple slices with a jug of home-made egg custard, or lamingtons – coconut-dusted squares of chocolate cake – to eat with a scoop of freshly churned strawberry ice cream made with berries picked that very morning. And to cheer us on our way on the bus, a pound or two apiece of the beautiful dark-red cherries.

On our return to the bus, cheeks bulging, I slip into a vacant seat next to a well-upholstered middle-aged woman travelling alone like me, who has been partaking of Kate's lamingtons with particular enthusiasm.

Her name is Muriel and she is indeed an expert on what can be considered Australia's national cake. The cake's invention, continues Muriel, can be credited to Lady Lamington, wife of a Governor of Oz in the days of old Queen Vic. There's an affection for British royalty in Tassie, though this does not extend to British politicians responsible for the carnage of both world wars in which so many of Her Majesty's loyal subjects came to grief.

I must not take such references to heart, she continues kindly, since it's well known that many English soldiers suffered the same fate. I agree that this is true. Anzac biscuits and lamingtons are just two of the many reminders of wartime that pop up when nobody's looking.

We move to safer territory, recipe-swapping, and embark on an in-depth discussion of whether or not a drop of vinegar or a pinch of salt increases the volume of the whisked egg whites when baking soft meringue for a pavlova. Muriel goes for vinegar and I vote for salt. Passion fruit is a must for the filling; kiwi fruit can only be considered acceptable in New Zealand.

This evening – the high spot of the journey – is a night in a lodge in the wilderness, convict territory.

To prepare us for the experience, Margie decides to alert us to the perils of the wild lands of the west with a dissertation on what really happened in those far-off days when Tassie's cuisine was not all about strawberry ice cream and chocolate cake.

Let there be no misunderstanding: the convicts were starving so they ate each other.

Never mind if nobody else wants to talk about it; Margie considers it her duty to do so.

Teachers don't talk about it in school, but it's there for anyone to read in the diaries, the stories people kept in a locked box under the family Bible so nobody knew the truth.

And this, proposes Margie, is a truth that needs to be acknowledged, whether people want to believe it or not. Much as Nelson Mandela obliged his nation to acknowledge both sides of the story, truth and reconciliation is a two-way conversation.

'We all know what we did to the people who were here before us. What we don't want to know is what we did to ourselves.'

Margie offers this insight into island history, she continues, because the blame goes both ways. Feed a man on slops not fit for pigs and make him work till he drops and he'll die. And if he doesn't die, he'll eat whoever dies ahead of him. And if he's not yet dead, he'll help him on his way.

'If you treat a man worse than a dog he'll behave worse than a dog. The ones who managed to escape into the forest had to eat to live.'

We are still and silent, hoping the story will end right here. It doesn't.

'What else could they do? What would any of us have done?'

We hope the question is rhetorical. It isn't.

'First they took out the outsiders, then the weaklings, and then it got so bad none of them slept at all in case they woke up basted on the barbie.'

Margie waits for a reaction to the joke. Nobody laughs. Basted on the barbie is not what any of us would wish to wake up to.

'What we need to acknowledge is that the ones who got out were cannibals and everyone knew it. Any of them could have been your granddad or mine.'

Margie takes a deep breath and returns to the fray. She is not a woman to let us off the hook just yet. The story has a happy ending – of sorts. The last ship to be built was stolen by the last of the convicts, who sailed the vessel all the way to the coast of Chile. This was all the more remarkable since the ship's stores were no more than were sufficient for the short voyage round the coast to Sydney.

The story doesn't end here. As soon as the ship docked by the quayside in Valparaíso, the Spaniards clapped the convict crew in irons and sailed them right back. Meanwhile, word got out and by the time the ship sailed into Sydney harbour, the crowds went wild and carried the convicts up to the courthouse in triumph. The judge congratulated all present on an excellent result, everyone went home for dinner and the delicate subject of the ship's stores was not mentioned at the time or thereafter.

What happened can be taken, says Margie, with a sideways glance at me as the representative Pom – I'm used to this by now and react with a cheerful wave – as a prime example of Aussie virtues of resourcefulness and willingness to flout authority. This is as much a part of Tassie's true identity as the jokes about growing two heads.

Laughter breaks out. The atmosphere lightens just in time for our arrival at our billet right in the middle of the very forests through which the cannibal convicts escaped.

Sunsets are spectacular everywhere on the island, but in the west, a coastline rimmed by pink granite cliffs capped by dense green forest beneath which blue waters churn white, the sun drops like a stone in a blaze of ruby and gold to the end of the world.

The stormy west coast is mountainous, heavily forested and still sparsely inhabited, attracting backpackers and nature-lovers to camp out on the beach or take advantage of the little settlements of rough shelters left over from the days of the convict shipbuilders. One or two of the abandoned settlements have been converted into boutique hotels, where adventurous chefs from the mainland are experimenting with forest gleanings.

As soon as the bus turns off the highway on to a bumpy forest track through eucalyptus woods, it comes to a halt at a pretty whitewashed lodge surrounded by a cluster of log cabins. When we descend from the bus and make our way into the lodge to collect our room keys, Margie has an announcement. There is news, both bad and good.

The bad news is that the chef is away on the mainland at a bush-tucker conference, where his expertise in forest gleanings is expected to cause a sensation. The good news is that, to make up for any disappointment caused by the unavailability of the featured expertise, drinks are on the house and dinner is on the barbie.

Mention of the barbie gives pause for thought. But with good humour and Tassie's appetite for indelicacy restored, the announcement triggers a short burst of tasteless barbie jokes.

Dinner on the barbie, Margie continues with a frown at the more unruly of the jokesters, will feature hamburgers and sausages with – accompanied by a quick glance in my direction – a vegetarian option.

I laugh appreciatively as a demonstration of a Pom's ability to take a joke.

'Good on you,' whispers Muriel, patting my hand. Muriel is an enthusiastic admirer of *The Two Fat Ladies*, recycled on loop on Tassie's TV station. When I admit to a passing acquaintance with the famous ladies, both sadly deceased, our friendship is sealed.

The mood among the group is further lifted by cans of cold beer and glasses of chilled white wine embellished with small blue flowers. These I know to be a member of the flax family, one of the few edible plants recognised by the settlers, valued for its oily little seeds as a source of frying-oil.

Muriel, asked for confirmation, agrees that this is indeed so, although her mother told her that pounding the tiny seeds was hard work for little gain. Her grandmother, she adds, used the fibrous stalks for weaving sturdy linen cloth of a far higher quality than is available today.

Refreshed and cheerful, the company disperses to inspect the accommodation in anticipation of unlimited free drinks and a hot meal of recognisable provenance.

The cabins have been comfortably modernised and equipped with en-suite shower rooms. A shower is more than welcome, and by the time I rejoin the group, the party is already in full swing. Inspecting the offerings on the barbie, I skip the meat and go for the vegetarian option sizzling in a pan set over the coals. This, a combination of eggs, cream and greens cooked like a Spanish tortilla, is dished up on a thin sheet of paper-bark. This is the only forest gleaning – other than the flax flowers now in evidence as pretty little arrangements on the tables – not subject to government inspection unless certified by an expert such as the absent chef.

Looking for somewhere to sit and eat my portion of frittata, I see Muriel wave me to her side, patting a vacant place on the bench.

'Sit here, my dear, and tell me all about yourself and why you're here.'

I explain about forest gleanings and how much I had been looking forward to sampling the chef's much-praised menu on behalf of the sophisticated readership of *Country Living*, the magazine to which I contribute a cookery column. The magazine is popular in Tassie and Muriel is pleased by the connection. This exchange pleases us both, the frittata is very good, and I retire to my bed under the eucalyptus trees to the strains of 'Waltzing Matilda' rendered by a male-voice choir that would not have disgraced itself at a sing-along in my local pub in Wales.

I wake just before dawn. My fellow explorers are still asleep, so I set out in the direction of the ocean with my sketchbook, intending to catch the sunrise. In the forest around the cabins, my bird-watching binoculars pick up the quick movements in the branches of unfamiliar birds with familiar names – pink-breasted robin, forest raven, magpie-lark. Once out of the woods, the landscape opens up into rolling dunes in which sunburst clumps of enormous grasses bunched together like Martian wedding-bouquets have found a foothold in the sand.

The grasses have needle-sharp tips, tearing flesh and skin. I'm glad to reach the safety of the shoreline. In my days as a botanical and bird artist, I spent many happy hours at the Natural History Museum in London, where I made drawings of the stuffed birds and animals on display. Among the panoramas of Australia's marsupials, I made a particular study of those that had vanished soon after the settlers set about eliminating the competition. The most haunting of these was the Tasmanian Wolf, the island's largest predator, last of its kind, snarling from behind the glass at the species responsible for its fate.

I tread cautiously, conscious of reports of recent sightings of a hyena-like creature rattling dustbins in urban backyards. The *Hobart Examiner*, carried with me on the bus as a source of more up-to-date information than my guidebook, indicated that abalone thieves were not the only source of anxiety among the populace. Tasmanian Devils had to be hiding out somewhere, possibly right here.

Muriel greets me with some anxiety on my return from my dawn raid on the flora and fauna to join the breakfast queue. She too had been worried about the possible presence of man-eaters in the woods – two-legged or four – and I am happy to have found a friend.

Better still, Muriel promises to send me her prizewinning recipe for lamingtons as soon as she gets home, and I, in turn, promise to include it in my column, editor willing. Editors, we agree, are as bad as tour guides when they get the bit between their teeth.

We are on our way bright and early in the bus, rattling back to the main road through the eucalyptus forest and down the coast through fertile farmland until we turn towards the ocean. Today's excitement is Jim's Oyster Farm and we have a date to go out on the oyster flats to collect the raw materials of lunch with the proprietor himself.

Muriel is not convinced by the notion of eating anything raw, let alone alive and quivering, and is hoping for something in the way of oyster fritters, or possibly oysters in cheese sauce bubbled up under the grill, as her mother prepared them on the rare occasions when wild oysters were available in Hobart. Oyster farming has greatly improved the availability of fresh oysters, so she is looking forward to recreating a recipe from Constance Spry for macaroni cheese with oysters which she remembers from her childhood in the 1950s.

I, on the other hand, like my oysters as nature delivers them, freshly opened on the half-shell with a squeeze of lemon and a fistful of Black Velvet – a pint of Guinness and champagne in equal measure – while perched on a high stool at the bar in Wheelers in Soho in the old days, when the world and I were young. We all have our memories, and this is mine.

Right now, decanted from the bus, we are braving the wind-swept estuary to meet the proprietor of Jim's Oyster Farm. Margie has already put her charges in the picture. Supplier of the most succulent bivalves ever tasted to eager customers as far away as Sydney and Melbourne, Jim is a hero whose mission is to change the world. He may be a man of few words, continues Margie, and he doesn't talk about himself, but even though he may not wield financial muscle or make speeches or lobby politicians, what he does is already a game-changer among those who do the real work of farming the sea.

The man in question – arms akimbo over his oilskins, lux-uriantly bearded, weather-beaten and young for a man who has already achieved such a formidable reputation – is leaning by a battered hut with 'Oyster-shack – visitors welcome' roughly scrawled in blue paint above the door.

Tassie's oyster farmers – Jim himself and a few hardy entrepreneurs established along the coast – co-operate with the tourist industry by offering trips to the oyster beds to sample the shellfish freshly shucked in situ. The idea has been a success. Popular with the tour-bus operators, it provides an additional source of income for the oystermen both in and out of the tourist season.

First we are to inspect Jim's oyster nursery, a line of tanks in the shed.

Jim breeds his own stock, harvesting the tiny spat – infant oysters no bigger than a pinhead – and coaxing them tenderly to toddlerhood, moving them on to the flats only when conditions are right.

For a man of few words, Jim is surprisingly eloquent when it comes to baby oysters. Young oysters don't like sudden surprises – anyone who understands the oyster's natural life-cycle can see the stress-marks on their shells. They're like children, not ready to leave home until they're teenagers, and even then you have to keep an eye on them.

Now, for those of us who wish to take advantage of the authentic experience of oyster gathering, our chariot awaits. Jim quickens his pace as we reach the oyster-barge. The vehicle, a rusty platform resting on tank-treads, is clearly his pride and joy.

'It may be ugly but it does the business,' he says, patting what looks like a steering wheel with obvious affection. 'We modelled it on a D-Day landing craft in the movie with Tom Hanks.'

We climb aboard, arrange ourselves cautiously on the wooden benches that line the sides, the engine splutters and the vehicle moves forward with surprising smoothness on to the mud flats without a shudder.

I take out my sketchbook and settle back contentedly to record the scene as best I may – never mind that the paper is already speckled with droplets of rain, this is what I came for, an experience I can write about and the readership will love. I am already working out the shape the article will take, describing in my head the wild beauty of the place, seabirds sailing overhead, the silence of this windswept estuary between reed beds and wooded hills and the jagged outline of twin headlands, the distant murmur of waves breaking against invisible rocks.

Spars of ancient shipwrecks punctuate the muddy shoreline among the reed beds, reminders that this is the final resting place of the Roaring Forties, the winds that sailors dread. For those who survived to make landfall, Tassie is the last port of call before the ocean turns to ice. One of our number, an experienced yachtsman, tells us that, even with modern navigational aids, ships lose all knowledge of where they are. There are stories of shipwrecked sailors convinced they've made landfall on the shores of Africa.

We reach the water's edge. Jim cuts the engine and waits for his passengers to hear the silence.

When he speaks, his voice is soft. 'Now you can see it as we do. This is who we are and why we're here.'

As if to confirm his words, the sun – until now no more than a soft glow on the southern horizon – breaks through the bank of cloud and turns the ocean into dancing pools of light.

'We chose this place, just as the Old Ones did before us. We come for the beauty of it, the cleanest waters, the freshest breeze.'

When he speaks again, he's smiling, no longer the taciturn fisherman reluctant to engage in idle chitchat, but a man who knows his place and finds it good.

'Sometimes I come here when there's no need to work the beds or gather the crop, and stand on the edge of the ocean where the Old Ones stood, and feel their presence, and know just as they did that the world is beautiful and strange.'

Another pause and a smile, broader this time. 'And of course we come here for the oysters – the best you'll ever taste.'

Laughter greets this sudden flash of salesmanship. The spell is broken. Jim swings over the running board, hauls up a netful of rough-shelled, saucer-shaped bivalves, takes a head count of his passengers, removes a short-bladed knife from a holder on his belt, and begins to shuck.

One by one his passengers accept their offering, tip back throats, and swallow. I am last to receive my shell, preoccupied with tucking away my sketchbook safely in my pocket.

'Here. Taste.'

Jim leans towards me, smiling. Gently cradled in his out-stretched hand is an opened oyster on the half-shell, pearly and luscious and almost translucent. The flesh is soft and sweet and salty in my mouth, and the taste is creamy and silky and a little metallic, incomparably delicious.

Jim sees the pleasure on my face, and laughs.

'That's good.'

The engine ignites, our companions are waiting and the rain is falling in earnest.

Later, back at the rearing shed where the infant oysters are coddled in their tanks, he finds me. Muriel has told him I'm writing an article for a magazine. Tourism is important to the oyster farmers and he wants to make sure I get the story right.

'It's not only what we can do for the oysters but what they can do for us. They teach us to be patient. They come to maturity in their own time, reminding us to enjoy what we have, of our good fortune in living here in peace and tranquillity in this beautiful place.'

The future is as uncertain for the farmers as it is for the fishermen. 'Everyone knows what's happening out in the wild. Everyone in the industry, wild or farmed, knows it's bad. And everyone knows what needs to be done.'

He shakes his head. 'We can all see the changes. We see it in the estuary when we look at the oyster shells. We can read what's happening out there like a book. We all know what works and what doesn't. And we know that if what we do works for us, it works for the oysters.'

When he continues, his voice is sombre.

'It's not ignorance. It's not that we don't understand what has to be done. But we have to take action right now, before it's too late. The technology is already in place for farming the seas and restocking the wild.'

Jim's enterprise is already breeding scallops and bringing on young lobsters for release into the wild, and, he adds, there's work being done in the North Atlantic on turbot and cod. If the sea is farmed in ways that don't wreck the seabed or poison the oceans or interfere with breeding in the wild – and there's no doubt it can be done – fish stocks will restore themselves with or without human assistance.

Marketing is the key. As long as farmed fish is seen as inferior and restaurateurs continue to list line-caught and wild as a desirable element in the seafood they sell, things won't change.

'There is a middle way. Salmon farming has moved in the right direction – a lot of it is now free-range and organic. We start our own young salmon in the shallow water in the estuary and then move them gradually into big pens in the ocean where they swim against the tide. With the marketing it's a matter of how you see it. Everyone accepts rope-grown mussels and no one expects wild oysters, so we know it can be done.'

There is also a need to bring farmed fish to market – not only oysters and mussels – at a price that makes it uneconomic to source them from the wild. Abalone is a case in point. If there was enough farmed abalone to satisfy the market – and no one has yet worked out how this can be done – there'd be no money in stealing and the thieves would vanish overnight.

Farmed scallops are still expensive to produce and sell, but one day – not this year but maybe next – oyster farmers will be able to bring farmed scallops to market at a price which will send the dredgers packing.

More controversial is the farming of seahorses for export to China's oriental medicine trade. Dainty little creatures with long snouts and enquiring eyes that float upright among coral reefs, seahorses are already being successfully grown in tanks in disused warehouses by the quayside in Hobart and sold at high prices into an ever-expanding market. The problem, much like the trade in rhino horns and elephant ivory, is that seahorse stocks are already seriously depleted in the wild, and once they've disappeared from the wild, any hope of using their charms to encourage conservation of their habitat will soon vanish altogether.

'We need to do what we have to do and we need to do it now – all of us, all over the world, or those who come after us will never forgive us.'

Jim's impassioned plea is still ringing in my ears as we reach our final destination, the waterfront at Hobart. By the end of the journey, we are no longer a busload of strangers but family. We will all miss Margie, but her message has been taken to heart. I am no longer the alien Pom but an honorary Tasmanian, as will soon be confirmed when I take a glance in the bathroom mirror this evening and find I've grown two heads. Muriel has acquired a dozen of Jim's finest and is already planning a party to sample her macaroni dish and promises a full account of its reception.

The Hobart waterfront sparkles in sunshine. I provide myself with the latest issue of the *Hobart Examiner* and settle down at a harbourside café for a slice of home-made cheesecake and a cup of strong English tea.

Hot news in Hobart is that the harbour's deep-water dock is now open for business and will be celebrated by the arrival this very evening of a three-thousand-passenger cruise-ship. The visitors will be welcomed with a brass band, an exhibition of sheep-shearing and a market with local produce, as well as free tastings of the best the wineries can offer. This is my last day on the island; I can live without the wine and, as a long-time resident of shepherding country, have witnessed enough sheep-shearing to last me a lifetime.

The inside pages of the *Examiner* bring news of a matter close to my heart – and by association, I hope, the magazine's readership. A truffle-oak plantation has come into production after seven years of anxious expectation. Truffles, a high-value crop for those who have the patience to wait, require the restoration of woodland, even if the trees are not native.

It is confidently believed, the paper reports, that the tubers – *melanosporum*, the Périgord black, second in value only to *magnato*, the Piedmont white – are of sufficient quality to fetch high prices as far away as Italy and France. Seven years is a long time to wait for a commercial crop to come to maturity, and even then, in the *Examiner*'s opinion, such time-wasting methods of production may not be advisable or even excusable. There are grants available for promoting new products that might be, on mature consideration by the powers-that-be, better spent on seahorses.

The man who can provide the information on all things to do with exotic fungi is Dougie, Hobart's mushroom king. Dougie, I am informed by a helpful lady in tourist information, will be able to tell me everything I need to know about the truffle harvest. If I wish to consult him and even take a tour of his mushroom sheds, this can be arranged this very day.

Dougie, summoned to provide information on Tassie's mushroom production for an important visiting journalist, is willing to oblige. The very picture of a successful Tassie entrepreneur in smart business suit, shirt unbuttoned at the neck to denote a relaxed way of life, Dougie arrives in a brand-new four-wheeler and opens the door with a flourish.

'Pleased to meet you, lady. Stash the clobber in the back and we'll take a tour.'

I mention my interest in truffle plantations. To be specific, I add as we speed through the suburbs, the black Périgord truffle, the only one of its genre in successful cultivation.

'Rubbish,' says Dougie. 'Pardon my French, but rubbish.'

Dougie delivers this assessment with such vigour that I decide to leave my questions until later – possibly never.

As we leave the outskirts of Hobart, the four-wheeler swings into a concrete yard and comes to a halt beside a huge and windowless warehouse which could easily swallow a whole forest of truffle oaks.

'This is it,' announces Dougie, waving a hand around the concrete battlements. Three more enormous warehouses form the other three sides.

'Follow me, young lady. You're going to have an experience you'll never forget.'

He shoots a heavy iron bolt on the sliding door and stands aside to allow me to enter. The open door releases a cloud of mushroom-scented warmth.

'Smell that,' he says, sniffing appreciatively. 'Pure profit.'

Profit shines moon-white in the darkness, eerie and silent. The scent is fresh and clean and faintly antiseptic.

Light from the open doorway falls on lines of plastic pillows stacked roof-high on slatted shelves.

'Recycled waste,' Doug adds, breathing in the aroma. 'Shit or crap or whatever you call it. Wonderful stuff. The Chinese have been on to it for centuries. Admirable people. Ever been there? No? You should. You'd be amazed by what they can do.'

The door clangs shut behind us and a switch flicks, bathing the stacks in a soft blue light. I follow as Doug strides down the aisles, halting to inspect first one stack and then another.

'This lot is the white-caps, standard stuff. We pick to order for button, mature or open-cap. Over here, we do the exotics. Oyster, straw, shiitake, the ones the Chinese have been growing for centuries and the rest of us are just catching up on.'

The straw mushrooms are slender little toadstools crammed together on artificial logs in clumps. The chefs love them, but the main market is Japan, though Dougie has yet to achieve the volume for export.

Cropping is monitored electronically, dictating the number of pickers bussed in every morning from the line at the employment office in downtown Hobart, mostly immigrant Chinese on minimum wage.

Dougie has come to a halt at a pile of logs. 'See these,' he says, poking at a bundle of what looks like reddish tree-fungi. 'We're working on a new variety the chemists have just come up with. We're calling it beefsteak. It looks and tastes a lot like meat.'

I don't point out that beefsteak mushrooms have been gathered in the wilds since my ancestors and his were running round the wildwood, painting their faces with woad.

Dougie sighs contentedly. 'Treat a mushroom right and you know where you are. Not like that other rubbish. Sure it's romantic. But who gives a recycled excrement for romance?'

Well, Jim, for one.

'We can do anything we want in here. Anything the chemists come up with, we can grow it. You won't even know we've done it. Remember that next time you pick up a box of what says it is wild woodland mushrooms in the supermarket; don't think that's what you're getting.'

He doesn't take risks, protects his investment, feeds it, waters it and cares for it, providing everything it needs to make his money grow. Politicians understand the power of money. Money dictates the future. And the future is right here, right now in this glowing mass of man-made nutrients, this precious source of money shimmering in the darkness.

Soon there will be no more need for unskilled labour in the sheds. Everything will be done by robots and profits will soar.

I listen in silence. All at once the warmth of the recycled air feels cold on my skin and I need light and air and sunshine.

Dougie follows me as I head for the door, snapping the heavy padlock in place, leaving his windowless growing-machine to return to silence and darkness.

As we drive back together into Hobart, Dougie is no less certain than Jim about the need to change the world.

'Our children will thank us for what we've done. Hunger will be unknown, our seas will be clean and our landscapes unpolluted. This is the future – we're too far gone to turn back.'

Dougie may well be right and Jim wrong. When all our food is grown in a man-made circle from production shed to powerhouse to water-pump and back to its own beginnings, our children's world is saved. Romance is no match for reality. There may well be no room for romance in a world where half go hungry and the rest stuffs itself to bursting, I reflect as I watch the towering cruise-ship discharge a thousand well-fed tourists for the evening's gastro-entertainment.

Cast the bones, read the runes, consult the oracle. But if the battle is already lost and the inhabitants of this beautiful planet find no further use for the good things of land and sea, the sun will spread its warmth over barren pastures and spill its light into an empty ocean. And our children, yours and mine, will never know the sweetness of a ripe strawberry still warm from its bed, or pluck a cherry from a tree, or taste the soft salt flesh of an oyster fresh from the sea.

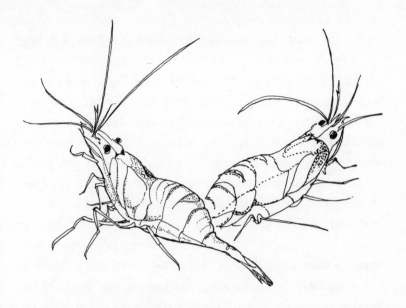

SEARED SEAFOOD SALAD

A fresh seafood salad made with just-cooked shellfish and crust-aceans (except crab, which is not firm enough) is briefly marked on the grill and served warm. Ready-cooked seafood won't cut the mustard.

Serves 2 as a starter
2 tablespoons olive oil
100 g raw prawns or shrimp, heads on
100 g shucked queen scallops, sliced if large
100 g small squid or cuttlefish, cleaned but left whole
100 g firm-fleshed fish fillets
juice of ½ lemon, plus ½ lemon to serve
pinch of chilli flakes
12 mussels or large clams, in their shells, soaked to de-sand
2 generous handfuls of rocket or other mustardy leaves
sea salt

(recipe continued overleaf)

Preheat a heavy iron griddle pan.

Toss the prawns, scallops, squid or cuttlefish and fish fillets in a little olive oil – just enough to give them a shine. Cook them quickly in batches in the hot pan, allowing only 30 seconds on each side. Transfer to a bowl and dress with a little more olive oil, a squeeze of lemon, a pinch of sea salt and a scattering of chilli flakes.

Meanwhile, cook the shellfish – mussels or clams – either on the griddle pan or in a splash of water over a high heat in a closed pan.

Toss the seafood, including the mussels or clams in the shell, with the rocket, dress with a little more olive oil, heap on 2 plates and serve each portion with a quartered lemon.

MACARONI CHEESE WITH OYSTERS

The oyster's not much to look at in the hand: a pair of rough-ridged shells clamped tight shut. To prize these apart, you need a strong fist, a thick cloth and a short stubby knife to go in through the hinge. And suddenly there you have it: a mouthful of pearl-grey flesh bathed in salty juices to cook in a cream sauce folded with macaroni and crisped beneath the grill under a crust of parsley, butter and bread-crumbs.

Serves 4–6
8–12 oysters
350 g macaroni or any tubular pasta
salt

For the sauce
75 g unsalted butter
50 g plain flour
600 ml full-cream milk
1 tablespoon double cream
few drops Worcestershire sauce
salt and pepper

To finish
2 tablespoons fresh breadcrumbs
1 tablespoon grated Cheddar cheese
1 tablespoon finely chopped parsley
1 large knob unsalted butter

Open the oysters and loosen them from the half-shell, saving the fish and the juice.

Set the macaroni to cook in plenty of boiling salted water for 18–20 minutes – or according to the instructions on the packet – until just tender.

Meanwhile make the sauce. Melt the butter in a heavy-based saucepan. Stir in the flour and let it fry for a moment until it looks sandy – don't let it take any colour. Allow the pan to cool while you heat the milk in another pan, removing it from the heat just before the milk boils. Whisk the hot milk slowly into the butter and flour, return the pan to a gentle heat and stir with a wooden spoon until the sauce is smooth, no longer tastes of raw flour and coats the back of the spoon. Stir in the reserved oyster juices and the cream. Taste and season with salt, pepper and a shake of Worcestershire sauce.

Preheat the grill to its highest setting.

Drain the macaroni, fold half of the sauce into it and spread it into a large pie dish. Make indentations in the surface with the back of a spoon and drop an oyster into each dip. Top with the remaining sauce, sprinkle with breadcrumbs tossed with the grated cheese and parsley, and dot the surface with butter. Slip the dish under the grill or in a very hot oven to crisp and brown and bubble.

ANZAC BISCUITS

Oatmeal and coconut biscuits baked hard and crisp for ease of transportation were sent to men as iron rations by the wives of Australian
soldiers fighting in both world wars. Anzac biscuits are still a popular snack in the bakeries of Tasmania.

Makes 12
100 g plain flour
100 g caster sugar
75 g rolled oats
75 g grated coconut
100 g butter
1 tablespoon golden syrup
½ teaspoon bicarbonate of soda

Preheat the oven to 140°C/Gas 1.

Combine the flour, sugar, oats and coconut in a large bowl.
Melt the butter with the syrup. Dissolve the bicarbonate of soda
in 2 tablespoons of boiling water and stir it into the melted
butter.

Fold the wet ingredients into the dry to make a softish mixture
(you may need more water or oats).

Drop teaspoons of the mixture on to a buttered baking tray.
Bake for 30 minutes, until firm and golden.

Transfer to a baking rack to cool. Store in an airtight tin and
serve, re-warmed in the oven if they've lost their crispness, with a
good strong cup of tea.

APPLE SLICE

A buttery cake mixture with a handful of oats for crunch, baked with a layer of cinnamon-dusted apple through the middle – simple but good, particularly with thick clotted cream or a spoonful of home-made strawberry ice cream.

Makes 12
225 g softened butter
225 g soft brown sugar
2 eggs
225 g self-raising flour
2 tablespoons rolled oats
1 tablespoon wheatgerm
2–3 tablespoons milk

For the apple filling
3–4 cooking apples or 4–5 crisp green eating apples,
   peeled, cored and diced
4 tablespoons soft brown sugar
1 level tablespoon ground cinnamon

Preheat the oven to 180°C/Gas 4.

Beat the butter and brown sugar together until light and pale, and gradually beat in the eggs. Fold in the flour along with the oats and wheatgerm. At this point the mixture will be quite dry.

Press half the mixture into a Swiss-roll tin. Spread with the diced apple and sprinkle with half the sugar and half the cinnamon. Add enough milk to the remaining cake mixture to make a dropping con-sistency. Spread this mixture over the apples and sprinkle the top with more cinnamon and sugar.

Bake for 25–30 minutes, until well risen and brown. Cut into a dozen squares and serve warm.

LAMINGTONS

Fist-sized sponge cakes – call them fairy cakes at your peril – covered in chocolate icing and dusted with coconut. Their invention is ascribed to the wife of Baron Lamington, Governor of Queensland when the Queen Empress was on the throne. Lamington fund-raisers are a regular feature of Australia's charity circuit. The method works best in a food processor and requires all the ingredients to be warmed to the temperature of the blazing Queensland summer before they're combined for the batter.

Makes 24
4 large eggs, unshelled
250 g self-raising flour
1 teaspoon baking powder
250 g caster sugar
250 g butter, softened
½ teaspoon vanilla extract
1–2 tablespoons milk

For the coating
175 g butter, softened
250 g icing sugar
2 heaped tablespoons cocoa powder
100 g desiccated (shredded) coconut

Preheat the oven to 180°C/Gas 4, and butter and line a rectangular cake tin measuring roughly 25 x 15cm (or equivalent).

Warm the eggs by placing them in a bowl of hot but not boiling water. Wait for exactly 2 minutes and then crack them into a measuring jug. Whisk until thoroughly mixed.

Sift the self-raising flour with the baking powder into the prewarmed mixing bowl of the food processor and stir in the sugar. Make a well in the middle, drop in the softened butter, half the egg mixture and the vanilla. Beat in the processor for one minute, when the mixture should change to a lighter colour and become thick and creamy. Add the remaining egg mixture and beat for another 30 seconds. Add a tablespoonful or two of milk if the mixture is too stiff to drop easily from the spoon.

If preparing by hand, whisk the eggs in a warm bowl until light and fluffy. Combine the flour with the baking powder and sugar and fold it into the whisked-up egg. Melt the butter and fold it into the mixture with the vanilla extract. Fold in a little milk if the mixture doesn't drop easily from the spoon.

Spread the cake batter into the tin and level the top with a spatula. Bake for about an hour, until well risen and firm to the finger, testing for doneness with a skewer or a sharp knife – it should come out clean rather than sticky. Leave to cool a little, then tip the cake out on to a rack. When perfectly cool, use a sharp knife to cut the cake into a dozen perfect cubes.

Meanwhile, make the coating. Beat the butter in a warm bowl until really soft. Sift in the icing sugar with the cocoa powder and beat until light and fluffy.

Cover the tops and sides of the sponge cubes with chocolate icing and dust with coconut.

RIVERS

TO OUR NOT-SO-DISTANT ANCESTORS, LACKING the convenience of motorised travel by road and air, rivers served as highway, trade route and larder. It's no accident, therefore, that the great cities of the world grew and flourished at the mouths of rivers.

One waterway is much like another at its source – all it takes is a belch and a bubble and a trickle of silver. Thereafter, the path the river carves for itself defines its character and that of those who settle along its banks. My own early schooldays were spent within sight and sound of the River Plate, where it spreads itself in a wide arc into the South Atlantic. The river rises in the jungles of Brazil, carves a broad path through the Argentinian pampas, Paraguay and Uruguay, and meets the ocean between two harbour ports established under Spanish colonial rule, Montevideo and Buenos Aires. The two are very different. Even I knew, at school in Montevideo in the early 1950s, that while Uruguay's capital was a sleepy backwater, Argentina's capital was a hotbed of excitement. Buenos Aires had magnificent shops, a glamorous if notorious first lady, Eva Perón – even a branch of Harrods. The difference was geographical. Montevideo is in reality a seaport, sited at the furthest edge of a 200-mile-long river that measured 140 miles at its mouth. Buenos Aires was (and is) a river port situated where the waterway becomes a trade route, the main highway into the interior. Uruguay, herself a major producer of meat from cattle and sheep for export to Europe, channelled all her trade through Buenos Aires, enriching her sister country while impoverishing herself.

In Europe, differences between the Danube and the Rhône are similarly geographically dictated. The Danube rises in the mountains of southern Germany, gathers strength from its tributaries as it flows through Austria, Hungary, Slovakia, Serbia, Bulgaria and Romania, until its waters drain through a vast region of un-navigable marshland into the Black Sea. The Rhône rises in the mountains and forests of Switzerland, and flows west and south through the French heartland until it spreads itself through a broad sandy delta into the Mediterranean. Both are navigable along much of their length. Given the energy and inclination, an adventurous water rat might travel from the Black Sea to the Mediterranean and home through the Dardanelles without the need to set foot on dry land.

This happy confluence of waterways led to the establishment of trading posts at points of intersection between river and sea. From trading posts grew towns and from towns grew cities. Great cities are like rubbish dumps, messy and unpredictable but infinitely capable of re-invention. It's no accident that the great capitals of the world are sited at – or close to – a river-mouth. Both the Rhône and the Danube were protected by vast un-navigable deltas, a natural line of first defence against invasion. The shifting sands at the mouth of the Rhône protected medieval France from invasion from the southern shores of the Mediterranean at a time when most of Iberia was under Muslim rule. The mouth of the Danube was protected by her vast un-navigable marshlands from the fierce nomadic horsemen who roamed the steppes of Asia.

Security and prosperity – derived, at first, from the imposition of harbour dues and the granting of safe passage – allowed the development of an independently wealthy merchant class in the river cities. Later, as trade grew in importance and sophistication, great fortunes were made from warehousing, ship-victualling and manufacturing. Prosperity brought leisure and an appetite for learning. Those not actively involved in trade and industry became bankers and lawyers, founders of the schools and universities that attracted philosophers, artists and craftsmen.

Travellers, whether rich or poor, needed to eat and sleep, and this too was an opportunity for the citizens of harbour ports to sell their services. While the traditions of the countryside required the provision of hospitality without payment, the citizens of the river ports turned their responsibilities as hosts to profitable account. Hostelries and drinking dens evolved into wine bars and restaurants. Cities such as Lyon and Vienna became centres of gastronomic excellence as a result, not least, of a sophisticated citizenry prepared to pay good money for the skills of innovative cooks. Meanwhile the poor had access to the leavings of the rich. You will find offal dishes in ship-victualling ports – salt-barrellers were paid in part with butchers' innards – as well as dishes prepared with salt cod, the fasting food of Catholic Europe. Once a taste becomes established, it remains popular long after the need has vanished.

If the economies of nations are built on the provision of goods and services, without the watery highways that provided their trade routes, the civilisations of the world might never have flowered.

Rhône

I DO LOVE A RIVER-CRUISE, I REALLY DO. IT'S partly the element of surprise – you never know what's around the next bend – and partly the feeling that nothing can possibly go wrong when the men and women in uniform are in charge. I am here, as usual, for the food. Not, this time, in order to experience something I know nothing about, but as a lecturer, one of three on the cruise, charged with explaining the gastronomy of Provence to an audience of some hundred and twenty paying passengers embarking on a leisurely cultural meander in a luxury river-barge up the Rhône from Avignon to Lyon.

I am not entirely responsible for enlightenment, but I come well recommended since the biography pinned up on the ship's noticeboard explains that I have already written and illustrated a book on the basic recipes of the French kitchen. Excursions with local guides are arranged at each stopping point. On non-excursion days, the lecturers are expected to deliver illustrated talks on the wine, architecture and – my responsibility – food of the region through which we are passing. There's certainly plenty of wine and architecture, but appreciation of the culinary habits of Provence is uncommon in the rest of France. Unless, that is, discussion stretches to the gastronomic joys of Lyon, second only to Paris in its reputation for culinary excellence, which is actually in the province of Burgundy and so doesn't fit within the brief. No matter. No one is obliged to listen to any of us or leave the comforts of our floating hotel for the uncertainties of the shore unless they choose.

Everyone is in holiday mood as we assemble on deck for instruction in what to do if our transport, due for retirement at the end of the voyage, should happen to sink into the slow-moving current of the Rhône. It's mid November and an unscheduled dip is not what any of us would wish. Many of the passengers are travelling as couples or groups of friends and are happily exchanging memories of previous excursions while strapping themselves into life-jackets and cracking jokes about not swallowing the water if you land in the drink.

Our tour leader's name is Suzie. Severely tailored and impeccably groomed, Suzie delivers a short burst of instruction on what to do if the sirens sound. We of the lower decks are to exit via the staircase in good order and find our colour-coded muster point on deck. Some of us aren't listening and are called to order. Suzie is not a woman to tolerate levity on matters as important as personal on-board safety. Suzie's lecture having been concluded, the captain will be hosting us at a champagne reception in the lounge before we proceed to dinner.

I worry a little about dinner. I have been hoping for a Provençal menu but the bill of fare appears to lean towards

Scandinavia, land of the Viking longships. Cautious enquiries reveal that the vessel is victualled in Sweden, the crew is Bulgarian and the kitchen staff is Filipino.

The delta of the Rhône spills its waters into the Mediterranean by way of the Camargue, a vast expanse of vineyards, market gardens, reed beds, lagoons, rice paddies, eel canals, bull pastures, marshes and dunes which together make up one of the last great wildernesses of Europe. The Camargue starts at Arles, point of departure for our voyage upriver through the vineyards of Macon and Burgundy until we reach the chestnut forests of the Ardèche.

I have happy memories of the Camargue as a wild and lonely place, breeding ground for birds and mammals found nowhere else in Europe. Many years ago, when my children went to school in the Languedoc and I was working as a natural-history artist and needed raw material for my paintings of botany and birds, I would pack the four of them (and sometimes their father, Nicholas) into our camper van and head to the reed beds and mud flats for a happy weekend pursuing the flamingoes, spoonbills and storks at nesting time. The entertainment for the children – consolation for long schooldays – was a chance to ride into the reed beds on sturdy white ponies with the cowboys of the Camargue and be gone for the day, returning at sunset hungry and tired and ready for whatever I'd cooked up on the camp stove – maybe a *pot-au-feu*, beef broth thick with vegetables, to eat with a garlicky aioli, or something hot and peppery with plenty of wine and herbs and good bread from the bakery to mop up the juices.

Levels on the upper Rhône, Suzie informs us when we gather for the captain's party, are reported as high enough to endanger navigation. As a result, there is a possibility that our vessel, though of comparatively modest size and low to the water, may not be able to slide under the bridges that span the water at Avignon or Lyon. If so, no doubt the distinguished lecturers will be more than capable of providing entertainment.

I haven't yet met my fellow lecturers, wine writer Bill Knott and architectural historian Huon Mallalieu. But I do know that both have other skills – Bill is a professional chef who writes about food, and Huon's area of specialist expertise is nineteenth-century watercolours. In other words, ideal partners on a trip such as this. Bill is a man for the good life – cheerful, confident and happily anarchic. Huon is cautious and serious, as befits a cultural historian.

I quickly establish that Bill and I are natural allies, prepared to skip ship at the first opportunity and head for the nearest watering-hole on shore. Bill loves his food and knows his wines – cheap as well as classy – and was a cash-strapped university student in Lyon around twenty years ago. He is thirty years younger than me, knows his onions and – as a chef rather than cook like me – can chop them too. In other words, the perfect companion for a trawl round the cheap and cheerful end of the catering trade in a region I know and love but rarely have a chance to revisit.

As we enter the cocktail lounge for the captain's welcome drinks, Bill rejects his glass of champagne in favour of the wine list. His reasoning – a quick aside – is that it's always wise to identify the good stuff and have a word with the wine waiter before anyone else does. This is promising. Even more promising is Bill's enthusiasm for oysters, foie gras and *confit d'oie*, all of which, we agree, can confidently be expected in the markets of the Rhône valley in midwinter.

Huon and I share a clan, the Huguenots – French Protestants thrown out of Catholic France in 1685 for refusal to toe the official line – accounting for the non-Englishness of our family names and making us instantly identifiable among other members of the clan. My own family name, Longmore, was easy to spell and thoroughly English before I changed it on marriage – with the result, perhaps, that I'm more than usually conscious of the origins of my adopted identity.

So when Huon greets me warmly as a fellow Huguenot – even after three centuries, one Huguenot is always pleased to encounter another – I explain that I'm only connected to the mighty clan by marriage. No matter, he tells me kindly. The club is not so exclusive that wives cannot claim kinship. We slip into discussion of Huguenot characteristics as experienced by those who marry into the clan. Among these are an admirable ability to upset intellectual apple carts, an unwillingness to conform and a taste for political naysaying if the situation warrants it (and even if it doesn't).

Huon's interest in his own line of descent, as befits a historian in his middle years already contemplating his legacy, lies in the origins of the clan. The Mallalieu family, he explains with pride, were among the earliest of those who fled religious persecution in France after the Revocation of the Edict of Nantes, an event and date engraved on every Huguenot heart. The Luards, I might like to know, left rather later, in the early 1800s, when they established themselves in the vicinity of Soho Square, London's red-light district, an area for which I have an enduring affection since it was where I was working when I met my Huguenot husband. I was not, I hasten to point out, a working girl in the old sense of the word, but was on secretarial duties at *Private Eye*'s offices on Greek Street when Nicholas took over the proprietorship.

Huon admits himself too young to appreciate such memories. But I might also like to know, he adds thoughtfully, that when the time comes, the name Mallalieu opens all doors at a well-regarded Huguenot old folks' home in the Home Counties, where writers are particularly welcome and bursaries are possible, particularly when Huguenot memorabilia are included in the package in the form of diaries, letters and unwanted family portraits – it is amazing what people store in their attics.

Bill, sipping thoughtfully at his restorative Bloody Mary, suggests that the Huguenot wine cellar might be less than adequate since Huguenots were as puritanical as their co-religionist Presbyterians, possibly even teetotal.

We are all agreed that you're unlikely to find a well-stocked wine-rack in a Huguenot old folks' home, let alone a slice of seasonally fattened goose-liver with a sliver of Périgord truffle, as anticipated at some point during the course of the voyage.

Credentials are established. Our collaboration promises well.

The following day, the first of our sightseeing programme, the sky is blue but the air is cold enough for snow.

Suzie, ever present on the intercom as well as at the morning briefing in the cocktail lounge, advises wrapping up warm, wearing stout shoes and not forgetting umbrellas. Our tour guide, Adrienne, will be waiting for us when we disembark. We will recognise her by her red coat. She, no doubt, will recognise us from our unmistakably British uniform of stout shoes, heavy coats and neatly furled umbrellas. I reflect as I watch Huon and Bill, somewhat the worse for wear after a heavy cocktail-sampling evening, head for the bar and a quick pastis and a restorative espresso.

I love city tours, however many times I've taken them, and wouldn't miss one for the world – and anyway, I don't like pastis. Adrienne is dark-haired, bright-eyed and immaculately chic, and is indeed wearing a coat of appropriately cheerful hue. No one but me speaks French, but Adrienne speaks beautifully accented English – a pleasure in itself. The accent of Provence, much like Catalan, comes from the *langue d'òc*, outlawed in favour of Parisian French, the *langue d'oïl*. The old language of the troubadours disappeared underground and was – and is – still spoken in the upland farmhouses of the Languedoc, where my children attended a year of secondary school and weekends were spent, if not in the Camargue, playing chess for the school team in and around the towns of Provence.

A Monday in November is not a good day for sightseeing anywhere in France, Adrienne explains apologetically, since many of the sites of architectural and archaeological interest are closed. It is our good fortune, however, that the impressively restored and recently reopened Roman amphitheatre is ready and waiting. I decide there is just enough time for a quick water-colour of the undeniably magnificent pillars before I join the tour in the arena. Over thirty years of intermittent visitings, I've never seen the amphitheatre without its scaffolding. I can't remember a time when some part of the theatre, used for con-certs throughout the year and bullfights in the summer, had not been undergoing restoration.

Today the dazzling white marble columns are stripped of their scaffolding under a cloudless sky. The wind is ferocious, more than a match for Adrienne's efforts to inform her charges of the magnificence before them.

'What you are now seeing is the largest and most famous amphitheatre outside Rome,' shouts Adrienne into her micro-phone. 'Here is seating for twenty thousand spectators.'

The tiers of seating are pristine and so are the newly restored columns, now relieved of their protective cladding. Unfortunately the columns funnel the wind directly into the amphitheatre and Adrienne's audience is already retreating to the shelter of the entrance – the place where the gladiators sallied forth to do battle with lions.

'What we are now experiencing is the famous mistral,' shouts Adrienne. 'This is wind from the north, all the way from the snowfields of Siberia. When the wind comes from the north the air is cold and the sky is blue. The wind from the south, which comes from the deserts of Africa, is warm but brings clouds and rain.'

This, no question, is the wind from Siberia.

'The mistral is not so bad in summer,' says Adrienne by way of consolation. 'We are glad of it because it cools the air. But in winter it goes through the skin like needles.' Adrienne turns up the collar of her coat and pulls on a woolly hat before she resumes the microphone.

'When I was a little girl, *maman* would make my brother and me wrap up warm when the mistral blew and be sure to eat a good breakfast of *café au lait* and *pain perdu*. This is coffee made with milk and a slice of bread dipped in egg and milk and fried in butter. It is very good. I hope you did the same.'

This is meant kindly and we murmur appreciatively. I am beginning to enjoy the infantilisation of the seventh age. There's something comforting in being told exactly what to do and when.

We set off obediently in a raggedy wind-whipped crocodile towards the newly restored town centre for a brief view of the architectural ensemble during which I make an unsuccessful attempt to unseat Huon and Bill from the comfort of the Café du Forum to join the gang. Huon and Bill are old hands at the lecture game. No sense in putting in his own pennyworth, says Huon firmly, when the local guide is doing just fine.

For the rest of us, there is an opportunity to purchase Van Gogh memorabilia in the courtyard of what was once the city's lunatic asylum, where the painter of idyllic views of the windy mountain, Mont Ventoux, was incarcerated when misery and madness led him to slice off his own ear, an event recorded in paint.

The one-time lunatic asylum is a surprisingly homely two-storey building, roofed in terracotta and built round three sides of a courtyard with an arched walkway fronting a line of monk-ish cells with wooden doors. The courtyard is planted with dusty lemon trees, un weeded flowerbeds and unclipped box hedges. Details of the architecture are picked out in red and yellow. A staircase leads invitingly to the upper floor and the cells that line the walkway.

The interior, Adrienne regrets to inform her charges, is unavailable for public view since it is occupied by municipal offices. We may, on the other hand, purchase postcards of the artist's work at the kiosk.

The truth, Adrienne tells me when I seek her out in the hope of a glimpse of the cells, is that the asylum is closed to visitors because the town's reputation might suffer if the brutality of the treatment handed out to nineteenth-century lunatics was generally known. Nineteenth-century Arles's reputation for breeding more than her fair share of lunatics was not helped when Vincent, the city's most famous adopted son, chose to present himself on canvas with one ear missing and a bandaged head. While the mistral was – and still is – blamed for crimes of passion, the relatively high number of those incarcerated for madness might also have had something to do with a closed society that believed in magic and witchcraft.

The evidence for this is to be found in my favourite museum in all Provence, nineteenth-century Provençal poet Frédéric Mistral's Musée d'Arlatan – closed on a Monday, of course – which houses, among other domestic memorabilia, a well-preserved collection of dried toads, shed snakeskins, mole paws, rabbit scuts, wax dolls stuck with pins, and dehydrated extra digits – fingers, toes – along with all the other paraphernalia essential to the preparation of spells and potions.

Spells and potions remind me of my missing fellow lectur-ers. I skip the raggedy crocodile weaving its way home for the buffet lunch and afternoon siesta. Instead, I head back to the Place du Forum, where Bill and Huon are moving on to contemplation of the lunchtime menu. The Place du Forum is graced with a life-size bronze statue of Frédéric Mistral himself. Monsieur Mistral – an adopted name that reflects his land of origin – is held responsible for the revival of the Provençal language and culture and, as far as I'm concerned, for his encouragement and support of Jean-Baptiste Reboul, author of *La Cuisinière Provençale* – first published in 1897– which was my own introduction to the depth and breadth of the domestic cooking of Provence.

Bill knows the town from student days. He has, I am happy to observe, the nose of a truffle-hound for the only restaurant worthy of the name in an out-of-season gastronomic desert, the Bar Taurino. The bullfighter's bar, naturally, is within a trumpet-blast of the amphitheatre. The walls are plastered with bullfighting posters from the past – classicist Antonio Ordoñes and his son-in-law Paquirri, showman El Cordobés, gypsy genius Curro Romero – all familiar to me from my time in Andalusia. In Arles as in Andalusia the annual bullfights held at *feria* time were a reason for celebration even for those who couldn't afford to attend the fights, since the bull meat sold cheap from the butcher the following day was the only meat the poor could taste all year.

The Bar Taurino, true to tradition, does beef two ways: stewed with rice or grilled with chips. It doesn't do art-on-a-plate. The regulars like plain food and plenty of it. There are two choices for each course. We order the *salade camargais*, an uninspiring plateful of cold rice, anchovies, chunked tomatoes and raw onion. The main course is a distinct improvement: the chef-proprietor's mother's recipe for *bœuf camargais*, shin of beef cooked very slowly in a *daube*, the Provençal earthenware stewpot, with red wine, cinnamon and cloves.

'Perfectly acceptable,' declares Bill, pouring himself a glass of *vin ordinaire*, the rough red wine of the Rhône. The dish comes with rice. Bill, observing a regular at the next table eating off-menu *steak-frites* with a creamy sauce, summons the chef-proprietor and orders double portions of chips with sauce. The proprietor is disbelieving. Chips and *sauce Roquefort* with *bœuf camargais* is the craziest thing he's ever heard. He and his regular customer find this hilarious proof of the horrible combinations *les Anglais* are prepared to put in their mouths. He is wrong. Chips and sauce is more or less perfect with *bœuf camargais*.

The Bar Taurino, apart from its gastronomic attractions, offers a clear view across the square to Van Gogh's Blue Café.

The café, no longer blue, has been repainted in tasteful shades of elephant-grey. At the entrance is an easel on which is propped a gilt-framed copy of the original, just to remind passers-by what they're missing.

Coffee is not so good at the Bar Taurino. Far better, explains the proprietor, that his valued customers who have invented a new dish – *bœuf camargais avec sauce Roquefort* – should make their way to the specialist coffee emporium round the corner, a new addition to the town's gastronomic opportunities, leaving the proprietor to shut the kitchen and return to the real business of the bar: Pernod over ice and hold the water jug.

The coffee emporium is tiny and very narrow. Coffee purchasers can choose from fifty varieties of bean and have them ground to order. Coffee is also available for immediate consumption at the counter. There is, however, no coffee-roaster, a serious shortcoming in a high-class purveyor of coffee.

'The neighbours are ignorant and won't permit it,' says the coffee-seller sadly. 'Can you imagine?'

We agree that not one of us, if resident in the neighbourhood, can imagine objecting for a single instant to the fragrance of freshly roasted coffee wafting down the street, even if frozen mid-puff by the mistral.

There are also teas, herbal or English, flavoured with vanilla or orange zest or bergamot. English rather than herbal is fashionable in Arles right now.

A customer hesitates over the purchase of a Chinese stoneware teapot with a raffia-bound handle – the perfect vehicle, she explains to anyone listening, for her favourite infusion of lemon balm, *verveine*, which has eclipsed the Proustian *tilleul*, lime blossom, as the nation's favourite tisane.

I observe that lemon balm grows like a weed in my garden in Wales.

'How fortunate you are. I drink it all day long and so should you.'

'You drink it for pleasure?'

'Certainly not. For the nerves.'

Trouble with the nerves ranks alongside digestive difficulties in France's lexicon of ills to be cured by infusion. If tea-drinking in France is strictly medicinal, pleasure derives from coffee. We order and drink tiny cups of very strong, very dark Nicaraguan brew and adjourn, at the tea purchaser's suggestion, two doors down to the best pâtisserie in Arles.

Fashions in tea, coffee and pâtisserie, as well as ballgowns, take their lead from Paris. The fashion for Parisian baker Ladurée's *macarons*, bite-sized multicoloured almond meringues sandwiched in pairs with buttercream, went global in the 1990s, spawning *macaron* outlets in the same fashionable shopping streets as Prada and Hermès from Hong Kong to Moscow to Rodeo Drive, attracting very thin, very elegant ladies of a certain age who forgo the latest diet for just a little taste of something perfect.

Me too, as it happens. I blame my maternal grandmother – a pampered belle from Baltimore – for the happiness I take in the sugary little frivolities available in French pâtisseries. When I was no more than six or seven, my grandmother's kitchen included a French *maître-pâtissier* – and if this sounds a little on the extravagant side of normal, I can only say that my maternal grandparents were the beneficiaries of a very large fortune, the entirety of which, unfortunately for their descendants, they managed to unload in a single generation.

Monsieur le maître-pâtissier taught me kitchen French and allowed me to help prepare his exquisite haute-cuisine desserts: light-as-a-feather profiteroles stuffed with vanilla ice cream to be swamped in a dark river of melted bitter chocolate. Teatime treats were millefeuilles, buttery layers of crisp brown pastry sandwiched together with thick golden custard and home-made strawberry jam, and little raspberry tarts made with shortcrust pastry so light and crumbly it only just held its shape in my fist. Thereafter I was hooked, unable to pass a pastry shop without making a detour through the door.

Those who entertain in France think it no shame to order their dessert from the best pâtisserie in town, reasoning that specialist skills are best left to those who have the time and training to produce the perfect *tarte aux pommes* or *rum baba*. Some of the specialities are available everywhere – madeleines, florentines, *sablées* – while others remain strictly regional. Close your eyes and with a little practice you can tell exactly where you are from the fragrance drifting from the ovens at the back of the shop – if not, you're in the wrong shop. The trick is to know what to expect: *calissons* perfumed with orange-blossom water in Aix; apple-stuffed turnovers, *chaussons*, in Savoillan; almond cookies, *nougatines*, in Montélimar.

In the pâtisserie in Arles, I am looking for *navettes*, boat-shaped shortbreads flavoured with aniseed, though, says the saleslady, I might like to try the new flavours – lavender, chocolate and chilli, citron, vanilla – recently added to expand the appeal.

'The customers demand variety. We must move with the times,' says the saleswoman, packing my ration neatly into a box.

The cruise-ship travels at night and all passengers, lecturers not excepted, must return in the evening by ten or miss the boat and catch a taxi to the next port of call: the ride of shame. It is our last day in Arles. Before heading back to the ship, I need to visit a *confiserie* in the old part of town where I have already noticed hand-made chocolates on display in the gleaming plate-glass window. What I have in mind is a little tasting menu to carry back to the ship for the lecturers and favoured passengers (as yet unselected) to enjoy at leisure. Sweet things must be shared.

My eye had first been caught in passing by a little pile of hazelnut fondants, *menchikofs*, finger-shaped and dusted with very dark cocoa.

I choose a dozen and add a little bag of pistachio-studded nougat from Montélimar and a handful of dark chocolate medallions dotted with almonds and raisins.

The medallions, says the saleslady, slipping the little discs into just the right size of cellophane bag, are *mendiants*, a Christmas speciality of the *maître-chocolatier*'s own devising. They represent the alms due to the begging monks who came to the door for admittance on Christmas Eve. You could not refuse to give alms to a begging monk, even if all you had was a crust of bread.

'*Goûtez, madame*. One must always taste before one buys.'

I taste. The chocolate is indeed exquisite – smooth, dense, bittersweet and dotted with rough-skinned almonds and wrinkled raisins that taste of the sun.

I taste again, and in that moment I remember this place and when I came here once before and tasted the same tastes, and with the memory comes my daughter who died but was still, at the time, in the fullness of beauty and life. It's been twenty years since we – her father, brother and sisters – buried her in the little country churchyard with a view across meadows to the sea. Her disease was no fault of her own, unless picking the wrong lover at the wrong time sets her at fault. Unlucky, is all.

'No tears, Mother,' she'd say. 'No time for regret.'

She's right. I would rather remember my daughter in happiness than sorrow, in sweet things tasted in a place she loved and was happy and young and full of life. At funerals in more practical times, mourners were provided with little packets of seeds and sweetness – honey-sweetened grains, sugar-dusted mourning-cakes – to take home and share with others to bring happiness to memory.

'*C'est pour offrir?* Is it for a gift?' asks the saleslady. 'Would you like a ribbon?'

'Yes,' I answer. 'My daughter would like a ribbon.'

❧

Day four and we have a little trouble on our hands.

'This is absolutely not the norovirus,' Suzie informs us at the usual morning gathering.

Some of us may have noticed that we are not as numerous as usual at breakfast, and she wants to knock the rumours on the head.

The lecturers are unaware of any rumours, having spent the previous day on shore.

There are rumours, Suzie continues with admirable calmness, because, to put it delicately, a few of us have suffered digestive problems in the night.

Precautions are already in place to deal with what, we are assured, is sure to be a minor problem of brief duration. Sanitised hand-wipes are now required at all times but particularly when entering or leaving the ship. And we can no longer help ourselves from the breakfast buffet or pour our own coffee.

Those of us unaffected by what may or may not be norovirus digest this news in silence. I assume that, as meals are included in the not inconsiderable price of the cruise, everyone has been eating the same ship's menu. Apart, that is, from the lecturers who have been gallivanting around on shore eating heaven knows what.

We keep this to ourselves. Wisest not to admit that the previous evening the three of us – Bill, Huon and I – had skipped the on-board dinner menu of poached Alaskan salmon with cucumber in favour of *le grand aïoli*. Garlic, as everyone who

watches horror movies knows, is a well-known vampire repel-
lent and plague preventative, and I am reasonably confident that,
whatever is responsible for not-the-norovirus, we are not the
plague-bearers – rats returning to the sinking ship.

I share this view with a fellow passenger, a retired professor
of philosophy with whom I share a breakfast table. He has a
pleasantly gloomy view of human behaviour and relishes our
new status as plague-ship.

'Should it prove terminal,' says the professor, dabbing his
fingertips on a wet-wipe, 'as a philosopher I take the long view.
Sooner or later we'll all be dead.'

The dancing demoiselles of the bridge of Avignon, Suzie informs
those of us still standing when we assemble for our morning outing, can no longer do their dancing as the bridge is incomplete
and dangerous.

We all laugh appreciatively and no one mentions the not-
the-norovirus.

The city is walled, a fortified trading port which once held
the keys to the lower Rhône and access to the Mediterranean for
the nations of the north – Germany, Austria and the peoples
of the Baltic, as well as the Low Countries and Britain. Together
the three great arterial highways of Europe – Danube, Rhine
and Rhône – when nations were at peace, brought prosperity
and ease of trade to all.

Seven fourteenth-century popes took up residence in
Avignon, planting the vineyards of Châteauneuf du Pape and
building a vast papal palace within the city walls. Their pleasures as depicted in murals and tapestries were hunting, feasting
and the pleasures of the marriage bed.

Today is the feast of All Saints, a public holiday. France has
been a secular country since the Revolution but observes the

festivals of the Church with undiminished zeal. Avignon's housewives queue in the covered market for Sicilian and Tuscan specialities, Mediterranean fish, and fruit and vegetables clearly marked with place of origin. For those who just want to enjoy the company and the bustle, café kiosks offer seating where customers, on the purchase of a glass of beer or a cup of coffee, can break the mid-morning fast with food from the neighbouring kiosk – maybe a tranche of sourdough bread from the baker, a slice of salt-cured ham or a sliver of mountain cheese from the charcuterie on the corner.

Bill wastes no time in finding the oyster stall. The choice is take-home or opened to order. The tables are already crowded but the turnover is swift and Bill is persuasive. The only possible choice for the three of us – no man should eat oysters on his own – is a dozen apiece of naturally bred Atlantic oysters, Gillardeaux, with a side order of *fines de claire*, natives of the Île d'Oléron. In the hand, the shell of the Atlantic native is smoother and rounder than the larger and rougher-shelled, tear-shaped Pacific or Portuguese breed, *gigondas*. In flavour and texture, the natives are soft and pillowy and creamy, while the foreigners are chewier and the flavour is more like seaweed than sea spray.

The Gillardeaux are, naturally, twice as expensive as every other bivalve on the slab. We negotiate downwards and agree on a side order of winkles, the oysters of the poor. It takes dedication to pick a pint of winkles and no time at all to swallow an oyster.

Bill has serious wine-work to do thereafter. Leaving a respectable pyramid of debris on the Formica-topped table in the oyster emporium, we work our way up and down the narrow streets surrounding the market until we find Avignon's one and only *boutique en ligne*, a reference to the triple stack of gleaming wine-dispensers stretching the length of the narrow little shop, each with its own upside-down bottle. Here, for little more than

the price of a mouthful of oyster, the dedicated wine connois-
seur can sample every top-rated vintage produced by the
boutique winemakers of the Rhône.

Small-volume wine-producers care about what they do, just
as small-production oyster-farmers know their crop. Big-
volume winemakers, the famous names and producers of grand
crus, of which there are many in the region, are reliable but pre-
dictable. In a good year there is always the chance that the little
fellows will produce the wine writer's holy grail: the perfect
wine in the perfect vintage at the perfect price.

The experience is educational, or would have been had I
followed Bill's example and made my way methodically down
the stacks. At a wine-tasting I always taste and spit, saving a
swallow for the dessert wines. The final challenge is the digestif.
In a wine-growing region such as this, the preference is for a
bone-dry fruit brandy, *eau-de-vie de fruits*, distilled from the
winemaker's debris – skins, pips – combined with the orchard
fruits which ripen in autumn just in time for the grape harvest.

The appropriate technique for tasting a digestif, says Bill, is
to sniff, sip and suck. Simultaneous sniffing, sipping and sucking
takes practice, so we work our way through medlar, damson and
one flavoured with the bitter little fruits of the strawberry tree,
Arbutus, until we get to the pears. An *eau-de-vie de poire* is about
as good as an *eau-de-vie* can get. The variety is King William, a
particularly juicy and fragrant round-bellied pear with a charm-
ingly freckled golden skin – one needs to know these things. For
the digestion, I explain, holding out my glass for another little
taste.

Bill shakes his head. 'Wait till we get to the *cassis*.'

Cassis is a blackcurrant liqueur that makes even the least
acceptable white wine taste delicious. It takes its name from a
little town in the Mâconnais, a white-wine region known for
summer berries, where small producers work their magic.

Happiness is a mouthful of blackcurrant-flavoured sunshine. The industry was first developed in medieval times, the result of proximity to the Rhône. The waterway gave access to Mediterranean cane sugar and allowed the syrups to be exported directly into the markets of middle and northern Europe, where winters are long and sun in short supply. Central heating and cheap airfares haven't made much difference to the need for bottled sunshine.

Tasting proceeds. We are getting to the serious stuff, comparing the overblown rose fragrance of quince with the clean clear scent of the pears. As far as I'm concerned, there's no contest. Well, best take another sip of *cassis*, sweet as a baby's breath and good for the nerves. Or for the digestion. Perhaps it would even work against what's certainly not-the-norovirus.

Thereafter none of us three, not even Huon, care a fig for the magnificence of the Palais des Papes, still less for the historical significance of the Pont du Gard, our destination the next day and the subject of Huon's lecture that evening.

And anyway, nobody's computer seems able to upload a PowerPoint, though this might have something to do with the *eau-de-vie*, or possibly *cassis*. It's hard to be sure.

Not-the-noro has become the ship's mantra, whispered in corridors and muttered when passing on the stairs.

Meanwhile we three take sanitisation into our own hands with a basinful of ice cubes from the self-service ice machine in order to cool a litre bottle of the very best *eau-de-vie de poire*, which, being guaranteed at least 70 per cent proof, can be considered effectively antiviral if taken in sufficient quantity.

We smuggle the bottle, purely medicinal, out of Suzie's eyeline and decant the magic elixir into plastic toothbrush glasses by the soft glow of the night sky. All at once the moon rises over the medieval outline of a crusader castle on a hilltop. Closer inspection reveals this to be a decommissioned nuclear power station neatly positioned at a bend in the river where it broadens towards the quays of Lyon.

Self-medication by *eau-de-vie* keeps the three of us on deck until the small hours, when we're driven below by the wind from the south, which, as promised by Adrienne, brings warmth, thunder, lightning and rain.

The following morning we awake to find our luxury accommodation, as befits a plague-ship, double-parked against a rusting coal-barge moored to the wrong end of the crowded Lyon waterfront.

The omens are not encouraging. The skies are emptying into an already swollen river and the headcount at breakfast indicates that definitely-not-the-noro has claimed more than half our number, including my breakfast companion.

Bill, meanwhile, is planning for the arrival at Lyon airport of his fiancée and light of love, Tanya, escaping kitchen duties as chef-de-cuisine in a well-reviewed fish smokery with restaurant somewhere in the region of the Bristol Channel.

I, on the other hand, am planning the acquisition of raw materials for a demonstration of the whys and how-tos of the Provençal *réveillon*, the fasting supper of Christmas Eve. For this I will need cardoons and salt cod, neither of which are likely to be available in the ship's galley, even if the area had not been sealed off and under strict quarantine.

There's work to be done, ingredients to be acquired.

Bill leads the way to a busy open-air produce market under the railway arches by the bus station. Most of the sellers and their customers are North Africans. While a couple of the stalls are selling Moroccan couscous, Lebanese tahini and Tunisian harissa, most are heaped with the good things available in season from the pastures and woods of the Rhône valley. There are

furry heaps of rabbit and hare, little red-legged partridges with striped breasts and pale-blue back feathers, plump mallard and pheasant – all to be plucked or skinned to order. There is, too, wild fungi from the forests of the Ardèche: ceps, chanterelles, *pieds-de-mouton*. And cream, soft white cheese and butter from the pastures of the Massif Central.

Salt cod is available either ready-soaked or cut to order from huge triangular sheets. Cardoons, an oversized member of the thistle family which look like a gigantic bundle of furry-coated celery and taste like artichoke, are sold neatly trimmed or with full complement of bushy greenery. I buy ready-soaked middle-cut salt cod and untrimmed cardoons and carry my purchase home to the mother ship in triumph.

Lyon has always been a merchant city. Her quaysides provided safe haven for the ships of the Mediterranean and warehousing for their trade goods. The great fairs of medieval times took place along her banks. Her citizens grew rich on collecting taxes and imposing customs dues, provisioning ships with salt-meat packed in barrels, and from the silk-trade – cloth and ribbons. This happy conjunction of trade route, manufacturing base and access to the products of the fertile Rhône valley and the vineyards of Burgundy led, over the centuries, to the development of a culinary culture unmatched anywhere else in France, including Paris.

If the chefs of Paris take their lead from the palace cooking of pre-revolutionary France, the restaurants of Lyon are egalitarian, adapting but never abandoning the down-to-earth recipes of the bourgeoisie. Public catering in Lyon can be cheap, costly or takeaway. Presiding spirits are Mesdames Fillioux and Brazier and a gang of redoubtable women cooks known collectively as *les mères lyonnaises*. The original *mères* are long gone but their principles of good housekeeping – shop carefully and don't ruin good ingredients – are as useful now as they ever were.

The *bouchons* of Lyon serve a simple no-choice menu to the city's working population at midday and a glass of *vin ordinaire*, most likely from the proprietor's own vineyard, until sundown. Those too busy to go to a restaurant or shop and cook for themselves can avail themselves of the services of the *traiteur*, cooked-food shop.

The *traiteurs* of Lyon serve as intermediary between the city and the countryside, providing ready-cooked offal dishes, game pâtés, *quenelles de poisson* – delicious little fish dumplings – and a peculiarly Lyonnais concoction of fresh curd cheese mashed with herbs, *cervelles de canut* – silk-weavers' brains – so-called, according to the good folk of Lyon, either because the work addled the brain or because the weavers couldn't afford the offal.

Tripe and innards are the most popular of the reheatables – mostly because butchers' leftovers are always plentiful in a ship-victualling port, where prodigious amounts of meat were salted down for the transatlantic trade. Among local specialities still popular – judging from the queue in the *traiteur* – are *sabodet* (a pig's-head sausage); *tablier du sapeur* ('fireman's apron' – strips of honeycomb tripe fried in a jacket of breadcrumbs); and *gras-double* (matchsticked ox-tripe cooked in butter with onions and vinegar). These good things, along with the matured cheeses and salt-cured charcuterie, can be eaten standing at the counter or at a table with a glass of wine, or carried home to eat at the kitchen table instead of a meal in a restaurant.

Last time I was here – maybe five years ago – the fate of Lyon's venerable covered market, Les Halles, hung in the balance. The wholesale market had already been moved over to the suburbs, local street-markets organised by Algerians and Tunisians provided the city's immigrant labour with their groceries, and the site was ripe for redevelopment.

Thanks to public outcry – or pressure on the city council from regional or national politicians – the building was turned over to the city's most famous son, and is now reborn as Les Halles de Paul Bocuse, a vast indoor *traiteur* housing specialist outlets with famous names.

The French home-cook never pretends to have prepared something herself when she can boast of shopping in the *traiteur* sanctified by Paul Bocuse. Monsieur Bocuse is an entrepreneur, as every chef must be to escape the everyday labour of the catering trade at every level, high or low, even with modern kitchen equipment and working hours controlled by law.

While the rough and tumble of the fresh produce market is replaced by stalls selling *foie gras en croûte*, cured meats, smoked salmon and other delicacies that require primed credit cards, the underlying purpose of the market – a culinary exchange between town and countryside – remains unchanged.

The excellence of her table, superiority of her cellars and inventiveness of her chefs has much to do with the city's willingness to adapt to ideas from elsewhere. Gathered under the same restored roof are cheesemongers, chocolatiers, charcutiers, boulangers, pâtissiers, confisiers, wine merchants and a food court where all these good things can be sampled.

Pride of place right opposite the entrance is given to a marble and steel counter in which are displayed Lyon's most famous fast food: quenelles, finger-length dumplings prepared with fish flesh and cream, shaped by hand between two spoons and sold with their own little sachets of sauce Nantua, a strong reduction of crayfish broth and cream.

Despite their being twice the price of the commercial quenelle shaped by machine, the citizenry of Lyon knows what's good, and by midday a line has already formed. I join the queue and take my prize to a corner of a wine bar, order myself a glass of the house white and eat my quenelle, a little guiltily, still chilled from the paper.

The quenelle – now very much the aristocrat of the cooking of Lyon – had humble beginnings. For the fishermen of the Drôme, a rain-swept region of lakes and streams a hundred miles northeast of Lyon in the foothills of the Jura mountains, the quenelle and its sauce were a valuable source of income, the only way of bringing a perishable foodstuff to market in saleable condition. It is, in other words, the piscine equivalent of the *rillette*, potted pork preserved under lard, a preparation designed to add shelf life to a perishable foodstuff in a region not suitable for dry curing.

Lyon is goose-fat territory. In France you'll know where you are by the cooking fat: olive oil in the south, goose fat in the middle and butter in the north. With the festive season nearly upon us there is a brisk trade in the by-blows of the goose-fat trade – whole foie gras both cooked and raw, preserved as pâté, jarred with its own butter, stuffed into a goose neck or enclosed in a *magret*. There is also – half hidden beneath the counter – a bowl of trimmings for spreading.

The seller approves my choice. Spreadable foie gras is every bit as good as the other stuff. I must not, however, eat it with toasted brioche – why would anyone want to eat rich meat with even richer bread? – but consume it from the hand as the country people do, spread with its own golden butter on a thick slice of *pain de campagne*, deep-crusted sourdough country bread with a chewy honey-coloured crumb, not forgetting a little nip of *eau-de-vie de prune*, plum brandy, for the digestion. If there's anything that prevents the gourmets of Lyon from enjoying a surfeit of foie gras, it's the need to ensure good digestion.

Back at our plague-ship on the river, not-the-noro is keeping all but the most resilient cowering in their berths and the rain is still falling by the bucket-load.

Our brave quartet – Huon, Bill and his best-beloved Tanya, escaped from cheffing in a fish restaurant on the Severn Estuary to join us for the weekend, and I – gather under the tarpaulins on deck for a conference. We decide, in spite of the downpour, on an evening excursion into the city centre. With our mooring drifted three boats out – presumably to keep the rest of the river-barges well away from contamination – we are loosely roped to shore by rickety gangplanks slung across deserted decks to the cobbled quayside.

Bright lights beckon through rain-soaked streets and Bill is a man on a mission. We arrive at his favourite *bouchon* just as it's closing up for the day – *Bouchons* operate from the morning until early evening, the full working-day – the lunchtime trade has long finished wiping drops of *daube de bœuf* from its collective chin, and chairs are being stacked on tables.

Considering the weather and that we are visitors to his great city – only *les Anglais* would be wandering around in the pouring rain – the patron will allow us to take a glass of the house

Beaujolais at the bar before adjourning elsewhere. Every Lyonnais chef worth his salt cuts his culinary teeth on a potful of *coq au vin* brewed up in a tiny galley-kitchen in a *bouchon* before heading into the world of Michelin stars.

So where would the patron himself choose to eat, enquires Bill, if he wished to celebrate with friends the arrival of a beautiful fiancée in a city famed for its food? And if anyone thinks the lecturers (and fiancée) do nothing but think of what we're going to have for dinner, at least one of us has, I hasten to add, worked up a healthy appetite until closing-time in the Musée des Arts Décoratifs – silk and domestic artefacts respectively – followed by the three-mile hike back and forth from the plague-ship.

The patron considers Bill's question with knitted brow.

There are many restaurants and some of them may even be open for business rather than closed for *fermeture annuelle*, but, in his opinion, the choice would be his own favourite for a Saturday with the wife, Les Culottes Longues. As a reference to those opposed to the revolutionary sans-culottes – citizens too poor to own a pair of trousers who chopped off royal heads in 1798 for lack of bread – this is promising. The implication, we hope, is good food at bourgeois prices with a welcome absence of anything that smacks of molecular cuisine or art-on-a-plate.

'*On mange bien,*' says the patron. Then adds, '*Pas du tout moderne.*'

Eating well without modernity is a political statement in the city whose favourite son is a chef of such glamour and power his name is written in neon above the city's skyscape.

Les Culottes Longues offers its *menu du jour* from half a dozen main courses on the blackboard. The decor is 1980s flea-market chic. Dinner is served on scrubbed wooden tables with mismatched chairs. There are brass rails round the bar and a kitchen visible through a hatch. Once our custom is accepted –

not always the case in France's neighbourhood restaurants dependent on a regular clientele – we settle down at a shared table with one other occupant.

It's still early for dining by the standards of Provence but the restaurant is filling up rapidly, evidence that Lyon is a serious industrial city with habits closer to the hard-working north than the lotus-eaters of the south.

Our co-diner is thin and nervous and keeps glancing around the room like a terrier in rabbit country. He has a gold tooth and a diamond earring. He has, it seems, ordered off-menu and is rapidly working his way through an earthenware casserole of what looks like scrambled eggs but from which rises an unmistakable perfume.

'*Excusez-moi, monsieur,*' I say. '*Vous mangez des truffes?*'

Of course he's eating truffles. It's the season, isn't it? The gold tooth flashes and the dish is pushed towards me.

'*Si vous voulez, madame, goûtez.*'

The offer to taste is irresistible. I tear off a piece of bread and do as I am bid. The dish is about as perfect as scrambled egg can be when made with cream and fresh eggs from barnyard chickens, stirred over a gentle heat until softly set, then served in its cooking dish and showered with fine slivers of perfectly ripe truffle. It's the closest a person can come to gastronomic heaven.

Unfortunately, says the patron as we make anxious enquiries, there are no more truffles today, but if we care to return tomorrow at lunchtime, it's possible that the truffle-dealer will have brought fresh supplies. You never know with truffles.

By now my gold-toothed neighbour is well into his *foie gras poêlé*, a generous slab of fattened goose liver flipped on to a griddle just long enough to crisp the outside without allowing the insides to melt.

Foie gras, from my experience in the uplands of the

Languedoc where the fattened goose was a by-blow of a well-stocked barnyard, must be cooked either on the highest possible heat for the shortest possible time, or sealed in a jar – the original *sous-vide* – at the lowest possible heat, until the liver has set firm without losing the buttery golden fat which can all too easily separate into an oily pool. The latter method is traditional and it works, in spite of indications to the contrary.

I met my first fattened goose when my children were at school in Castelnaudary, a town famous for its *cassoulet*, a stupendous bean-pot for which the only absolute requirement is the white haricot beans of Soissons and a preserved goose joint from the confit pot. Other inclusions might be partridge, rabbit and perhaps a piece of salt-cured pork fat, *petit salé*, or a link or two of the all-meat sausage of Toulouse, but the only essential was beans and confit.

My farming neighbours kept a well-stocked barnyard and fattened up a couple of geese on leftover walnuts from the

distilling of *eau-de-vie de noix*, walnut brandy, a privilege that passed from one generation to another. The family kept one for their own confit pot, and the other – sometimes even two or three – was sold at the Christmas market in Revel. The liver was potted up under glass as a Christmas treat, while the feathers went to stuff pillows and bed covers, and the down was used to make waistcoats to keep the children warm when they walked through the snow to school.

But that was thirty years ago, and farming methods everywhere have changed, though less so in rural France, where the rules of inheritance mean that even city-dwellers keep a stake in the countryside, however small. There's a difference in both flavour and texture between commercially produced foie gras – much of which is sold as pâté, a convenient way of making the raw material go further – and *foie gras artisanal*, home-reared goose liver prepared under glass in the traditional way.

These musings are interrupted by the arrival of *monsieur le patron*.

'*Mesdames, messieurs?*'

The patron, a man of few words, arrives with pen poised over notebook to take our order. The menu is short and to the point. No need for fancy descriptions when the clientele knows what to expect of the season and the chef.

Salade lyonnais arrives as a generous heap of just-picked salad leaves tossed with olive oil, a few drops of wine vinegar, flaky salt and a generous scattering of crisp goose-bits, *gratons*, hot from the pan. This being midwinter, the season for game, a choice must be made between *civet de lièvre*, a huntsman's dish of hare cooked long and gently with wine and herbs for which the juices are thickened with the blood saved when the meat is prepared for the pot, and a classic dish of the chestnut forests of the Ardèche, wild boar with chestnuts, *marcassin aux châtaignes*, the chestnuts soft and floury and the meat cooked pink and tender with red wine, shallots and thyme.

Meanwhile, our truffle-eating table companion finishes up his foie gras with remarkable rapidity, rises, nods briefly in our direction and vanishes into the night.

'Drug-dealer,' announces Bill with cheerful conviction.

'How do you know?'

'No bill.'

Right. Next time I'll know.

꿔

Two evenings on, with most of the passengers recovered from what we no longer mention, it's my turn to sing for my supper with a demonstration of the preparation, appropriately enough considering the delicate state of most of my audience's digestion, of the Fasting Supper of the Provençal Christmas Eve.

This is no easy task, since the kitchen and dining room are both out of bounds and everything has to be done on a single rickety picnic-table with a two-burner electric camping stove in the lounge.

The traditional meal eaten in Provence on the evening before the Christmas feast is a penitential dish of salt cod with cream and olive oil, *brandade de morue*, designed to compensate for the rest of the year's indulgence in dishes such as, well, salt cod with cream and olive oil.

I contemplate the arrangement of catering-size cooking pot, tiny heat source and fire extinguisher. Bill volunteers as sous chef and I accept with alacrity. It's not easy to talk and slice and chop and whisk while keeping control of a pan of salted boiling water in which cardoons – the essential accompaniment – must be cooked just so.

I talk and peel and trim while Bill whisks and beats.

The ingredients, once combined by Bill in the correct order –
salt cod with cream and olive oil beaten until light and white –
do as they should. The cardoon stalks, trimmed of their bitter
little fringes of leaves and cooked until just tender in boiling
water, serve as scooping sticks. The delicacy of the salt-cod
cream and the earthiness of the bitter vegetable are proof, if any
is needed, that the cuisine of France at all three levels of excellence – peasant, bourgeois or palace – is unmatched anywhere
on the planet.

The audience queues for tasters, Huon disappears to prepare his lecture on the rococo in eighteenth-century art, and Bill
retires to the bar for a congratulatory whisky sour with his best
beloved.

Relieved to have completed my homework – albeit with
more than a little help from Bill – I order what I always forget I
don't like, Campari soda over ice with a twist of orange, and
take it up on deck where the rain has cleared and our floating
hotel has slipped its moorings to move smoothly upriver against
the current.

Rivers are soothing to the spirit, a reminder that the past is done
and cannot be undone. For the rest, guidance is best found in
advice offered by the Reverend Sydney Smith – wit, bon viveur
and preacher to fashionable London from the pulpit of St Paul's
in the 1830s. Among other useful suggestions offered to a
female friend admitting to low spirits is to admit these freely,
keep away from poets and others of a gloomy disposition, but
above all take a short view of life and look no further than
dinner or tea.

BRANDADE DE MORUE AUX CARDONS
(SALT-COD CREAM WITH CARDOONS)

Creamy salt-cod purée, very delicate, is the dish traditionally served in Provence at the *souper maigre*, the fasting supper of Christmas Eve, at which neither meat, wine nor sweet things can be served. You can buy your salt cod pre-soaked and ready to go; if not, choose a middle cut and soak it for 48 hours in several changes of water. It's very rich: a little goes a long way.

Serves 6–8
500 g salt cod, pre-soaked
1 onion, peeled and roughly chopped
2 bay leaves
2–3 fennel tops or 1 teaspoon fennel seeds
1 teaspoon black peppercorns

To finish
1 warm boiled potato, mashed (optional, but it helps the emulsion)
2–3 garlic cloves, peeled and crushed
300 ml extra virgin olive oil, warmed to body temperature
2–3 tablespoons warm cream

To serve
1 cardoon (whole head, trimmed)
1 tablespoon lemon juice or vinegar

Cut the soaked fish into 3–4 chunks and put it in a large pan with the onion and aromatics. Cover with water and bring gently to the boil. Remove the pan as soon as the water gives a good belch, and pour in a glassful of cold water. Leave for 5 minutes, then remove the fish pieces, skin and flake, discarding any bones.

Pound the flaked fish with the potato, garlic and a little of the oil, and mash thoroughly and vigorously. Beat in the rest of the oil

(recipe continued overleaf)

gradually, as if making a mayonnaise, adding the cream towards the end, beating until you have a very pale, thick, scoopable purée. You can do all this in a food processor, but the result will be noticeably smoother and whiter than if beaten by hand. Set aside at room temperature (a *brandade* should never be served chilled).

Meanwhile prepare the cardoons. Use only the tender inner stalks and trim off the little bitter fringe of leaf which edges the stalks. String the stalks as you would tough stalks of celery and cut into manageable pieces. Bring a pan of salted water to the boil. Add the lemon juice or vinegar and the chopped stalks. Bring back to the boil, cover with a lid and cook for 15–20 minutes, until perfectly tender. Drain well and serve with the *brandade* for scooping.

MARCASSIN AUX CHÂTAIGNES
(WILD BOAR WITH CHESTNUTS)

Wild boar, available in France through the hunting season from late autumn to the end of March, is the king of the chestnut forests of the Ardèche, prized above all other wild meat. Juniper and *serpolet*, a peppery variety of thyme, are the usual flavourings.

Serves 4–6
1.5 kg wild boar meat, diced
2 tablespoons plain flour, seasoned with salt and pepper
2–3 tablespoons lard or goose fat
3–4 garlic cloves, in their skins
100 g *petit salé*, streaky bacon or pancetta, diced
½ bottle red wine (Burgundy for preference)
1–2 sprigs *serpolet* (or thyme), leaves picked
½ teaspoon juniper berries (or 2 bay leaves), crushed
400 g fresh chestnuts, skinned, or 200 g dried chestnuts, soaked to swell
salt and pepper

To finish
2 tablespoons lard or goose fat
100 g fresh ceps or 25 g dried and soaked ceps, diced
3–4 anchovy fillets

Dust the meat with a little seasoned flour and fry it in a large casserole in the lard or goose fat until it browns a little – wild meat is
drier and firmer than farmed, so it takes less time to caramelise.

Remove the meat from the pan, add the whole garlic cloves and
bacon to the drippings and fry for a few minutes. Return the meat
to the pot, add the wine and bring to the boil to evaporate the alcohol. Add the herbs, season with salt and pepper and add enough
water to cover the meat completely.

Bring to the boil again, then turn down the heat and leave to
simmer gently, loosely covered, for as long as it takes for the meat
to be so tender it can be eaten with a fork – an hour or so – adding
more boiling water if it looks like drying out.

Meanwhile, cook the chestnuts in just enough water to cover
until tender – they'll take 10 minutes if fresh, 40 minutes if dried –
then drain and add to the meat when it's almost tender.

Prepare the finishing mix. Melt the lard or goose fat in a small
pan and fry the ceps until they begin to brown a little. Mash in the
anchovies. Stir the mixture into the casserole once the meat is perfectly tender. Serve with a salad of bitter winter leaves – endive or
chicory.

QUENELLES DE POISSON EN COCOTTE, SAUCE NANTUA (FISH DUMPLINGS WITH CRAYFISH SAUCE)

A workman's quenelle – baked rather than poached – as served at
lunchtime in the *bouchons* of Lyon with a little jug of sauce Nantua
and a helping of plain-cooked round-grain rice from the Camargue.

(recipe continued overleaf)

Serves 4

350 g raw, de-boned fish (pike, salmon, cod, haddock)

3 egg whites

½ teaspoon grated nutmeg

500 ml double cream, chilled

salt and pepper

For the sauce Nantua

50 g unsalted butter

50 g plain flour

1 litre strong fish stock

1 teaspoon paprika

2 tablespoons crayfish, shrimp or prawn meat, finely chopped

4 tablespoons crème fraîche or soured cream

salt and pepper

Put the raw fish into the food processor with the egg whites, season with a little salt, pepper and nutmeg, and process to a thick, smooth purée. You can do this by hand with a pestle and mortar – start with the fish and work in the egg white once you have a smooth paste. Cool the mixture for an hour or two in the fridge until well chilled, then blend it with the chilled cream – whizz for no more than 5 seconds, or work it in with a metal spoon. Chill again.

Preheat the oven to 180°C/Gas 4 and butter individual ramekins, set them in a baking tray of boiling water, and spoon in the mixture. Bake for 20–30 minutes, until well risen and browned.

Meanwhile, prepare the sauce. Melt the butter, sprinkle in the flour and stir until it looks sandy. Add in the stock, whisking to avoid lumps, and bring to the boil, then turn down the heat and simmer gently, stirring regularly, for 30 minutes or so, until the sauce has reduced by half its volume and is smooth and shiny. Stir in the paprika and the crayfish, shrimp or prawn meat, return to the boil, then remove from the heat, whisk in the cream, taste and correct the seasoning.

Hand the sauce round separately with the quenelles.

CERVELLES DE CANUT (SILK-WEAVERS' BRAINS)

Nothing to do with variety meats but a dish of fresh curd cheese softened with cream and flavoured with herbs, eaten with bread at the beginning or end of a meal. Among explanations offered for the curious name is that silk-weavers are soft in the head as a result of brain-addling dyes, or that the silk-merchants paid their workers so little they couldn't afford the cheapest cut on the butcher's slab. Poking fun at authority has always come naturally to the citizens of Lyon. Come the revolution, the Lyonnais have never been slow to throw up the barricades.

Serves 4
250 g fresh curd cheese
100 ml crème fraîche
1 tablespoon finely chopped parsley
1 tablespoon finely chopped chives
1 tablespoon finely chopped cornichons or pickled cucumber
salt and pepper

Combine the cheese and the crème fraîche, beat well to lighten, fold in the rest of the ingredients and heap in a bowl. Serve with hot baguette or crisp rolls and a salad of bitter leaves – radicchio, endive and chicory.

Danube

THE DANUBE'S DELTA, ON A RAINY DAY IN EARLY autumn after a long dry summer, is grey and ragged and inhospitable even to the few hardy birdwatchers, myself among them, who take to the canals in rusting paddle-boats in the hope of a glimpse of the wetland's wealth of waterbirds.

I have a particular interest in the avifauna of the last of Europe's untamed wildernesses. Before I embarked on a career as a food writer, to supplement an uncertain family income, I provided watercolour paintings of birds of prey – owls, eagles and hawks – to a Cork Street gallery, and the flowering plants of Andalusia for the botanical record at Kew. My preference was always for the avian life of the wetlands – the spoonbills, flamingoes and herons of the marshes of the Coto Doñana when we lived in Andalusia and the children learned their lessons in Spanish, followed by wet weekends under canvas in the

Camargue while our children endured a year of French schooling in the uplands of the Languedoc. In mitigation for such
arbitrary educational decisions, my own early education was no
different – and I had hopes that the intellectual gymnastics
required by learning your lessons in three different languages
would serve them well in later life. I have no idea if it did or
not – unless that none of the three have made the same choices
for their own children, my beloved grandchildren.

The Danube rises in the mountains of southern Germany
and flows through – or around or along – the borders of Austria,
Hungary, Serbia, Bulgaria and Romania before emptying its
waters into the Black Sea by the borders of Russia. Borders are
of no importance to the river's flow. The populations of the
towns and cities along her banks are a raggle-taggle mix of
people and nations, religiously and culturally diverse. Swabians
drifted downriver to tend the vineyards of Hungary; Saxons
came from Germany to farm the plains of Transylvania; Turks
planted the rice paddies of the Wallachia and established the
rose-water industry in the mountains of Serbia.

While the Rhône and the Rhine are accessible from the sea –
both are watery highways leading directly into the heart of
Europe – the delta of the Danube, though navigable throughout
most of its length, is stoppered up at the mouth, serving as a barrier
between East and West, protection against invasion from the fierce
nomadic horsemen of the steppes of Russia. Perhaps, had her marshlands been more hospitable, the warriors of Genghis Khan, diverted
towards the heart of Europe through the malarial plains of Hungary,
might have settled along her banks and never gone home.

Centuries later, the armies of the Ottoman Turks ignored
the delta, moving northwards to join the river where it broadens
to water the orchards and grain fields of Bulgaria and Romania.
Their garrisons, marooned in what they considered a gastronomic
no-man's land, taught local cooks how to prepare the sophisti-

cated dishes they ate at home. It was the Turks who taught the subject nations how to wrap the sturdy German dumpling in delicate Ottoman pastry. It was the Ottomans, too, who introduced the gardeners of Bulgaria to the fiery New World chilli. The Bulgarians, the horticulturalists of the Balkans, bred the fieriness out of the chillies and exported their skills upriver to the paprika mills of Hungary.

It was also the Ottomans who introduced the botanical riches of the New World to the Old. Within a century or two of their arrival on the quays of Seville, the revolutionary new crops of the Americas, including potatoes, maize, tomatoes, storable beans, marrow, pumpkins, fiery chilli-peppers – fast-growing and tolerant of latitude and climate – had spread throughout Europe, Asia and Africa. And if this seems geographically improbable, consider that an energetic water rat with a sense of adventure could travel from the delta of the Danube to the river's source in the Black Forest, splash along mossy pathways to the headwaters of the Rhône, follow the river's flow until the waters spill into the Mediterranean, slip along the northern shores of Africa and paddle home to the Black Sea through the Dardanelles – and all without the need to set furry foot on dry land.

The university of Pécs, founded on the banks of the Danube in southern Hungary in the fourteenth century, continues as best it may to fulfil its original function – the exchange of knowledge between East and West – in spite of the political turbulence endured throughout its history. At the time of my own brief visit, on a sunny Saturday in the autumn of 2013, I saw no evidence of disharmony between the congregations of the city's handsome baroque cathedral and the worshippers in her beautiful blue-domed mosque – the very reverse, since all were queuing happily for a mid-morning street snack.

Where town and country come together in the marketplace, the instrument for change is the street stalls, where food is prepared fresh to order and sold cheap to traders and their customers. Where there are immigrant or student populations crammed into overcrowded accommodation lacking cooking facilities, little family-run outlets are set up to serve customers yearning for the flavours of home. At first, many of the ingredients have to be imported, until farmers, observing a gap in the market, begin to grow what the newcomers want.

In cities with hungry student populations such as Pécs, the fast food available in the market when the traders pack up for the day is cheap, nourishing and hot. Treats – mostly deep-fried – are often sold from the same stalls later in the day, in the afternoon and early evening.

The street snack drawing a queue on a sunny afternoon in the cathedral square in Pécs goes by the name of *kürtőskalács*. At first sight, what's on offer looks like a cross between the German doughnut and the Spanish *churro*: a long thin rope of puffy dough wrapped round a tubular kebab-holder, hollow in the middle and slotted into a metal rod set over a charcoal brazier. Turned slowly, much like the method used to grill Turkish kebabs, the scent that attracts the customers is of vanilla, hot butter and caramelised sugar.

The queue includes students with overstuffed backpacks, churchgoers spilling out from the cathedral after a Saturday concert, and women in headscarfs with children who have just attended prayers in the mosque. Curious as to the method required to produce so unfamiliar a result, I join the line at the counter to watch the culinary process. As far as I can observe from the mixing, rolling and patting, the starting point is a yeast-raised bread dough enriched with egg and butter, much the same as Italy's festive *panettone* or Russia's wedding *babka* or the *kugelhopf*, the ring-cake that France's Austrian-born queen, Marie Antoinette, recommended with blithe unconcern to the angry poor of Paris as a substitute for a baker's loaf. The method of cooking, however, is distinctly Turkish. This may be coincidence or simply a solution to the problem of street-sellers everywhere – how to attract customers by appealing to eyes, nose and taste-buds.

At one euro for a fistful, it's irresistible. As for taste, texture and flavour – well, I was as hungry as a woman can be who's skipped breakfast in favour of a performance of something choral, tuneful and lengthy by the cathedral choir. My purchase is crisp, sweet and pleasantly doughy when dipped into a mugful of Turkish *salep* – hot milk thickened with powdered orchid-root – ordered at one of the little cafés that ring the main square.

As indeed – I reflect as I settle down with paints and paper on the steps of the war memorial to record the view of the university, cathedral and mosque – are the chips with ketchup available at the ubiquitous fast-food chain just opened for business in the old town hall on the far side of the square, attracting a rival queue, mostly teenagers.

The Danube served as both highway and larder to the people who settled along her banks. The river rises in the mountains of Germany, gathers strength in Austria, spreads itself into malarial marshland in Hungary, tumbles helter-skelter through the ravines of the Carpathians, meets the waters of its mighty tributary, the Sava, just below the fortress of Belgrade, before flowing onwards, broad and deep, through the orchards and wheat fields of Bulgaria and Romania until it turns north towards the Urals and vanishes at the edge of Russia into a vast wilderness of tamarisk, willow and roadbeds.

I met the river first in the early 1980s in Vienna, Budapest and Belgrade, while researching the cookbook I had long planned to write, *European Peasant Cookery*. And later – always with the joy of renewing old acquaintance – when travelling for similar purpose through Romania and Bulgaria. But it was not until the opportunity arose a couple of years ago to join a week-long river-cruise from Bucharest to Budapest that I had an opportunity to follow the river to her delta.

The delta of the Danube, unlike those of her sister rivers, Rhône and Rhine, remained un-navigable until half a century ago, when a chain of canals was hacked through the reed beds by convict labour from Russia and Romania. Even so, the narrow waterways need constant dredging and are navigable only when the rains have filled the upper reaches of the river to overflowing. The original purpose of the channel-digging was to link Soviet Russia with her satellite nations of the Balkans. Plans included a manufacturing centre to encourage settlement in the salt-mining town of Salinas; the establishment of rice plantations where rice had been grown in Roman times to avoid the need for imported rice from Turkey; and a nuclear power station on the Russian side of the delta at precisely the spot where the earth's tectonic plates are at their most volatile. Ambitions were abandoned with the fall of Ceauşescu and are unlikely to be revived as democracy finds its feet in Romania and Russia is busy elsewhere.

At the point where the river meets the borders of Bulgaria and Romania, it flows steadily eastwards through fields of sunflowers and maize, apricot orchards and vineyards until it finally spreads its waters into the delta at Salinas, capital of the region, once prosperous from the sale of salt but, with the delta's population reduced to a handful of fishing families, its industrial ambitions now abandoned as a jungle of concrete towers and warehouses.

This year, with the water level in the delta too low for navigation by our river-cruiser, we have been uploaded into buses in Bucharest for the drive through apricot orchards and maize fields until we reach the industrial edge of Salinas. Here some fifty of us brave souls, volunteers in spite of the unpromising weather, are decanted into the drizzle, ready for embarkation on a trio of rusting hulks roped together in the current by the quayside.

'Dearest ladies and gentlemen, *meine Damen und Herren* – please to believe that you are most welcome!'

The gloom of the day and the dark bank of cloud waiting to discharge its load over the already sodden marshland has not damped the spirit of Iuliana, our guide to the delta, a sparkling ray of optimism at the end of the visitor season. In the winter, as she has already explained through the intercom on the bus, the marshes are left in peace to the few fishing families whose relationship with the wilderness endures. Iuliana, curvy and pretty with bouncing curls and a technicolour dress sense, sets foot on the first of the rickety gangplanks without a backwards glance.

'Please all the people to follow me!'

This is easier said than done. The paddle-boats are roped together by wobbly gangplanks, and Iuliana jumps from deck to deck with the confidence of habit. Her charges, a small group of visitors and locals – three elderly British birdwatchers wearing binoculars round their necks, a family from Frankfurt and two young couples from Bucharest – make our way gingerly across the rocking planks holding on to rope handrails until we are all safely aboard the outermost boat.

Iuliana settles herself under the canvas canopy on deck and takes command of the microphone to deliver what turns out to be a trilingual explanation of what we are about to observe.

'We are commencing our tour of the delta, ladies and gentlemen,' Iuliana shouts into the crackling sound system. 'You may sometimes be seeing some fishermen with red hair and long beards who are fishing on the banks sitting in a wooden canoe. The wife has a round face and freckles but you will not see her as she is at home in Salinas looking after the children. If the fisherman fishes some fishes, the family will eat fish soup for dinner.'

The engine cranks into life, the paddle-wheels turn and our transport noses its way out into the sluggish yellow current.

At this moment the rain begins to fall in earnest and everyone but the birdwatchers and Iuliana, plugged into the sound system on deck, disappear below to take refuge from the rain with a restorative coffee in the cabin. The scent of Turkish coffee mingles unappetisingly with the petrol fumes from the engine, softened by the sweet-salt breeze and the grassy scent of the marshes.

This is a wilderness like no other I have ever encountered – more desolate than the wetlands of the Camargue, with their nesting flamingoes, or even, many years ago on a three-month crossing of the desert in the tracks of David Livingstone, the papyrus reed beds of the Okavango patrolled by fish eagles, or, more recently in my travels, the tangled rafts of the Everglades, home to alligators and pelicans.

I take advantage of the abrupt clearing of the decks and the absence of audience to take out my sketchbook, hoping for a glimpse of cranes, egrets, herons, harriers and anything else that has managed to escape the twin hazards of pollution and predation.

Iuliana settles herself on the seat beside me, observing the process of transferring technicolour paint to rain-soaked paper.

'You are an artist?'

Up to a point, I reply. I earned my living as a botanical and bird painter. But now I write about food and illustrate my own work when I get a chance. And when I travel, this is how I take notes, with images like this – sometimes detailed, sometimes just a reminder of where I am and what I see, but particularly what I eat.

'This I like very much. My brother is studying art in Bucharest, and he will like to know how you work. So quick.'

At the back of the book is a little sketch of fishermen cooking soup in a pot set on a tripod over a campfire.

'This is fish soup? What we Romanians call *ciorba de peste*?'

This, I confirm, is indeed the traditional riverbank cook-up found throughout the full length of the Danube, except that these fishermen are Hungarian and the soup is named for the *bogracs*, the iron cauldron in which it's cooked.

'You are making many such voyages?'

Whenever I can, I answer with a smile. But the sketch was made a few years ago when I was presenting a TV documentary on the paprika industry of Szeged. As demonstration of the excellence of the local industry, the fishermen were happy to cook their famous fish *bogracs* – the generic name for anything cooked in an iron cauldron over an open fire.

'This is making a little money for the fishermen from the tourists?'

It is indeed. Szeged's famous fisherman's soup is a fixture on the Hungarian tourist trail, promoted by the tourist authority in Budapest.

Iuliana nods. 'This is good business plan.'

Our conversation terminates abruptly as Iuliana springs into professional mode.

'Please to look to your left, ladies and gentlemen!'

Right on cue, we pass our first fisherman. He does indeed have red hair and a long beard and is sitting in a boat made out of a scooped-out tree trunk. Iuliana and I wave enthusiastically. The bird watchers are looking the other way.

'These people are Rus,' crackles Iuliana over the microphone. 'These people are Russian Orthodox and we Romanians are Eastern Orthodox.' She pauses, clicking off the microphone, then resumes. 'I can tell you that I was attending school with the children of the Rus when my mother was a schoolteacher in the delta. They have lived here for two hundred years because they were not allowed to worship as they wished under the Tsar. I say this because you must not think it was only Stalinists and Communists who oppress the people.'

This is a good joke and Iuliana laughs heartily.

'These people come here and we don't mind because they pay their taxes and of course they send their children to school.'

Romania is full of people who are not Romanian, continues our guide. There are Saxons in Sibiu, Hungarians in Timişoara, Slavs in Moldavia, and in Wallachia, by the Bulgarian border on the way to Turkey, there's a group of Turks who eat Muslim food and keep Ramadan and are perfectly well integrated into Romanian society. Then there are the travelling people, the *tsigane*. Nobody can do anything about them. When they come to the door, Iuliana's mother gives them money to go away, and that's the best anyone can do.

Iuliana switches off the sound system and returns to settle back beside me.

'You have many of these books at home?'

Indeed I do, hundreds. And I carry spares whenever I travel, some of which have sketches from previous visits.

'If you don't mind, please can I see?'

I hand over a nearly finished sketchbook carried for just such a reason, as a way of establishing common interest in how other people live and cook.

Iuliana flips through the pages with delight.

'Hah! I think that this is milking of sheep in our mountains of Carpathia? Am I right? And here we are again in Sibiu – this is how they build their houses and here is the big church with the clock. Sibiu is where my father's family lives. Did you taste their *sarmale*, the little rolls of rice and meat in cabbage leaf? This is what we prepare for weddings and other parties. In Moldavia they like their *sarmale* small enough to be eaten in a single mouthful. In Sighişoara they like them big enough for two bites, which is how my sister likes them. Her husband is from Moldavia, so every time they want to have a party, they have a fight.'

And Iuliana herself, how does she like her *sarmale*?

'Myself? I like them how my mother makes them in Timişoara, which is just right. You know the story of Goldilocks and the Three Bears, which was the first book in English that I am reading? My mother makes *sarmale* just right, like the porridge of the middle bear, which is how she will make the *sarmale* when I am married, though I have not yet chosen a husband.'

Does she have anyone special in mind?

Iuliana laughs and shakes her head. 'Perhaps I will find myself a nice polite Englishman who wears a bowler hat and carries an umbrella. You never know. Do you have a picture of a good husband for me in your book?'

I admit to a lack of nice polite Englishmen in my sketchbook. Fishermen maybe. And shepherds milking sheep. But none of these seem to fit the bill.

'You are right!'

Iuliana's peels of laughter send a pair of elegant little waders – redshanks by the look of their bright-orange bills and scarlet legs – skimming away across the water. I return to my sketchbook. When a bird is on the wing, the trick is to hold the image in the eye for long enough to put paint on paper.

Iuliana watches with interest.

'So quick. You always work like this?'

Fast and rough? Yes indeed. It's the only way to make sure I get what I need. Even though the images catch just one particular moment, the sketches tell me far more than the hundreds of images captured on a camera.

Better still, I add, sometimes they allow me to make a friend like Iuliana who can help me understand what I see.

Iuliana frowns.

'I can tell you what you are seeing right now, right here in the delta. There are no more fishes. Maybe some little fish for soup, but the big fish, salmon and sturgeon, the caviar-fish that could be sold for money, is gone. What good is soup-fish to a fisherman who has to pay bills for his family?'

So what will happen if the big fish never return?

Iuliana shrugs. 'The fishermen sometimes catch a little one, but they are too young to make caviar. The caviar-fish takes many years to make eggs, so the fishermen in the marshes will have to find other ways to earn a living. They don't want to go back to Russia where they come from, and they don't want to live anywhere else because that is their home.'

Iuliana pauses, then resumes. 'I am not Rus but I too am from the delta. My mother was a schoolteacher in a village until the school closed because there were too few pupils, and now she lives in Bucharest. But still she makes the best fisherman's *ciorba*, even though she has to buy the fishes in the market instead of waiting for my father to come home from the river, like your fishermen in the picture.'

She sighs. 'All this talk of *ciorba* is making me hungry. I wish I had some now.'

Ciorba, the Turkish name for soup, Iuliana continues, is one of the culinary legacies of five centuries under the Ottomans who ruled all of Romania. Perhaps, she adds thoughtfully, the connection is marketable – they had a reputation for the delicious things they ate. The garrisons of the Turks brought coffee and sugar and pastries perfumed with rose water, and taught their cooks how to prepare the good things they liked. And *sarmale*, of course, which are also made with vine leaves in summer and cabbage in winter. You can tell where you are in Romania – or Greece or Bulgaria or Serbia or anywhere in the Balkans – just by asking people how they like to prepare their *sarmale*.

This opinion having been delivered and digested, Iuliana walks over to the rail where the birdwatchers are sweeping the banks with binoculars. A rarity has been spotted. A gang of four squaccos – smallest and prettiest of the heron family, with pinkish-purple backs and black-spotted golden crests – are examining the current for signs of prey from a perch on an over-hanging branch.

Iuliana is not impressed by the diminutive fishermen.

'These birds are eating many fishes.'

When I take up my brush and make a few strokes, Iuliana shakes her head in disapproval. 'I do not like these birds.'

There are not enough fish in the delta to support the human fishermen who remain, and fishing-birds – of which there are, in Iuliana's opinion, too many – represent the competition.

The birds whose diet is under scrutiny are members of the last remaining breeding colonies in all of Europe. I have observed them before in the Camargue in southern France and in the delta of the Guadalquivir in Spain, where their presence is always a delight. Sociable little fellows, squaccos nest in mixed heronries with their larger relatives, storks, spoonbills and egrets. When their nesting companions disappear, so do the squaccos, and the sight of four in a row on a branch are, the birdwatchers and I agree, worthy of a tick on anyone's ornithological life list.

'We have very many of these in the delta,' says Iuliana dis-missively. If fish stocks continue to be depleted, soon even the Rus would not be able to survive in the delta. No one else would put up with the rain, the mosquitoes and the general discomfort of life in the marshes. And then there would be no red-bearded fishermen to entertain the tourists, could anyone ever persuade them to do so. Even if not and the fishermen preferred to keep to themselves, the marshes would be all the poorer for their absence.

And in that case, Iuliana's newly formulated plans for market-ing fishermen's fish soup as a tourist draw would be dead in the water, just like the sturgeon and the salmon and the birds and every-thing else that made the delta a pleasure for visitors and might, in time, be an opportunity to restore the delta to its former glory.

With the refugees in the cabin showing no signs of braving the elements and the birdwatchers contented with ticking their lists, Iuliana returns to musings on her childhood and that of her family before her. Life was better in the delta in her grandfather's day, when there was a living to be made in the marshes. In her grandfather's day, even in Iuliana's own childhood, there were birds and animals everywhere, the river was full of fish and the delta was populated with Turks and Ukrainians as well as Romanians and Rus. It was safe, too. Strangers and thieves didn't venture into the wilderness at night for fear of wolves and bears. Not that there were many of those left by the time the Russians went home, but the villagers encouraged the rumours.

By now we are proceeding at a steady pace through the mist and rain, sliding between chocolate-coloured banks on coffee-coloured water. In some places the bank has collapsed into the river, uncovering gigantic bare roots among which the white feathers of egrets shine like snow. A heron stands motionless at the edge of the water, one-legged and crook-necked, searching his mirrored reflection for prey.

'These birds are also eating too many fishes,' says Iuliana, switching on the microphone to alert the audience below as a marsh-harrier slips into view and disappears downriver. A flotilla of black and white guillemots rises untidily from the shallows and hurtles away, skimming low to the water.

'See everyone, is kingfisher!' shouts Iuliana, waving at a capsized tree.

Three pairs of binoculars – and my paintbrush – swing as one, catching a flash of metallic blue. The bird drops like a tiny torpedo into the water, emerges with a sliver of silver in its gun-metal beak and vanishes into the reed beds.

'Kingfisher is very nice bird. Very pretty,' says Iuliana approvingly. 'This bird is taking only small fishes and baby frogs, tadpoles, and there are many of these so we do not mind.'

Iuliana clicks off the microphone and returns to reminiscence. Even when she was a child, the river was full of the sturgeon, enormous fish with plenty of roe. In those days, the Russians came over the border to buy the caviar for roubles, some from as far away as Moscow.

Sturgeon makes good *ciorba*. The Rus made good *ciorba* with sturgeon, but theirs was never as good as her mother's.

'My mother's *ciorba* is made by putting plenty of bony little soup-fish in a big pot with water and not too much salt and boiling it up till the broth is strong. Then the small fish are taken out with a sieve and potatoes, and if you have big fish, this is cut in pieces and added to the broth. If there are no big fish, you add more potatoes. And since a *ciorba* must be a little sour, you must add a little vinegar.'

The vinegar, she continues, is not necessary if the cooking liquid is *bors*. This is not, as the name suggests, the Romanian version of Russia's beetroot and cabbage soup, but a cooking broth made in much the same way as *kvass*, by fermenting a handful of bran in water with a little yeast.

I lay aside my sketchbook and concentrate on her story. Perhaps it is possible that a fish soup, *ciorba de peste*, might be available in Salinas today? According to the guidebook, this is market day, and there might be one or two of the little restaurants that cater to market traders and their customers after the day's deals are done.

'Market is not in schedule,' says Iuliana decisively. Then, softening, 'But I will see what I can do for you in Bucharesti.'

She busies herself on the mobile phone as our transport returns to the quayside, the Germans and Romanians emerge from the cabin, and the ornithologists pack up their manuals and binoculars. Once we are all safely stowed in our seats on the bus ready for the return journey to Bucharest, Iuliana comes to find me at my seat.

'It is all arranged. You will meet with my cousin Codruta at the café at the British Council tomorrow at coffee-time. She works in the library there and teaches a class in English. I think you will like each other. She too is interested in the things that interest you – food and history – and she has a brother who is a chef in a restaurant.'

Romania and France have always had much in common, culturally and gastronomically. In the old days under the monarchy, Bucharest's French restaurants were famous as far away as Paris, and French was the language of the intellectuals of Bucharest before the Russians took over. French pâtisseries were the first to reopen for business after the fall of the regime, to provide the citizens of Bucharest with the delicate cream-stuffed cakes and pastries they loved and had never forgotten.

The dictatorship was a terrible time for anyone who remembered the regional diversity of the old days. Under Ceauşescu, all Romanians had to eat the same food prepared to recipes provided by the state. Never mind about the cooking of the Saxons, Hungarians, Turks and Slavs, everyone had to eat the same food cooked according to the official cookbook – so many grams of meat, so many grams of potato, so many grams of salt. All food supplies were the property of the state and were diverted to schools and workers' canteens. If you didn't work or go to school, you didn't eat. And to ensure no backsliding, all non-official cookbooks had to be turned in to the police station and burned in public in town squares. Naturally enough, the nation's grandmothers hid their household manuals under the mattress until the dictatorship collapsed and life returned to normal – more or less.

These days, twenty-five years after the fall of the regime, Bucharest has restored itself to elegance and Frenchness. Gap has opened outlets in suburban shopping malls. Prada handbags, Louboutin heels and Hermès scarves are on sale in the smart boutiques of the capital. Nevertheless, the city is still in a state of permanent makeover. The main square is heaped with rubble, the result of repairs to the sewer system, as it was under Ceaușescu, when the joke doing the rounds was that the reason for the excavations was that the murderous old dictator was trying to find his mother. Romanians have a dry sense of humour that served them well under Communism.

Research, for me, starts in the pages of Victorian and Edwardian travel writers, some of whom – mostly women – recorded what their hosts put in their mouths. Thereafter, for me, it's a matter of a willingness to talk to strangers encountered in places where natives as well as foreigners take refreshment. I usually settle down in a corner and paint. Sketchbooks and paint box are invaluable tools in opening up a channel of mutual interest.

Codruta comes to find me in the café attached to her offices. She is a history graduate, slender, pretty, dark-haired and earnest, employed by the British Council to catalogue the library and teach English classes to Romanians who wish to learn the language.

After preliminary introductions and talk of her cousin and her work as a guide to the delta, we turn to the main purpose of our encounter: the family's traditional Sunday lunch, *ciorba* with meatballs. It is not possible to invite me to the family home, since they live a hundred miles away in Timișoara on the Hungarian border, but if I wish to experience an approximation of the real thing, Codruta will be happy to accompany me to lunch at the Hotel Phoenician, where her brother is the under-chef and can be relied upon to cook a *ciorba de chiftea* according to the family recipe.

The Phoenician, a vast new hotel built of concrete, steel and glass for Russian apparatchiks in the Communist era, is marooned in the outskirts of a shopping mall. The dining room has a festive air, with tables draped in shiny green damask and gilt tablesettings among which a group of smartly suited dignitaries have already settled down to enjoy their platefuls.

Codruta advances purposefully towards the buffet, a magnificent self-service display in the next room, and searches through the bowls of cream-dressed salads, breaded chicken and chips in tomato sauce – 'peasant potatoes' says the helpful little label – until she finally lifts the lid of an ornate silver tureen.

'This is just what I have asked of my brother,' she says, inhaling the steam. 'This is *ciorba* prepared with *bors*, very traditional, very correct.'

Ladling out two steaming bowlfuls, releasing a yeasty, mushroomy fragrance, she tops each portion with a spoonful of soured cream.

'You must eat it like this, with apple-chilli.'

Apple-chilli, a small round capsicum, bright red and of a size to fit snugly in the palm, does indeed look like the roundest and rosiest of apples.

Codruta takes a mouthful of soup and a bite of chilli, and nods approvingly. 'First you take some soup, then some chilli, then soup again. Apple-chilli is not so very hot, very juicy, very sweet, very good for stomach.'

I follow her example as soon as we settle down at a table. The famous soup is a clear straw-coloured broth with a pleasant rather beery sourness, in which have been poached tiny bite-sized meatballs speckled with grains of rice and something green and scented which my taste-buds tell me is lovage, a peppery relative of the celery family that grows enthusiastically in my garden in the Welsh uplands. The flavour of lovage is stronger and ranker than celery – though I sometimes include it sparingly in vegetable soups – but the sharpness of the broth and the delicate flavour of the meatballs suit it to perfection.

'Delicious,' I say, as I mop up the last drops from the bowl.

Codruta smiles. 'I shall be happy to tell my brother of your appreciation.'

I should understand, she continues, that the method of souring a *ciorba* is important. If vinegar is used, the soup is Bulgarian, even though Romanians use it too. If lemon juice is used, it's Greek. If the souring agent is sumac – a powder prepared from sour little fruits of a shrub endemic to the southern shores of the Mediterranean – it's Turkish. If the sour flavour comes from *bors*, as now, it is Romanian or Russian or Turkish, where it is used to add depth to a cooking broth as one might add wine.

Since *bors* takes several days to prepare, it is possible, she adds, to buy it as a soup-cube. And when the cook is in a hurry, as her brother is today, a soup-cube is perfectly acceptable.

I agree that the *ciorba* is delicious, in spite of the soup-cube, and would be happy to be able to congratulate the chef in person. Unfortunately this is not possible owing to Romania's strict interpretation of rules governing hygiene in commercial kitchens.

'This comes from the time of the dictatorship,' Codruta adds. 'At that time, you must understand, everyone had to take their midday meal at their place of work – schools as well as factories – in government canteens. At that time the market-places were closed, government supermarkets were the only places you could buy food, and people were forbidden to cook at home. But Romanians don't always do what we're told, and people went on growing food in little patches of earth hidden behind the houses and carried on preparing the dishes they liked to eat according to who they were.'

Codruta glances around to see if we are overheard, then continues, 'One day the government decided the people were disobeying orders to eat only Communist food prepared according to the government manual. They were still cooking Romanian *ciorba* or Hungarian goulash or Saxon dishes prepared with sausage and sauerkraut and all the other dishes that remind people who they are and where they belong.'

She pauses, smiling at me. 'Can you possibly imagine what it would be like if English people were forbidden to eat shepherd's pie, or roast beef with Yorkshire pudding? If you do, you will understand how angry it made the people. But we couldn't protest because the secret police were everywhere. So when everyone was told to bring their household books to the police station – the handwritten ones that were like the family Bible – we did as we were told.'

'That must have been hard.'

'It was. Even though I was just a little girl, I knew how much pain it caused my mother and grandmother when the police made a big bonfire of all the books in the market square and the children were taken to watch. But what I didn't know was that everyone gave the police a book that didn't matter and hid the real one under the mattress. So when the revolution came and the dictatorship ended and the markets were open again, there was food to set on the table and everyone brought the books out from under the mattress and nothing was lost.'

She frowns, then lifts her head and smiles. 'Perhaps, as a mother and grandmother yourself, you would have done the same?'

I hold out my hand to take hers. I feel it every time, I reply, whenever my own children or grandchildren are gathered together under my roof. The dishes that speak to the heart are those we remember from childhood, that remind us who we are and where we come from.

Codruta nods. 'I hope you will not forget the meal we have shared today when you return home to your own country. There are many opportunities for friendship and understanding between the nations of Europe, and for that we have reason to be thankful.'

Another pause. Then, slowly: 'This is why this dish we have shared today is so important to us, and why it should never be forgotten.'

CIORBA DE PESTE (FRESHWATER FISH SOUP)

A simple soup prepared using the Danube's bony young river fish: pike, tench, roach, bream, catfish, carp, small sturgeon, whatever swims into the net. Save any larger fillets to poach in the broth at the end.

Serves 4–6
2 kg small river fish
1 kg onions, peeled and finely chopped
1 kg potatoes, scrubbed and sliced
1–2 tablespoons vinegar or lemon juice
salt

To serve
fresh red chillies
1–2 tablespoons hot paprika or chilli powder

Rinse and gut the fish but leave the heads on and do not scale. Remove and reserve any meaty little fillets.

Pack the small fish into a large saucepan with about 2 litres water and a teaspoon of salt. Bring to the boil, turn down the heat and simmer uncovered for 50–60 minutes until the fish is absolutely mushy.

Strain the broth through a sieve or mouli, pushing through all the little threads of flesh but leaving the bones behind. Return the broth to the pan and add the chopped onions and potato slices. Bring to the boil, turn down the heat and simmer gently for another 20–30 minutes until the vegetables are perfectly tender.

Taste and add salt – river fish have no natural salt, so extra salting is usually necessary. Stir in the vinegar or lemon juice, just enough to add savour. If you have any reserved fish fillets, slip them into the boiling broth just before serving.

Serve ladled into bowls with chopped chilli on the side. If using dried chill or paprika, stir it with a ladleful of the hot broth and hand round separately.

BORS (WHEAT-BRAN BROTH)

Bors, a mildly fermented wheat-bran beer, is used for sharpness and flavour in a *ciorba* ('sour' soup), much like wine in grape-growing regions. You can find commercially prepared *bors* sold in concentrated form as a soup-base in Polish, Russian and Turkish delis as well as in Romania. The flavour is surprisingly mushroomy, umami-laden, with a touch of sweetness and just a little sourness, as if someone had added a glass of sharp white wine.

Makes 2 litres
250 g wheat bran
1 hazelnut-sized piece fresh yeast or 1 teaspoon instant yeast
2 tablespoons cornmeal
2 litres spring water

Start 3–4 days ahead. Combine 2 tablespoons wheat bran with a cupful of warm water and add the yeast. Leave to froth for a couple of hours, then drain and reserve the bran, discarding the liquid. Put the remaining dry bran in a clean bowl with the cornmeal. Boil the water and pour it into the bowl. Mix and leave to cool to body temperature, then stir in the yeasty bran.

Cover with a clean cloth and set aside for 3–4 days in a cool place, stirring regularly, until delicately soured. Strain into a clean glass jar, store in the refrigerator and use as required.

To start another batch without yeast, reserve a cupful of the strained bran and proceed as above, adding the yeasted bran to the new batch at the stage when the bran-and-water mixture has cooled to body temperature.

CIORBA DE CHIFTEA (SOUR SOUP WITH MEATBALLS)

Tiny meatballs poached in a clear broth soured with *bors* – wheat-bran beer – this is a party dish to be eaten with a generous dollop of soured cream and a bite of apple-chilli.

Serves 4–6
For the meatballs
350 g finely ground beef, lamb or pork
2 heaped tablespoons (uncooked) risotto or pilau rice
1 small onion, peeled and grated
1 egg, beaten
1 generous handful of chopped dill or fennel tops
1 generous handful of chopped parsley

For the broth
600 ml chicken or beef-bone broth
600 ml wheat-bran *bors*, or water and white wine
  plus 2 tablespoons wine vinegar

To finish
1 heaped tablespoon shredded lovage or celery leaves
soured cream
fresh red chillies

Work the ground meat with the uncooked rice grains, onion, egg, half the dill and half the parsley until well blended and smooth. Roll into balls about the size of a walnut.

Bring the broth to a boil, gently slip in the meatballs, return the pot to the boil, turn down the heat and leave to simmer without bubbling for 30–40 minutes, until the meatballs are tender and the rice is cooked through.

Strain the *bors* into the broth (or add the wine, water and vinegar) and reheat to boiling point for a couple of minutes.

Finish with the shredded lovage and the rest of the parsley and dill. Ladle into bowls and add a dollop of soured cream. Serve the fresh red chillies separately, one for each person.

SARMALE (STUFFED CABBAGE ROLLS)

Sarmale is the generic name throughout the Balkans for little rolls of leaves – cabbage or vine – filled with rice and meat known as *dolmades* to the Greeks and *dolmasi* to the Turks. The wrappers are preserved under salt for the winter and the sizes of the rolls vary according to size of leaf and regional preference, as do the flavouring ingredients. Iuliana's mother's recipe includes tomato in the stuffing and is sauced with soured cream.

Serves 6–8
1 large green cabbage
2 carrots, scraped and finely chopped
2 sticks celery, finely chopped

(recipe continued overleaf)

For the filling
4 tablespoons seed oil (sunflower or pumpkin)
1 medium onion, peeled and finely chopped
2–3 garlic cloves, peeled and chopped
250 g risotto or pilau rice
1 large ripe tomato, skinned, de-seeded and diced
1 tablespoon finely chopped dill
1 egg, lightly beaten (optional)
salt and pepper

To finish
300 ml soured cream

Trim the base of the cabbage and place the whole head in a large bowl. Pour in a kettleful of boiling water and leave it just long enough to soften the bases of the leaves, then drain. Remove about 18 of the large outer leaves and lay them flat, ready for stuffing, pressing down with the flat of your hand. Cut out the hard stalk and discard, shred the remaining inner leaves and put them in a large casserole with the carrot and celery.

Heat the oil in a frying pan and fry the chopped onion and garlic until soft and golden – don't let it brown. Add the rice and stir it over the heat until the grains turn translucent. Season and add enough water just to submerge the grains. Bring to the boil, turn down the heat and simmer for 10 minutes, when the grains will be chewy but most of the water will have been absorbed. Tip the contents of the pan into a bowl. Work in the tomato, dill and egg thoroughly with your hand, squeezing to make a firm mixture.

Drop a tablespoonful of filling on the stalk-end of each leaf, tuck the sides over to enclose, roll up neatly and transfer to the bed of cabbage in the casserole. Continue until all the mixture is used up. Add enough water to cover the stuffed leaves, bring to the boil, turn down the heat, cover with a lid and simmer gently for about an hour, until nearly all the liquid has been absorbed. Spoon the soured cream over the top and serve warm.

DESERTS

IT'S FAIR TO SAY THAT NOT EVERYONE HAS THE
opportunity to cross the great Kalahari Desert in much the same
way – give or take motorised transport – as Dr Livingstone,
celebrated author of *Missionary Travels and Researches in Southern Africa* in the 1850s. Still less would anyone choose an unruly
group of gun-toting hunters, trackers and wilderness addicts as
company, even if such an expedition were possible in the
twenty-first century.

The Kalahari, a vast wilderness of cracked red earth and
grey thorn-scrub a thousand miles from north to south as the
eagle flies, separates the marshes of the Okavango Delta from
the grasslands of southern Africa. Beneath the desert, trapped
by a layer of impermeable rock, a water-table renewed annually
by the floodwaters of the delta supports an extraordinary variety
of desert creatures as well as a sparse population of nomadic
hunter-gatherers. These, the San people, are of small stature,
apricot-skinned and so perfectly physically adapted to their
surroundings that they can endure long periods without food
or water.

I had no business, with family commitments not yet dis-
charged, to accompany the family breadwinner on a two-way
crossing of a trackless wilderness under conditions, in 1978,

designed to mirror those encountered by nineteenth-century missionary-explorers. The expedition, a dozen full-grown men (and one woman) crammed into a pair of ancient Land Rovers and a back-up truck with camping gear, was a motley crew of hunters, trackers and ne'er-do-well friends (and wife) of the writer. Wife's responsibility was the provision of a pictorial record suitable to such a nineteenth-century undertaking, no easy task in a vehicle rocking and rattling from dawn to dusk.

We slept under the stars, hunted for the pot, baked bread in an earth-oven dug in a termite mound, roasted guinea fowl over the campfire and avoided, where possible, the wrong side of lion, elephant and buffalo. Now and then, when our hunters had been particularly successful and there was enough fresh meat to dry as biltong, the San would make their presence known. A curl of smoke from a campfire, a line of footprints leading into the bush, were an indication that our companions in the wilderness were prepared to trade. Their temporary encampments, grass-thatched shelters set around a central hearth-fire, showed no evidence of personal possessions. The San travel without encumbrance, material or emotional. All members, old and young, are required to contribute to the welfare of the group. Those with skill in handicraft – carving in wood and bone, curing animal-skins, leatherwork – were particularly valued since their goods served as currency.

Goods set out for exchange for brightly patterned cotton handkerchiefs as well as our leathery strips of sun-dried meat were beautiful rugs made with soft pelts of jackals and wild-cats, ostrich-shell beads strung on slender leather thongs, quivers and arrows bound with zebra skin, intricate little carvings of birds and animals in wood and bone. While meat and cloth were the main attraction, when I set to work to record the scene with paint on paper, an enthusiastic audience passed my sketchbooks from hand to hand, identifying images on previous pages and showing me which among the furs was a jackal pelt and which of the artefacts was carved from an antelope's horn. Later, under similar circumstances, travelling in remote regions such as the highlands of Ethiopia and the wildernesses of northern India, my sketchbooks served much the same purpose, as a way of communicating without a common language.

Trade is the lifeblood of desert-dwellers. For thousands of years the nomadic San occupied vast territories unchallenged, a reason for their survival as hunter-gatherers well into the second half of the last century. In the more overcrowded regions of the world, similarly nomadic peoples were obliged to settle down as pastoralists and farmers. Nevertheless, both Ethiopians and Gujaratis remain travellers by tradition, establishing the great trade routes that linked Asia to Africa to Europe. Gujarat traded with the seafarers of Portugal and from thence to the ports of the North Atlantic and the Baltic. Caravans from land-locked Ethiopia traded with Egypt and onwards to the great medieval fairs of France and Germany. With the market traders came the storytellers – minstrels, tellers of tales from faraway places – links in the chain of human knowledge. The scholars of Imperial China followed the merchants of the Silk Road to learn from the philosophers of India. Students in the great universities of Europe were taught to question the nature of the universe by the mathematicians of Damascus and Granada.

The desert is a demanding taskmaster. But for those for whom nature provides, living in harmony with the planet is not a lifestyle choice but the raw material of life itself.

Gujarat

THE FRAGRANCE THAT FLOATS ACROSS THE SHIMMERING acres of salt flats on the breeze in the Little Rann of Kutch is unmistakable.

'These people are harvesting cumin, my lady.'

The speaker, Devidas, employee of the tourist board in Ahmedabad, capital of the north-western region of India, is charged with accompanying me, as a visiting journalist, to places that, in Devidas's opinion, no sane person would wish to visit.

The Little Rann and the Great Rann of Kutch do not feature prominently on the list of India's popular destinations for Western tourists – in spite of the rarity of the last remaining herds of wild Asiatic asses and the last of the Asiatic lions – but they are most certainly on mine.

For the first two days of our association, Devidas, rightly in his view, sees it as his responsibility to deliver the usual itinerary of temple-visiting and admiration of architectural splendours. I, on the other hand, wish for wilderness, markets and people.

'I question the wisdom of this choice, my lady.'

I have already given up trying to convince Devidas that I have no claims to ladyship of any kind, inherited or earned. And since Devidas speaks very fast and supple Indian English, I am not always able to catch the subtleties of his drift.

Today I have had my way, and Devidas has agreed to inspection of the salt flats of the Little Rann in the company of Muzaid of Rann Riders, a new enterprise offering nature-lovers and birdwatchers accommodation in luxurious wattle-and-daub cabins modelled on the safari camps of South Africa.

Gujarat's two great wildernesses, the tourist board decides, are suitable for development as luxury destinations for nature-lovers in much the same way as the safari parks of Africa present their game reserves. This decision is responsible for my presence with notebook and sketchbook on the salt flats of the Little Rann on behalf of the readers of *Food and Travel*.

Muzaid, as manager and part-owner of Rann Riders, has driven over from his home in Dasida, the nearest town, to open up the camp and provide overnight luxury accommodation unavailable elsewhere. Muzaid has also been at pains to point out, as he gives me a brief tour of the facilities, that it is his cousin the Rajah who actually owns the camp. This is not to say that this particular Rajah is one of your palace-dwelling Moguls of the type you find in Rajasthan, but a working citizen of the egalitarian state of Gujarat, doing the best he can for his family in the India of today.

'This is how we are in India – hierarchical, given that there's always an obligation to look after family – which is why it is myself rather than my royal cousin who is privileged to enjoy the beauty of this place and the pleasure of excellent company such as yours.'

Muzaid is charming, handsome and very much a son of the Mogul Empire, followers of the Prophet who ruled Hindu India for three hundred years before losing out to the garrisons of the Queen Empress.

Devidas, on the other hand, is a modern citizen of urban India, distrustful of the countryside, with a little too much good living under his belt, teetotal and vegetarian even though his favourite fast food is breaded chicken nuggets from Chicken Shack in Ahmedabad.

The two men are not destined, it seems to me, to be soul mates.

The salt-cured cumin of the Little Rann is harvested at the end of the dry season, just before the monsoon rains fall, as they do in roughly one year in three. The breeze from the salt flats blows through the ripening seed-heads when the salt dries out the pans to form a thick crust, which is raked by hand into glistening pyramids of crystallised salt.

Proximity to the salt flats delivers cumin of unusually high quality, esteemed for strength, fragrance, resistance to insects and an almost indefinite shelf life. In flavour and scent, this diminutive pink-flowered member of the aniseed family is unmistakable. A sunny blend of liquorice, cinnamon and clove, it is the fragrance that rises from every kitchen in India as well as throughout the Arabian peninsula and much of the Middle East.

Used medicinally, cumin encourages appetite and aids digestion. It is the basic flavouring for garam masala, the spice mix used to perfume everything from the sophisticated sauces and stews of the Mogul kitchen to the simplest dish of dhal and chapatti, the daily dinner of the poor and those who choose to live in simplicity. It's also the flavouring in chai, India's milk-based tea, sold from roadside stalls to the millions of travellers and pilgrims who wander the length and breadth of the land on foot.

Little else can be found in the Little Rann that's useful to man or his domestic animals apart from the salt and ragged clumps of grass that serve as fodder for scattered herds of the last of the wild Asiatic asses. A dozen or so of the handsome little beasts, their coats a dusty pink picked up from the parched red earth of the desert, are grazing on new growth along the edge of what looks like a dried-up riverbed.

Survival, I say to Muzaid, seems a miracle in such a desolate landscape.

The river wasn't always dry. When Muzaid was a boy the river never ran dry unless the rains failed for many years in a row. But now that the river has been taken further up the flow to irrigate farmland and supply water to the cities, the government pays money to the villagers to dig waterholes for the asses and satisfy the conservationists.

'Conservation is a political issue in India. However much we're told by you in the West to preserve our tigers in spite of the villagers they kill, it's only when we ourselves decide we don't want to lose what we have that our politicians take notice.'

The only commercial crop available from the Little Rann consists of vast deposits of sea salt, tip-tilted by the ocean when the earth's tectonic plates clashed together to form the Himalayas. The care of the salt flats and the raking and drying is the ancestral right of a single family living in ramshackle huts by the pans for six months at a time, rotating their tour of duty with fellow family members.

'The work is hard and the pay is low but the labour is hereditary – and that counts for much even in the India of today. Perhaps it could be compared with your miners who couldn't bear to leave the coalmines whatever the dangers and wanted their children to work as they did.'

Today in the last of the summer sunshine, the cumin is ready for harvesting. Brightly dressed women and children working in pairs are tossing forkfuls of golden seed-heads high in the air with wooden pitchforks, separating the grain from the chaff as it falls in a glittering arc into shallow woven baskets. The scent carried towards us on the breeze is of new-mown hay, fresh and sweet and dry. The winnowers work together in silence, keeping the rhythm, bending and swaying like dancers. Meanwhile their menfolk, reed-thin in loincloths and heavy boots, are raking a thick crust of snow-white salt from the mud-rimmed pans into shimmering heaps of crystals.

'These people are tribals,' Devidas announces with confidence. 'Tribal is what we in India call people who live traditionally because the other word is not polite.' There are many such linguistic pitfalls to trip up the unwary as India rids itself of its socially divisive caste system. We both know that the other word is 'untouchables', an outdated caste to which no one belongs.

Devidas, born and bred in Gujarat's densely populated capital, has a town-dweller's distrust of inhospitable places. Surely by now, two days into our trip, I would agree there was no need to leave the city at all? There are so many pleasures available in Ahmedabad that there can surely be no need to travel elsewhere.

'All in due course, Devidas,' I answer soothingly, flicking paint on to paper.

Devidas heaves a sigh of resignation, and borrows my bird-watcher's binoculars to inspect the group of harvesters and deliver his verdict on their activities.

'These people are throwing the cumin up in the air and catching it in baskets.'

Meanwhile, Muzaid has already swung long khaki-clad legs out of the vehicle and is striding purposefully towards the harvesters. It's clear from the enthusiasm of the greeting that the relationship is warm.

In the old days, Muzaid admits when he returns to rejoin his passengers, the arrangement was undeniably feudal. But there was mutual respect, and even as India changes, respect remains and the relationship continues. As middleman for the sale of the harvest, Muzaid makes sure the crop fetches good prices in the marketplace and that the villagers benefit from the income derived from the tourists who come to spend their holiday dollars with Rann Riders.

The rains came early this year and the cumin is plentiful and well ripened and will fetch a good price.

'Taste this – see what you think.'

In Muzaid's outstretched palm is a little heap of greeny-yellow grains. I set down my sketchbook, accept a pinch and rub the grains between my fingers, releasing the fragrance. The scent is fresh and grassy, but the flavour, when tasted, is peppery and rank, unfinished, as if the raw material is not yet cooked.

'What's missing?'

Muzaid smiles. 'You're right. I'm used to eating them fresh – it's the taste of my childhood.' The final stage is yet to come, he continues, when the seeds are spread in the baskets and left to dry in the sun, a slow process compared to what happens when cumin is prepared commercially. The cumin of the Little Rann is sought after not only for its excellence but also its rarity, since only a few bushels are harvested every year.

'We Gujaratis love to trade; we're always looking for the best price in the best place. It's in the blood. When I came home from boarding school in England for the holidays, my father took me to the marketplace every evening to listen to the dealers talking about where they went and the deals they did. Their stories were magic.'

Gujarat's merchants travelled east along the Silk Road, through the passes of Afghanistan and west to the shores of the Mediterranean and into Africa. Gujaratis were trading with Portugal well before Marco Polo found his way to China. Cumin from Gujarat was used to perfume dishes served to the diners of imperial Rome.

These reminiscences are interrupted when the vehicle rolls to a halt beside an untidy clump of dried-out plant stalks just before we turn into the campsite. Muzaid reaches through the wound-down window and snaps off one of the stalks. It is thick-walled and hollow and the scent of aniseed is unmistakable.

'When I was a boy, my father used a hollow stalk like this to carry hot coals to light the campfire when we were hunting in the desert.'

In a moment, he is out of the vehicle and scraping the earth around the root of the clump with a hunting knife. A slash of the blade produces a trickle of milky sap.

'It's what we call *hing* – asafoetida. I don't like it myself, but I am Muslim and this is used in Hindu cooking to give the flavour of onion. If you ask me, onion is better.'

'This is not exactly so, my lady,' Devidas remarks without raising his voice above a whisper. 'But because Mr Muzaid is our host and courtesy is due, we will not quarrel when the milk is already spilt.'

This evening, for my further instruction in the ways of Gujarat's countryside – though possibly because the kitchen's closed –

Muzaid has arranged for us to take our evening meal in one of the scattered communities of Rabari, desert nomads who settled the Little Rann many centuries ago and still live much as their ancestors did, keeping goats and gathering foodstuffs from the wild.

'Perhaps so, but I am presenting my excuses, my lady,' says Devidas.

Muzaid ignores this negative appraisal. Rabari cooking is of particular interest for its inclusion of herbs and berries as flavourings that even one who has lived here all their life cannot identify for certain.

Devidas remains unimpressed. 'These people eat only roti and dhal.'

We must arrive at the village after sundown, Muzaid continues, which is when the fires are lit and the pots are set to simmer in the communal cooking area.

'This, my lady, is because these people have no toilet facilities inside their houses but must do their business without privacy where they do not like people to watch,' says Devidas. And anyway, it is his duty to check the itinerary with head office and make sure everything is ready for tomorrow's departure for an even bigger and more desolate region, the Great Rann of Kutch.

It's as plain as the nose on his face that Devidas is not an admirer of deserts and those who dwell therein. I, on the other hand, am delighted with our day in the salt pans with the cumin-harvesters and even more so with the prospect of an informative evening and the company of my courteous host.

*

On the way to the village as the sun dips towards the horizon, Muzaid pulls into the side of the track and trains his binoculars on a reed-fringed pond. A raft of waterbirds – mostly mallard and garganey – are drifting tranquilly on the dark surface. To me, this is an extraordinary sight in a desert region, but Muzaid is unimpressed by the gathering.

While the main draw for nature-lovers in the Little Rann is the wild asses in the breeding season, in a good year, when the rains have filled the reed-fringed pools from the edge of the desert, the wilderness provides a haven for nesting birds. Rosy-feathered flamingoes migrate from the deserts of Africa to build their drip-nests from the red earth turned to mud by the monsoon rains. Egypt's sacred ibises and China's demoiselle cranes take up residence among the reed beds to feast on hatches of tadpoles and frogs.

'Such a pity we've just missed the crowd. I was hoping the ibises and flamingoes would still be rearing their young. My ancestors used to hunt them with golden eagles. Eagles are fearless hunters – I once saw one attack a wolf.'

'Who won?'

Muzaid considers the question with a smile. 'Let's just say that both held retreat to be the better part of valour, as your Mr Kipling says. I wish our politicians would do the same.'

Muzaid is in thoughtful mood as we rattle along the dusty track, bouncing in and out of the ruts. There are divisions between Muslim and Hindu opening throughout India once again. There is no solution to an intractable problem. If Pakistan is Muslim and India is Hindu and no one wants to be the first to offer compromise, sooner or later war is inevitable. Meanwhile, Gujarat is a frontier region, as it has always been, with friends and family on both sides of the border.

'Perhaps you will see this in the Great Rann, when you travel there tomorrow, or perhaps not. My father always told me there's no place safer in all the world than a hundred miles behind a warzone. And trouble never starts in the countryside but in the cities where many people gather.'

I am relieved that Devidas is elsewhere, or he might well have tried to cancel the trip. Muzaid, having delivered himself of this gloomy assessment, is once again in good humour.

'Enough of politics and talk of what most certainly will not come to pass. What you and I who are both travellers will share tonight is travellers' food. Rajasthan, where my ancestors settled, has meat-eating warriors' food. Gujaratis are peaceful vegetarians and their food is suitable for a nomadic way of life. Did you know our trading partners were the Portuguese, the greatest travellers the world has ever known?'

He glances across at me, smiling. 'We are not newcomers to your world. Our dhows were sailing into the West long before the Portuguese or even you British found us. Our ancestors protect us – even I who follow the way of the Prophet believe our forefathers will return in time of trouble to guide us. We are not afraid of anything in this world or the next.'

My host falls silent, as do I, both of us lost in our own thoughts as night falls and the stars begin to appear in the sky. Desert horizons slip over the curve of the earth to infinity by day. At night, when the moon rises, the arc of the heavens is as brightly lit as day.

The village is in darkness but for the glow of embers from the cooking fires. The air is already heavy with scented steam and the appetising fragrance of roasting grains. Rabari women, bright as butterflies in crimson silks and beaded bangles, squat down beside the coals, patting out millet dough for roti and keeping a watchful eye on the cooking pots. Goats, sheep and wild-haired children are everywhere.

One of the cooks, a young girl with long dark hair tied back with a flower-printed kerchief, rises gracefully to offer me a freshly cooked roti wrapped round a little scoop of dhal. I hesitate, reluctant to take food out of the mouths of people who have so little.

'Eat,' says Muzaid. 'Sharing food with a stranger is an obligation and a blessing.' I accept gratefully. I'm hungry. The roti
tastes good – chewy, rough-textured and blistered by the fire,
and the scooping dhal is sweet and soft and flavoured with
cumin. There is, too, a dish of chickpeas stirred with mustard
greens, and something simmering in a double-handled, raw-iron
skillet, which I don't recognise at all.

'This is a dhal made with roti,' Muzaid explains. 'I will ask
Sarina to explain how she makes it.'

At first the information is given reluctantly, and then, as
Sarina demonstrates the action with her hand, with increasing

confidence as she waits courteously for her words to be translated.

'Sarina would like you to know that she learned this dish from her mother, who learned it from her mother and from her mother before her, so you can be sure it's very old indeed.'

Sarina nods and smiles, watching the effect her words are having as her hands continue to work the roti dough, pushing with the palms, fingers held delicately aloft. Tearing off a piece of dough to demonstrate the texture, she pats it smooth, talking all the while.

Rolling up her sleeves, Sarina rinses her hands in a bowl of water set ready, and indicates I do the same. Muzaid continues with the translation as Sarina slows her movements to allow me to follow her instruction. 'First the flour must be clean and dry when you measure it into the bowl. To make sure there are no lumps, rub it between your fingers, like so.' Sarina's fingers are supple and the flour rises and falls in an airy shower. 'Now you must add warm water just hot enough for your hand to feel the heat, and work it with the heel of the hand till it comes together softly, like so. Now you must work it like this with your fists till it's smooth as a baby's cheek.'

Sarina kneads the dough on the board with her knuckles, fingers bent to make a fist.

'Now you break it into little pieces – like so – and roll them out like so. See? There's the first one. Now you try.'

I knead and pat and roll. Mine is not perfect: it comes out a little too thick and oval rather than perfectly round. I try another, an improvement on the first.

'This is what Sarina says you must know if you want to pre-pare a dhal with roti,' continues Muzaid. 'First you must make some roti-bread, as you have done just now, and dry it in the sun. When you are ready to cook, you must tear it into small pieces. Then you must cook the pieces in a little oil with onion

and chilli and cumin. Then you may add a little water and whatever vegetables you please. And you must finish it with this
herb – I think you know it well.'

I taste. The herb is cilantro, leaf-coriander. When added to
the roti, it occurs to me that there's a similarity in flavour and
texture with *açorda*, a bread-risotto prepared in Portugal.

Muzaid is watching me with amusement. 'Sarina would like
to know if you have enjoyed your meal?'

Indeed I have, I answer with enough enthusiasm for my
words to need no translation.

'If this is so, perhaps you might care to express appreciation
with a token. It has to be something of your own as money is
never acceptable in exchange for hospitality.'

I hesitate. I have left all my possessions back in the camp and
I have nothing to offer except, I suddenly remember, a faded silk
flower pinned on to a pull-on cotton hat of the kind you can fold
up and tuck away. The flower belonged to my daughter – Francesca
was not yet thirty when she died – and I take it with me whenever
I travel, thinking to carry her with me in my heart. It's time and
not before time. I unpin the blossom and hold out my hand.

Muzaid asks me no questions about the gesture, but his
silence is companionable as we drive home through the darkness
of the night. For my daughter's sake and mine, I am glad of the
company of strangers and the silence and the stars and curve of
the heavens and the night.

Early the next morning, with scarcely time to snatch a mouthful
of croissant and coffee – Muzaid explains that he likes his guests
to feel at home first thing in the morning – Devidas announces
our immediate departure.

The reason, he explains, is that we have great distances to
cover before we reach the city of Bhuj, capital and gateway

to the Great Rann of Kutch, and we must find safe haven before nightfall.

'I believe no time must be lost, my lady.'

Devidas shakes his head vigorously, head-shaking in India being an indication of agreement rather than dissent.

I am beginning to understand that Devidas does not share his countrymen's appetite for travel. He is a homebody. In the city he lives with his mother, brother and sister-in-law in one of the more sought-after of Ahmedabad's suburbs. The women of his household are all excellent cooks, more than capable of preparing the traditional dishes of Gujarat without stepping outside their own front doors, as can be observed from Devidas's expanding waistline.

'This is a most important duty, my lady. As I am sure you understand since you are yourself no doubt an excellent cook when you are in your own kitchen and cooking for your family.'

We agree that there is nothing more important than setting good food on the table to feed your family – or anyone else's, for that matter.

'Cooking is not a skill I possess, my lady. This I believe to be fortunate since it allows me to truly show my appreciation of what my mother and my aunts and my sister-in-law do so well.'

The balance of our relationship restored with Devidas's customary blend of charm and good manners – he has his prejudices, but these are never overtly expressed – we proceed on our journey from the Little Rann to the Great Rann in good humour. The journey takes six hours by road and is well peppered with hazards. The middle of the two-lane highway is frequently occupied by a herdsman carrying his shoes on a pole over his shoulders behind a flock of goats, or an ox-cart swaying beneath a skyscraper of cotton-balls, or – once – a group of beautifully dressed women carrying stones in baskets on their heads.

Devidas slows down for a closer look.

'These women are starvation women. They must pay for their rations from the state – the millet for root and mung beans for the dhal – with work on the roads. These people are poor and the men do not work. These are not good men. What can you do?'

Last year the city centre of Bhuj, regional capital of the Great Rann of Kutch, a glory of eighteenth-century palaces, was reduced to rubble by an unusually violent clash of the earth's tectonic plates. Thousands of lives were lost. Rehousing is in progress, though this time the buildings are single-storey dwellings outside the city walls. The citizens, however, prefer to camp among the rubble – lighting cooking fires in the street and cooking among the ruins – and have refused to take up residence in the brand-new houses, preferring the devil they know to the one they don't.

The old city – as much of it as is still standing – is entered through a triple-arched gateway that marks the limits of where people were permitted to build before the earthquake.

Headquarters have advised Devidas of the need to acquire permits from the military in Bhuj before continuing into what is now a militarised zone aimed at discouraging incursions into Indian territory from Pakistan, which is in dispute with its neighbour over Kashmir. If it's not Kashmir, says Devidas gloomily, it's Bangladesh. And if it's not Bangladesh, it's Pakistan's support of the Taliban in Afghanistan.

But mostly it's Kashmir, an insoluble problem left by the British when they drew pencil lines on the map and left the nations of their Empire to fight it out among themselves.

The army office that issues permits to enter the military zone is open for business – never a certainty in India – so I hand over money and passport and watch Devidas vanish into the prefabricated warren of government offices.

Negotiations, Devidas adds with relish, will be protracted and the outcome uncertain.

I settle down to sketch the avifauna – sand-martins darting in and out of the walls, a white-ruffed vulture with bright-pink wattles perched on a dead branch of an upturned tree. One of the humpbacked cows that are everywhere in India watches me through lowered lashes, chewing thoughtfully – although heaven knows what there is to eat in this parched and barren landscape.

I am just dipping my brush in the water-container, ready to make the first mark, when a door opens to release a crowd of excited children let out from school for the mid-morning break.

'English lady, how are you?'

'Very well indeed. And how are you?'

'How you! How you! How you!'

Delighted mimicry gives way to enthusiastic phraseology.

'Jump up! Jump down! Nose, ears, head, feet!'

This is demonstrated several times before the mood switches to more practical matters.

'Who are you? How old are you? What is your name?'

As soon as I answer, my young audience is delighted to discover that the fillings in my Western teeth are made of gold. Real gold, the stuff that shines like the sun and is an essential element of every young bride's dowry.

Word travels like wildfire that here is a visitor of unimaginable wealth and prestige who not only carries her savings in her mouth but shares a name with the Queen of England, and may well, considering her independent air, be Her Majesty herself.

'Again! Again!'

I open and shut my mouth on demand. Noblesse obliges: my namesake would have done no less. Fortunately – or I might well have found myself obliged to spend the rest of the day with a gaping jaw – the bell in the schoolroom clangs to summon the children back to their lessons at the moment that Devidas re-emerges waving a fistful of papers.

My guide's negotiating skills have triumphed over all obstacles. Our permits are secured and permission granted to proceed. This is something of a surprise, I point out, since – without wishing in any way to diminish his success – as far as I am aware our itinerary was established in advance and all the necessary authorities notified. Official questions had to be asked and answers verified with his employees in Ahmedabad. Information has been flying around like birds on the wing on a warm evening in search of insects in the desert. Devidas is capable of quite a poetic turn of mind when the need arises.

'You are not taking account that this is India, my lady,' says Devidas happily. 'It is the problem of left hand and right hand. This is most certainly important problem in Gujarat when we are so far away from Ahmedabad.'

I ignore the propaganda and examine the permissions. These extend as far as the villages of the Banni, the limits of the inhabited region of the Great Rann, and allow us to travel within the no-fly zone that separates India from Pakistan. Devidas is looking increasingly cheerful. Warzones, like storm clouds, come with silver linings. Owing to the presence of the military, the road will be in a good state of repair, the villages have access to water from a tap, and mobile phone reception is known to be the best in the state.

As we proceed smoothly down the miraculously bump-free highway, we pass a flock of goats followed by their herdsman talking animatedly on a mobile phone. The goats, practised in the ways of the military, move tidily off-road to allow a convoy bristling with hardware to pass at speed. The tranquillity of the desert is disturbed at intervals by the whine of warplanes patrolling the no-fly zone from the safety of the skies.

The border is a hundred miles to the north of us, the situation is currently stable, and Devidas has taken to winding down the window and waving cheerfully as more military transports speed past.

There is, however, a curfew in place and Devidas is anxious to arrive at our destination, the tourist village of Hodko, before dark.

A curfew imposed by the military?

'Not because of the military, my lady,' Devidas answers cheerfully. 'Because of the wolves.'

There are wolves?

'This is true, my lady. And lions, too, but they are very far away and the government protects them.'

And does the government protect the wolves?

Devidas frowns. 'This is a question I am not able to answer, my lady.'

Questions Devidas is not able to answer, I have observed during our week's acquaintance, indicate political hot potatoes. There are many of these that emerge when the interests of the city do not coincide with those of the countryside, such as predation by protected species – tigers, the last remaining Asiatic lions of the Great Rann, and possibly, presumably, wolves – which is a problem for the rural population that does not affect those who live in the cities and wield political power.

The sun is already setting when we arrive at our destination, the tourist village of Hodko, an enclave of mud-brick dwellings surrounded by a thick wall of acacia thorn that mirrors – at least architecturally – the non-tourist village of Hodko, whose self-sufficient way of life it is designed to support.

The manager of tourist-Hodko, a pretty young woman in jeans and white T-shirt emblazoned with the name of the village, appears from her office to greet us. She has been informed of our arrival and announces herself delighted to welcome us.

Her name is Nicole Patel and she is, she explains, a volunteer worker on a fellowship from the University of Chicago who will be happy to demonstrate the good work her NGO is doing to improve health and well-being among the impoverished villagers of the area. One of the attractions of tourist-Hodko to outsiders within India itself, she adds, is the chance to experience the traditional cooking of the self-sufficient villagers of the Banni at a time when India is enthusiastically exploring her roots.

There is paperwork to be completed, continues Nicole, as she leads the way into an office by the gate. No doubt I will already be aware that nothing in India happens without everything in triplicate.

Meanwhile, there is literature available to read at my leisure to explain that the mirror-village of Hodko is a pioneering example of the kind of low-impact, high-value tourism the regional government is anxious to promote. The enterprise offers local employment as a practical solution to the problem of staffing in a remote location such as the Great Rann, at the same time as providing non-tourist Hodko with a share of the profits from visitors.

It is as well for the regional purse, adds Nicole, that the enterprise is funded and run by a non-governmental organisation such as hers, as the cost would otherwise be prohibitive.

The mirror-village of Hodko, she adds as she completes her form-filling, attracts internal rather than international tourism, as it does throughout Gujarat, although there are hopes that this will change. Today, it being Friday and the start of a holiday weekend, there are visitors from Delhi taking a weekend break. The attraction is an exotic location that can be experienced without leaving the country. Facilities, thanks to the presence of the military's fast broadband and excellent television reception, allow guests to maintain contact with the outside world in safety and comfort.

Devidas expresses his pleasure with a happy shake of the head.

Nicole leads the way across the courtyard of beaten earth towards our accommodation, a cluster of what look like traditional village *boma*, dome-roofed, mud-walled dwellings much like others we have passed along the road.

'I'm sure you must be tired and in need of a shower.'

The exteriors have been freshly whitewashed and newly decorated with elegant stylised patterns picked out in mirror-work, but the interiors have been fitted out with everything that might be expected of a modern hotel in Ahmedabad, right down to the hand-woven bedspreads and jasmine-scented toiletries in the adjacent shower-room.

Nicole points out the attention to detail in the cool interior. The traditional fretwork – piercings in the walls – lets in light and air, and the hand-stencilled borders are in traditional leaf-and-flower patterns.

My readers, Nicole continues, might like to know that the enterprise also offers instruction weeks in mirror-work, jewellery-making, weaving, pattern-painting and pottery led by experts from the sister village, non-tourist Hodko. There are plans for marketing the villagers' skills on the internet, including lessons in mud-work and the construction of dwellings such as these, which have proved remarkably resistant to earthquakes.

'I hope you will be comfortable. We are proud of our guestrooms, all hand-built by local craftsmen from the villages. Dinner is in an hour and we have a special surprise for our visitors. Please listen for the bell.'

Traditionalists would certainly not approve of the copycat dwellings, but comfort – at least for me and certainly for Devidas, who disappears into his own mud-walled dwelling with a cheerful wave of the hand – is reason to be grateful.

I shower, change swiftly and set off to enquire of Nicole the whereabouts of the kitchen. I am hoping for a chance of hands-on tuition in the traditional cooking of the villages of the Great Rann.

Nicole is busy unloading boxes from a van on to the communal table under a tarpaulin. She sets down the box and turns to me with a smile. 'You'll be happy to hear we have a wonderful surprise for you and the rest of our guests this evening – a traditional Kutchi *balti*.'

I agree this does indeed sound wonderful. Perhaps it could be arranged for me to witness – or even assist – in the preparations?

Unfortunately this is not possible, as the meal arrives ready-cooked from non-tourist Hodko. On the other hand, says Nicole, observing my disappointment, I might like to watch the preparation of the roti, the flatbreads that are cooked fresh and are always the most important element in any meal in India.

The roti-maker of the evening is known to be particularly skilled at producing the perfect balance of chewiness, nuttiness and elasticity in her flatbreads, and she will be cooking on the open fire on an earthenware bake-stone, just as she does in her village.

I return with my sketchbook and paint box at exactly the moment when a battered army vehicle with 'Hodko Tourist Village' over-painted on the military insignia rattles through the gate.

The driver begins to unload silver trays on to a wooden table under a tarpaulin beside the dining area while our bread-maker, a motherly old lady in an impeccably pressed blue-and-white overdress, spreads a cotton sheet on the ground in front of the fire and begins her preparations. As she works, I make notes in my sketchbook. Wholemeal roti is the simplest of all flatbreads, and as with all such simple preparations, excellence depends on the skill of the cook. While I'm well used to baking yeast-raised bread in my kitchen at home, unleavened bread is a skill I've never mastered – and probably never will.

Rapidity and sureness of touch can only come with a lifetime's experience, as I know well from accepting many an invitation to emulate a skill. My notes, when deciphered by the light of a hurricane lamp in the *boma* after the generator is switched off at midnight, are lengthy and detailed.

First there must be the correct proportion of hand-milled flour to salted water, to make a soft dough that can be worked to silky smoothness with the heel of the hand. When the texture is judged correct, the baker breaks off pieces the size of a pullet egg and swiftly works them smooth. Speed is essential. Then, with rapid movements of a rolling pin on a wooden board, each piece is rolled in turn with perfect accuracy to a size convenient for the hand.

Once all are prepared, the bake-stone is set over the camp-fire – actually a stick-fire lit in the cooking area in the middle of a sandy depression – and heated to the correct temperature. Once this has been tested with a hand held horizontally over the surface, the flattened discs of dough are flipped on one by one. Each is toasted on one side only and stacked in pairs, brushed between the layers with melted white butter. The task is completed with extraordinary swiftness and grace.

'Bravo! Such expertise is wonderful to behold, is it not?'

It seems I am not alone in my admiration of the bread-maker's skill. One of the other guests, an elegant middle-aged woman in a beautiful dark-red sari, has been watching the work with equal interest. Her English is perfect and I'm glad to find a friend who shares my enthusiasm.

'You are the journalist from England, are you not? You are the only one of us who isn't – how shall I put it politely? – one of the natives. And I can see you're interested in the cooking.'

She presses her palms together and bobs her head in the traditional greeting between strangers.

'My name is Indira and I am from Delhi. If you are alone, perhaps you would care to sit with us, my friends and I, so we can enjoy the meal together.'

I accept the offer gratefully.

Devidas has already disappeared, in search, I suspect, of access to fast broadbrand and a well-earned rest from his charge's endless questionings.

He has my sympathy. My maternal grandmother, irritated at having to take care of a schoolgirl when she was having her clothes fitted in Paris, told me that curiosity killed the cat. She was wrong. Curiosity is a gift, a treasure, a compass by which to set a course.

A bell rings to summon the rest of the guests, some of whom – a family group with two well-behaved teenage children, a young couple and half a dozen smartly dressed middle-aged women, including Indira – are already clustered around the table where the trays are laid out in rows.

Each tray has been provided with an array of little bowls. Indira guides me through the recipes. Here is okra, *bindi*, cooked with chilli and cumin; these are fritters, *pakora*, prepared with millet and onion. Here is potato with cumin, and this, a soupy yellow dhal with nigella seeds, has been stirred with the white goats' milk butter used to brush the roti. And this little pile of bony joints is chicken stewed with cinnamon and chilli.

I might be surprised, she continues, by the presence of chicken since I will already be aware that most Gujaratis follow Gandhi's example and stick to a vegetarian diet. This is not so in the big cities such as Mumbai and Delhi, where all but the strictest Hindus eat chicken and fish.

In the tribal areas of the Great Rann, she continues, some villages are Hindu and some are Muslim. Hodko is a Muslim village that serves a *balti*. Had Hodko been a Hindu village, the meal would have been a *thali*. This can be confusing for the visitor, Indira explains, but there are other indications of differences.

Among these are certain spices when treated in a particular way. I can assume that if the cumin is toasted in a dry pan and used to finish a dish, the family is Hindu. Cumin tossed in hot oil before the cooking liquid is added is the Muslim way of doing things. This culinary rule is by no means set in stone and every household has its own preferences, but as a general rule, preliminary frying and the use of an iron pan is Muslim and simmering with a liquid in a cooking pot is Hindu.

Devidas, arriving late to the party, inspects the array with disapproval. He has already told me that Muslim food is too greasy for a Hindu. His face brightens, however, when he spots a dish of what looks like hand-rolled noodles in a caramel-coloured sauce.

'This is what we call *idli*. It's very special. All Indians love it,' says Indira, observing Devidas's enthusiasm with a smile. 'Please to help yourself.'

Devidas cups his hand, bends his head and, in a flash, the mouthful is gone. 'This is very good, my lady, very good. There is nothing more delicious in all India. Do as I do, cup your hand.'

'Like so?'

Obediently I cup my hand.

'Not quite.' Indira places her right hand beneath mine to form a double cup and squeezes gently. 'You must close the fingers tight, like so. Now take it up with the hand, like so. Now bend your head and take it with your tongue, like so.' I do as I am bid. When I raise my head, most of the buttery sauce has trickled through my fingers and into the bowl.

Indira laughs. 'It will come. This is hard for you but easy for us. It's natural because it's how we use our hands, like making roti – our fingers just make the shape.'

Later that evening, with Devidas retired early to his billet, I join Nicole and Indira and fellow guests for a nightcap round the hearth-fire. The temperature drops sharply in the desert at night, and the warmth of embers is welcome.

All the other guests are from Delhi, mostly in finance. Hodko is expensive, so only the rich can afford it, and talk soon turns to ways in which the villagers can be encouraged to earn money for the things they need. English is the common language – the rapid-fire colloquial Indian version that can be hard to follow for those unaccustomed to its cadences – although this may well be a courtesy to my presence as the only member of the group with no alternative.

Poor people such as the tribals, there's general agreement, don't want to live in the old way once they experience the new. Television and mobile phones are undeniable improvements to the traditional way of life in the villages, and to pay for service, once the military are no longer providing it for free, you need an income, however small.

For an income, everyone agrees, you need a business. For a business you need a bank. Indira herself is in micro-finance. Even her name is an indication of the desire for change: many girl babies of her generation were named for Mrs Gandhi. Microfinance, she continues, works well because it is paid to the women. Women are social entrepreneurs, as she is herself.

'Is this not also true in Britain?'

I hesitate. Women are nowhere near parity in Parliament and as leaders of industry, and this, I admit, is proving hard to change.

Indira laughs. 'We in India are showing you the way. Some of us here are independent women, are we not? We are travelling alone and we have no fear.'

She holds up her hands. 'Look at me. I have gold rings. I own my own house. My first micro-loan bought me a basket. Then I bought a pushcart. Now I own my own shop. If you help one woman, you help the whole family. And women can reach other women. It affects everything – health, childbirth, education. We are making progress. There is no alternative. Women can no longer be treated as the property of husbands and fathers, worthless unless protected by a man – this is the source of all our problems.'

Another member of the group of middle-aged women travelling on their own, Sonali, is not sure that change is always for the better. Even here in the Great Rann, where life is still lived much as always, pleasures are no longer as simple as when she was a girl.

'I myself was from one of the villages of the Banni, but I was fortunate to marry a husband who made enough money for us to live in Delhi. I am grateful he left me well provided for in my widowhood. But I still have pleasant memories of my childhood. I remember when my grandmother made butter, her arm bracelets made a special sound as she churned, and then we always knew there'd be something delicious for dinner. This was her role, and I never heard her wish for any other.'

Sonali smiles and glances round at her audience. 'And I remember that my grandmother taught me that when a woman goes to meet her husband before she is married, she walks on tiptoe so her anklets don't betray her.'

Indira smiles. 'And when she goes to meet her lover, what then?'

Sonali rises to the challenge. 'This won't happen. She will be too busy churning the butter.'

I wake late to the rattle of the returning army truck. This time there are two vehicles. The second, open-topped with benches for passengers on either side, looks like a safari jeep. An excursion to the real Hodko is available for those who wish to take advantage of the opportunity. Safari jeeps bring thoughts of wolves.

Devidas anticipates a busy morning on the internet. 'You need have no fear, my lady, that I will not be accompanying you,' he tells me. 'This place is very wild but the army will protect us.'

Nicole shepherds the rest of her guests into the vehicle. We must understand, she explains when we are all settled in our seats, that the villagers do not usually welcome outsiders. But she has managed to convince the villagers that since each village specialises in a particular handicraft, direct selling will be to everyone's advantage by cutting out the middleman. Some of the villagers are potters, some weavers, some metalworkers and others, Hodko among them, specialise in embroidery.

'I advise everyone to open their purses,' she adds with an encouraging smile. 'There will be many bargains.'

First we should know a little of the remarkable construction methods of the village. Hodko's round-walled, mud-brick *bomas* are roofed with tiles supported on wooden struts drawn together like the closed petals of a flower – a construction that ensures the petals fall outwards when shaken by an earthquake, leaving the inhabitants unharmed. The traditional building material, mud strengthened with fibrous cow-dung, is similarly earthquake-proof, crumbling when the walls collapse and re-usable after the monsoon. From an architect's point of view, though the mud walls would be no defence against bombs should war break out in earnest, since all the building materials are recyclable, reconstruction would be quicker, easier and cheaper than with conventional buildings.

There are many additional lessons to be learned from traditional methods of construction. Interior walls are lime-washed, a natural disinfectant. Pigments traditionally used for decoration are prepared with home-grown chilli and turmeric and recyclable mirror-work, allowing restoration of beauty as well as shelter.

Technology has already changed ways of building. The struts that support the petal-shaped roofing are made of beaten metal rather than peeled branches bent to shape, and the tiles are industrially moulded concrete rather than hand-made pottery.

The traditional patterns of intertwining chillies, flowers and leaves and sprouting wheat-grains – the paisley pattern – are painted around windows and door with shop-bought paints.

Change is here to stay. Money is needed not only to buy materials for construction, but for mobile phones and televisions as well as oil, salt and spices. And even an idealist such as Nicole cannot disagree with the value of medical attention and the pro-vision of care in childbirth. The young are hungry for what's advertised on their screens, even though their parents are still self-sufficient in the basic necessities of food and shelter.

Preparations for meals, as in the Rabari village of the Little Rann, take place in the open air. The cooking fire is lit in an earthenware fire-bowl which is open on one side, the heat of the flame controlled by pushing the sticks into the coals. Others are double-bowled, shaped like a footprint but with one wall taller than the other, allowing the cooking utensils to be placed closer or further from the fire. The vegetables which make up the bulk of the meal – potatoes, aubergines, radish greens, tomatoes, gar-lic – are grown in an enclosure just behind each *boma*, protected from the goats with a barrier of cut acacia thorns.

I abandon the rest of the party to their bargaining for the beautiful embroideries to inspect the contents of the cooking pots, making notes in my sketchbook. My rough sketches, I have found, are a diversion for those involved in the more serious business of the cooking itself, ensuring a friendly welcome and answers to questions.

Today I am taking note of the ingredients and the way they're used. Little yellow potatoes stored in a wire basket hung on a hook on a rafter are set to simmer in a sauce of peanut oil, garlic and tomato to produce a scooping-dish, *aloo ki kari*, to eat with roti. At another fireplace, radish greens, well rinsed and shredded, are stirred into hot oil with crushed cumin seeds and a handful of salt and allowed to soften in the heat. In the scraped-out

ashes of a third cooking fire have been set half a dozen aubergines, a double-purpose crop since they can be dried for storage,
which are left until soft and squishy and blistered black.

'*Bharta*, my favourite,' says Nicole, leaning over my shoulder to inspect the quick rough sketch of aubergines roasting over
the flame. 'When they're ready, you scrape the pulp of the skin
and mash it in hot oil with garlic and ginger and maybe a little
chilli. It's delicious.'

Nicole volunteers as translator of my questions to the cooks
in exchange, she suggests laughingly, for the aubergine sketch. I
agree without hesitation – I can always take a copy and goodwill
is more valuable than marks on paper.

Millet is grown as a crop-share with the landowner because the
tribals are not traditionally land-owning – a political weakness,
Nicole adds in a quiet aside, which allowed others to claim ownership, a situation which suits the state since landowners can be taxed.

Three or even four crops a year are possible in Great
Rann. In a year when the rains are good – three in every five on
average – four acres and one crop-share is enough to supply a
household of six adults and their children and pay the landowner.

In a bad year, the state steps in and pays famine money to
families in distress, demanding work for the public good in return.
If the rains have failed, mothers and daughters – the famine women
passed on our journey – repair the roads. The milling of the grain
is paid for in cash. Households keep their own grain and bake their
own supplies of roti, both dried for storage and fresh. Three
milk-goats, productive for half the year, are sufficient to supply a
household with fresh milk and curd cheese, and for the preparation
of butter stored as ghee. The buttermilk provides minerals and
protein, and the ghee is used to enrich rather than fry.

Goats' milk is particularly rich, more so than cows' milk, but
less than buffalo. A litre of goats' milk can be turned into half its own
weight of butter in less than a half-hour if the churner is skilled.

When the butter comes, adds Nicole, you'll hear a soft bumping sound. The churn is a metal pot with a wide-mouthed neck that supports a wooden paddle attached to a spindle – a string wound round the paddle like a yo-yo – pulled back and forth until the fat separates from the liquid and the butter comes as lumps of semi-solid butter melted down for storage as ghee. The buttermilk is drunk fresh and cool, or hot and spiced. Nothing is ever wasted. Goat dung, the other end of the milking-cycle, is used to heat the bake-stone for the flatbreads – roti or chapatti, it's all the same.

The interiors of the *bomas* are dusted, swept and spotless. Prized possessions and cooking implements are stacked round the walls on shelves moulded from the same building material as the walls. Possessions are a visible show of wealth. Embroidered covers for beds and furniture are a young woman's dowry. Work begins as soon as a little girl is able to hold a needle, and the embroideries are folded and stacked on a shelf against her marriage day, a source of wealth.

As she watches her visitors bargain for the beautiful handiwork spread out for sale on sun-bleached cotton sheets in front of each *boma*, Nicole admits to mixed feelings about the influence the tourists will have on village life if her plans succeed.

'Tourists bring money and choose what they buy as well as what they eat and wear and take home as presents. In Hodko, for instance, where the handiwork is Muslim, the embroidery has lots of little bits of mirror. In a Hindu village, it's plain. If the one sells better than the other, the one that's not successful loses popularity with the embroiderers, whatever their traditions, and in time it will disappear, just as the culinary differences between Muslim and Hindu are already disappearing. Perhaps this is good, perhaps not. Religious prohibitions preserve a way of life but the consequences are unpredictable.'

Indira breaks off from her bargaining to join the discussion.

While her family are devout Hindu and never eat meat, there are many who do, and she herself has many Muslim friends who are happy to enjoy the vegetarian dishes she sets on the table. The same is true of embroideries. Everyone knows the difference between Muslim and Hindu handiwork and she herself has an outlet in Delhi which can sell everything she buys from both sides of the religious divide. The money the villagers receive, particularly the women, can give them independence and political influence. Western tourists, she says, can also be an influence for good. Westerners don't take sugar in the chai available by the glass at every roadside stall, and although Indians have a very sweet tooth, they follow suit because they think it's more modern. As a result their teeth are much improved and dentists are no longer kept busy repairing the damage. Instead they offer their services to whiten teeth because even the poorest want to look like Bollywood stars.

The villagers of the Banni have never had rotten teeth. Honey from wild desert bees has always been the sweetener and this is always in limited supply and not at all easy to gather.

While this may be true, reasons Nicole, what is also true is that, as more money comes into the villages, people prefer to buy jaggery – cooked-down crystallised palm-syrup – and the new generation of village children have to be sent to hospital with toothache and rotten teeth.

Next day we are due to return to the capital. The journey will be long and tiring but is eagerly anticipated by Devidas, who is up bright and early – long before anyone but Nicole and Indira are about.

On Indira's suggestion, I snatch a quick breakfast of leftover roti with ghee. By the time I reappear with my luggage to take my leave and send messages of appreciation to my fellow guests, Devidas is already filling the car with petrol at the expense of the NGO under Nicole's watchful eye. More forms will need to be filled in, as every penny must be accounted for.

Back in Ahmedabad – a journey that seems to take a quarter of the time it did on the outward journey – and safely delivered to my hotel, I am greeted by Devidas the following morning, the last day of my visit, with an invitation.

As promised, his mother, sister-in-law and brother, two nephews and their wives and three grandchildren will be delighted to welcome me to the midday meal in the family home. This is exactly what I had been hoping for, a chance to experience the urban cooking of the region in its proper setting. There is always a difference between the culinary habit of the city and that of the countryside, since urban cooks, shopping daily in the marketplace, have a wider choice of seasonal produce than country-dwellers.

I am invited into the busy lean-to kitchen, joining the senior ladies of the household – mother, aunts and daughter-in-law – to observe the preparations. Much is already under way. As a present, I have brought a pocket-sized cookbook of my own – *Classic French Cooking* – which carries my own illustrations. We lack a common language, so I take out my sketchbook and paints to show how the pictures were made.

The most important dish – apart from the flatbreads – is a *pilau dhal* – rice and lentils, the classic double act of the Indian kitchen – already prepared and awaiting its finishing ingredients: stems of green garlic, toasted cashews and fresh green lentils, tender and sweet as new peas.

Devidas's sister-in-law, Sarina, a handsome young woman with sparkling eyes and a ready smile, sets me a task. I am permitted to pod the lentils, two to each pod. My fingertips turn brown from the juices and Sarina, laughing, rubs off the stain with lemon juice.

The dhal and rice are ready. Last to be prepared is the *bindi bhaji*, okra fritters made with lentil and gram flour and flavoured with dried onion. Devidas is summoned to explain the onion. Spiced, fried, sun-dried onion flakes acquire some of the characteristics of *hing*, an expensive ingredient which keeps more or less indefinitely when stored in lump form and doesn't release its pungent odour until crushed and heated in oil, when it becomes wonderfully mild and gentle. Dried onion, while not permitted to high-caste Hindus, delivers mildness and gentleness but without the expense.

There are two kinds of chutney to be prepared, one fresh and scoopable, and one dry and suitable for sprinkling. The two together, explains Devidas as the fragrance of mint and sesame rises from pestles and mortars, is for balance and additional protein that can be lacking in a vegetarian diet. The sprinkling chutney, roasted sesame seeds pounded with chilli and salt, is for savour. The wet chutney, a raita, is prepared with home-made yoghurt stirred with little shards of fresh mint from the garden.

The meal, once set on the table and the family assembled, is consumed with remarkable rapidity. On a normal day the men, as the main breadwinners, are served first to allow them to return to their place of work without delay. Today, in deference to my presence as a female guest, we all eat together.

Sarina takes her place by my side and guides me gently in the delicate art of eating with my fingers from the communal dish set in the middle of the table. Ordinary households do not serve their food in separate little dishes, as happens with the *thali*. Eating must be done without finger-licking or straying into anyone else's portion. Everything is placed on the table at the same time and participants are expected to eat only as much as they need. Taking more than a single mouthful at once is bad manners, and heaping your plate, should this be provided, is even worse.

Eating with the fingers without giving offence has been a steep learning curve, and I'm pleased that my ability to scoop and suck is improving rapidly. Quite soon my table manners will no longer be a source of amusement and I might be almost presentable in polite company. When I share this thought with Devidas he laughs delightedly, translating my words for the benefit of the rest of the family, even though the younger members have a good grasp of my native tongue.

This is an important occasion, Devidas continues proudly, when an ordinary Gujarati household of modest means is honoured to welcome a distinguished journalist such as myself at the family table, thereby confirming the friendship between our two nations by the sharing of good fellowship – a situation all too uncommon in the world of today, when those who have lived in tolerance and mutual respect for many centuries find themselves at the mercy of the will of others.

I rise to my feet and reply with equal circumspection that I too am proud to represent my own great nation, which continues to celebrate a close relationship with a civilisation far older than her own. A civilisation, I continue, warming to my theme, that has proved so resilient over the centuries that the rest of the world cannot but admire and hope to emulate the philosophical and practical principles by which so many have lived in harmony with nature as well as their fellow man. This, I conclude, is the most important of the many lessons that India can teach the world as she moves into the new millennia.

With the speeches concluded and the meal finished and cleared – as an honoured guest, I am forbidden to help – Devidas suggests a tour of his mother's pride and joy, her vegetable garden. This turns out to be a double row of five-gallon oilcans stacked round a small paved courtyard just outside the kitchen door. The crops – fat little tomatoes ripening red on the stalk, clumps of golden lemongrass stalks, and bright-green bonsai trees of little-leaf basil – are chosen for physical and spiritual balance. The tomatoes, being sweet and juicy, are for pleasure; the lemongrass is used in a soothing infusion for health; while the basil is grown as a temple offering to ensure the household's spiritual welfare.

'It is natural among Hindus of north India such as ourselves to follow the principles of Ayurveda. These, as you will certainly know, my lady, mean that consideration is given to happiness, health and spiritual welfare whenever food is set upon the table, even if this is only roti and a pinch of salt. My mother has followed these principles all her life. And to make sure everything she cooks is fresh, she shops every day – sometimes twice a day, if the weather is hot. Everything must be carefully judged, as no food can be kept from one day to another, so there is very little waste.'

Furthermore, even the women who go out to work every day cook everything fresh at least once and sometimes twice a day.

Meals, however, are not usually the lavish feast we have just enjoyed. Sometimes the only hot food might be freshly baked chapattis to eat with a spoonful of yoghurt stirred with mint, and maybe a little chutney of ripe tomatoes. And anyway, in a household such as this, there is always a grandmother to help out with all the things for which nobody else has the time or patience. This must also be so in my own country, is it not? Is it not true that grandmothers are the most useful member of any household?

My reply – that I know this because I am seven times a grandmother myself – is greeted by the sisterhood of the kitchen with admiration and a warm embrace.

I rise to take my leave and offer gratitude and thanks. Sarina accompanies me to the door and walks with me a little way to find a tuk-tuk. She wants to reassure me that their meals are not always so luxurious.

'When it's just the family and we are not receiving visitors, we will eat perhaps one dhal and two or three vegetable dishes, something simple.'

I must understand, too, that nothing left over from a feast such as ours will ever be wasted.

'Anything we do not eat is given to the holy men and beggars who come to our door at sundown. It is a privilege to be generous, and we must be grateful to those who accept alms from our hands.'

If Gujarat is the poorest and least favoured by nature of India's regions, she is surely the richest in spirit.

GARAM MASALA (SEASONING SPICE)

This all-purpose seasoning mix – garam is 'hot' and masala is 'spice' – is the secret ingredient of the Indian kitchen, adding savour at any point in the cooking process but particularly as a finishing sprinkle. Feel free to experiment with the balance until you get it to your liking. Commercial blends are not a patch on your own, since there is no guarantee of the freshness of the spices and they often include unnecessary thickeners. Buy and store your spices whole and they'll last for a year.

Makes about 175 g
3 tablespoons cardamom pods
2 tablespoons coriander seeds
2 tablespoons cumin seeds
1 tablespoon whole cloves
1 tablespoon black peppercorns
1 finger-length piece of cinnamon stick or cassia bark

Crush the cardamom pods and extract the seeds, discarding the shells. Crush the coriander seeds and blow away the chaff.

Pack all the ingredients into a clean coffee-grinder and pound to a powder. You can do this by hand with a pestle and mortar, but the grind will not be so fine and it takes a lot of patience. Store in an airtight tin or jar for no longer than three months.

To use in a sauce, release the aromatic oils by toasting the mix for a few seconds in a dry pan, then add to whatever needs to be spiced – curries, chutneys, chai.

Possible additions are ground ginger, grated nutmeg, chilli powder, crushed fennel seeds and crumbled bay leaf. In savoury dishes, cassia is preferred to cinnamon. For sauces thickened with yoghurt or cream, omit the coriander and cumin. To spice a milk chai to accompany a festive dish of sweet rice, noodles or *idli*, the basic mix is nutmeg, cardamom, ginger and saffron. To use with clarified butter, ghee, allow the butter to brown a little before you add the spices.

ROTI (WHOLEMEAL FLATBREADS)

Unleavened scooping-breads – roti and chapatti – served fresh and hot from the bake-stone are the most important element in any meal in India, eaten in the morning, at midday and in the evening. In a well-ordered household, it's the privilege of the senior wife to prepare them herself and send them out as soon as they're done. You can vary the recipe with a handful of chickpea flour (*besan*) or any other milled pulses; for millet-bread, replace a quarter of the wheat flour with ground millet (*bajri*), a robust, sun-loving grain which flourishes in desert conditions and delivers a chewy, toasty flavour. The higher the proportion of wheat flour, the lighter the bread, though this is not always desirable, since chewiness and solidity is good when you're hungry and there's not much else on the menu.

Makes 16
500 g stoneground wholemeal flour
½ teaspoon salt
250 ml warm water
1 teaspoon vegetable oil

To finish
2–3 tablespoons melted ghee

Sift the flour with the salt into a large bowl. Make a well in the middle and add the water and oil in a steady stream, mixing with your hand, until you have a softish, sticky dough.

Dust the table with a little flour, tip out the dough and knead it thoroughly for at least 10 minutes. Or let the processor do the work: add the water gradually to the flour and stop as soon as it forms itself into a lump (a minute or two), then finish kneading by hand until silky and smooth.

Work the dough into a ball, cover with cling film or a damp cloth, and set aside for an hour or so – overnight is even better. Knead the dough for another minute or two, cut it in half and roll each piece into a rope as thick as your thumb. Break off a nugget the size of a walnut, work it into a little ball and pop the ball into a plastic bag to keep it soft until you're read to cook. Continue until the rope is all used up. Wait to bake until just before you're ready to eat, so that the breads are fresh and hot – now you understand why the women don't sit down with the men.

Dust a dough-ball with a little flour, press to flatten, and roll or pat into a thin pancake, about 15 cm in diameter – this is easiest if you sandwich it between sheets of cling film. Roll from edge to edge, beginning with the side nearest to you, pressing and pushing with a firm back-and-forth movement, until you reach the other side, then turn the dough a quarter circle and roll it again. Dust lightly with flour, drop it back in the bowl and cover with cling film. Continue until all the dough-balls are rolled out.

Heat a heavy iron pan or griddle and rub lightly with a scrap of linen soaked in oil or ghee. Drop the first flatbread on to the hot metal and wait until little brown blisters appear, about 1 minute – if the surface blisters black immediately, the griddle is too hot; if no black bits appear at all, it's too cool.

Turn and bake the other side for another minute, pressing the edges with a folded tea-towel to trap the air in the middle and create bubbles. Transfer to a basket lined with a cloth, and keep everything covered. Continue until all the flatbreads are cooked.

If you cook on gas, the roti can be puffed up before serving. Hold the roti in the flame for a few seconds, then turn it to toast the other side: magic. Good with a fresh tomato chutney: chopped ripe tomatoes with a little finely chopped onion and coriander leaf.

MOONG DAL KI ROTI (MUNG-BEAN WRAPPERS)

Poured pancakes made with a purée of mung beans, a variation on the usual scooping-breads, to be eaten with spiced yoghurt and a ginger and chilli paste.

(recipe continued overleaf)

Makes 8–10 pancakes

200 g yellow moong dal (mung beans)
½ teaspoon asafoetida (optional)
1 small green chilli, de-seeded and chopped
1 walnut-sized piece fresh ginger, peeled and roughly chopped
oil, for frying

Rinse, wash and soak the mung beans for at least 6 hours. Drain thoroughly, transfer to a food processor and grind to a smooth paste. Add the asafoetida (if using), chilli and ginger and blend thoroughly. Add enough water – about 150 ml – to make a thin cream.

Heat a heavy iron pan or griddle and rub with oil. Pour half a ladleful of batter on to the hot metal, wait for 3–4 seconds to allow the underneath to set a little, then, using the back of the ladle, spread the batter out in concentric circles, forming a pancake as wide as your hand. Trickle the surface with a little oil. Wait for 2 minutes until the top begins to dry, and then turn it carefully to cook the other side. Transfer to a cloth to keep warm. Continue until all the batter is used up and you have a pile of warm pancakes. To reheat, wrap in foil and heat in a low oven.

Serve as a starter with a yoghurt dip and a chilli-ginger paste, or as a main course with your favourite vegetable curry. Perfect, too, as a high-protein wrapper for vegetarian barbecued food.

BHARTA (SMOKY AUBERGINE DIP)

The secret is in the smokiness delivered by the roasting process – easily achievable over a campfire or barbecue, possible on a gas flame, impossible on an electric hob, and just possible under a grill or for a couple of hours at bread-baking heat in the oven.

Serves 4

3–4 large firm aubergines
2–3 garlic cloves, peeled and thinly sliced (optional)
1 teaspoon ground cumin
salt and pepper

Wipe but don't hull the aubergines. Make a few slits in the skin, push in the garlic slivers (if using) and set them to roast very slowly over an open flame, turning them regularly, until the flesh is perfectly soft and the skin blistered black. Cut the aubergines in half, scrape the flesh from the skin and pound it with a pestle and mortar along with the garlic (if using) until you have a perfectly smooth paste. Season with cumin, salt and pepper.

PILAU DHAL (BUTTERED RICE AND DHAL)

A simple combination of grains and pulses – also known as *khichree* – is spiced and enriched with butter to make it a festive dish. Dhal and rice counts as poor folks' food in the rice-growing area of India, but in Gujarat, which is not a rice-growing area, it's a dish for a celebration.

Serves 4–6
250 g yellow moong dal (mung beans)
250 g long-grain rice
1 teaspoon salt
1 teaspoon garam masala
1 teaspoon cracked black peppercorns
½ teaspoon ground turmeric
2 tablespoons ghee (clarified butter)

Soak the mung beans and rice together for half an hour, then drain.

Transfer the drained mung beans and rice with the salt, garam masala, pepper and turmeric to a large saucepan and add 500 ml water. Bring to the boil, turn down the heat, cover with a cloth and lid, and simmer until the rice and mung beans are perfectly tender – 30–40 minutes – adding more boiling water if necessary. The finished dish should be juicy but not soupy.

Stir in the ghee. Taste and correct the seasoning – you'll most likely need more salt.

ALOO KI KARI (POTATOES IN SPICED TOMATO SAUCE)

A spicy sauce for plain-cooked potatoes made with fresh tomatoes ripened in the sunshine of the Great Rann is cooked down until nearly caramelised with onion, garlic, chilli and cumin.

Serves 4–6
1.5 kg new or old potatoes, scrubbed and cut into chunks
1 large mild onion, peeled and finely chopped
2–3 garlic cloves, peeled and finely chopped
2 tablespoons ghee
1 kg perfectly ripe tomatoes, scalded, skinned and diced
1 teaspoon cumin seeds, crushed
½ teaspoon dried red chilli
salt

To finish
coriander leaves (optional)

Set the potatoes to soak in plenty of salted water while you prepare the sauce.

Fry the onion and garlic very gently in the ghee in a large saucepan, stirring regularly, until the vegetables soften – allow at least 20 minutes and don't let them brown. Add the chopped tomato, cumin and chilli, salt lightly and leave to cook right down over a very low heat into a thick, almost caramelised sauce – allow at least 40 minutes depending on the wateriness of the tomatoes. This sauce – also known as gravy, a relic of the Raj – can be prepared in advance.

Cook the potatoes in salted water until perfectly tender – allow 20 minutes. Drain, reserving a cupful of the cooking water. Dilute the sauce with enough of the reserved water to coat the potatoes. Finish with a sprinkle of fresh coriander leaves – or not, as you please. Save any leftovers to set out in the desert as an offering to whoever might be in need, human or otherwise.

Amhara

'PLEASE TO INFORM ME IF THIS IS CORRECT?'

The speaker pushes my notebook across the table for approval. His name is Endele and he is a third-year archaeology student paying his way through university in Addis Ababa by acting as a government guide to travel journalists such as myself and photographer Rod.

I glance down at the careful copperplate.

'*We are eating Ethiopian National Food in Enkukutash Restaurant in the town of Bahir Dar which is located beside Lake Tana in the province of Amhara which is in the mountains of Ethiopia.*'

Perfectly correct, I agree. And – apart from the fact that Ethiopian National Food has not yet arrived on the table and I'm hungry – just what I'm looking for.

Endele nods in satisfaction. Bespectacled and serious, with a round, earnest face and a habit of thinking very carefully before he replies, he has so far proved a model of political discretion. Not even our accommodation – a crumbling state-owned hotel built under the previous regime as a holiday destination for Russians and Cubans – draws anything but an apologetic shrug of the shoulders. Democracy is not nearly as efficient as dictatorship. And when Mengistu's paymasters went home as the Soviet empire crumpled, their leisure facilities were left lying empty and unappreciated and in need of an upgrade in the plumbing and catering department.

This is the second day of our highland adventurings, and Endele is experiencing some difficulty finding public eating places away from the capital, Addis Ababa. There are, he explains, always one or two modest establishments in every town of any size which serve honey beer, *tej*, and ladies offer entertainment of a nature not found at home. But since Ethiopians maintain a wide network of cousins and other relatives who can be expected to offer hospitality and shelter, there is little need for public eating places suitable for foreigners such as Rod and me. And even restaurants such as Enkukutash can be closed down by the government at a moment's notice.

'Let's hope it's still in business when my article appears,' I observe cheerfully.

Endele shakes his head. 'Who knows what will happen tomorrow? We are a people as old as the mountains, yet we live like birds, looking for somewhere to settle at nightfall.'

As a government employee, Endele is careful to avoid offering an opinion on anything that might be taken as political, even a statement as elliptical as this. The problem is clearly acute, and I have taken to referring to the president as David Beckham and the government as Manchester United. However, since we are six hundred miles from the capital and a government edict banning the private use of mobile phones has just been published, communication with his bosses, the Tourist Authority in Addis Ababa, has been temporarily suspended and Endele has allowed himself a little latitude.

Assorted National Food is the generic name for a wide variety of little dishes served with injeera. A large, floppy, yeasted pancake about as wide as a man's arm that serves much the same purpose as India's chapatti or roti and the pitta breads of the Middle East and Iran, injeera is generally accompanied by a wide variety of scoopable foodstuffs. While Amhara's economic importance is reflected in the use of Amharic as Ethiopia's national language, there are many regional differences in what might be served with injeera, although the basic culinary method is much like that of India – careful spicing and a strong tradition of cooking for health and well-being as well as to satisfy hunger.

Endele was born not far from where we are now, on the Ethiopian side of the Rift Valley, where the bones of a race of grain-eating, hunter-gathering hominids, our earliest ancestors, lie buried. And since injeera is made with teff, a hardy variety of millet never altered by cultivation, it's possible to imagine that our ancestors took advantage of the same food source. Ancient beginnings ensure that Ethiopia's civilisation is one of the oldest in Africa, perhaps the most ancient of all. A mountain kingdom without access to the sea, fertile in parts and arid in others, her vast inland water-source when it overflows with the winter rains provides the river Nile with her headwaters. The founder of the nation, legend has it, was the love child of King Solomon and the Queen of Sheba. Her population is three-quarters Christian, one-quarter Muslim, plus the remnants of a small population of Jews who practise a form of Judaism so ancient that scholars in Israel, asked to adjudicate on the suitability of Ethiopian Israelites for citizenship, at first refused to recognise it.

Ethiopian National Food does not easily reveal its secrets. Injeera, the main element, serves as both plate and scoop, obscuring the identity of the little scooping purées dotted round the edge. As a result – although I can identify the scent of cumin, ginger and cinnamon rising in puffs of steam, I don't trust myself to describe all the little dishes accurately, let alone negotiate alternative modes of Amharic spelling – I have turned over my note-taking to Endele so I don't get everything wrong. Mistakes are easy to make when you're a foreigner – a know-nothing *farange*.

Photographer Rod, in the opinion of our commissioning editor, is an old-style safe pair of hands, well accustomed to getting what's required. This is reassuring. I have learned over the years that words on paper, however eloquent, are of little importance where there are photographs to tell the story. Right now, Rod is hard at work with a great deal of undoubtedly expensive camera equipment, gathering local colour on the other side of the road, photographing a crowd of brightly dressed men, women and children milling around outside a handsomely frescoed baroque church much like those to be found in any small town in southern Italy. The gathering, explains Endele, is outside the church of St George. The saint himself is depicted on horseback in armour while plunging his sword into the scaly breast of a fire-breathing dragon. Today, he continues, is the feast day of Ethiopia's patron saint, accounting for the popularity of the restaurant, currently full to bursting.

I suspect Rob of deliberate avoidance of another helping of Ethiopian National Food. Injeera's beery, yeasty sourness is undeniably an acquired taste unless known and loved since childhood. Meanwhile Endele is carefully transcribing the menu into my notebook. A graduate student in archaeology at Addis University, Endele is paying his way with occasional work as a government guide. By the standards of his famous countrymen – the tall, lanky, ebony-skinned long-distance runners who claim all the medals at the Olympics – he's of medium height and build, with a round face and the pallor of a man who works all day in a library, an impression of studiousness reinforced by scholarly reading glasses mostly perched on the end of his nose or pushed up on his head.

Apart from archaeology, his degree subject, Endele's interest lies in stories of rap-singers, Premier League footballers and the British royal family, news of whose activities is unavailable from Ethiopia's state-censored news outlets. For myself, Endele is the source of far more than the raw material of a couple of thousand words for a magazine; he's the key to how people live now at this particular time in this particular place. Right now, set on the table in front of the two of us – I have little expectation that Rob will join us – is a half-metre-wide pancake, puffy and yeasty, round the edge of which have been placed little dabs of technicolour stew. No eating utensils have been provided. Instead, following Endele's example, I learn how to tear off small pieces of the section immediately in front of me, scooping up a morsel of stew, wrapping it up in a little parcel and conveying it neatly into the mouth with the utmost delicacy using only the fingertips. Mine are clumsy. Eating with the fingertips, right hand only, is a skill denied to *farange* such as myself, but I persist.

'*What we are eating today is injeera with* w'ett, *which is Assorted National Food,*' continues Endele in my notebook. '*We are also eating* bozena shiro, *which is also* w'ett *but is made with fava or pea flour.*'

I'm glad of Endele's enthusiasm. If my brief as a journalist is to report on facilities and food for adventurous European tourists in a little-known region of Ethiopia, without Endele I would have had little hope of local colour.

Endele continues with his task.

'*Injeera,*' he continues, '*is a special Ethiopian bread which can be eaten with small amounts of stew. Injeera is prepared with a grain called teff, which is found nowhere else in the world but Ethiopia.*'

My experience of injeera is limited to today and yesterday – and I fully expect the same thing tomorrow – but I am already beginning to enjoy its oddly active flavour.

While the commonest form is the colour of stoneground unbleached bread, this varies from ivory to grey to terracotta depending on the original colour of the grain. Botanically, teff is a particularly hardy variety of millet. When pounded to a flour, mixed with water and allowed to ferment before baking, it becomes a sole-food, capable of sustaining human life without additional nutriment. As with other flatbreads of similar purpose, injeera serves as both plate and scoop for small amounts of something fiery which, in Ethiopia, goes under the generic title of *w'ett*. There is also *t'ibs* and *alich'a*, dishes of lesser import and muted fieriness.

I've never had a problem with unfamiliar foodstuffs; the very reverse. When travelling for work – or even pleasure (it happens) – I look for the market rather than the museum, eat at street stalls rather than restaurants, find out where the market traders take their midday meal and where families take their

Sunday lunch. And I spend far too much time wandering around supermarket shelves and poking around in freezers looking for the ready-made dishes familiar in the region that tell you just what the locals really like to eat.

My own children, when young and not yet free to choose their own menu, complained that their mother would put anything in her mouth just because it was there – and quickly learned to do the same. Chickens' feet in black bean sauce are no problem when you're hungry, which my four children certainly were when competing with siblings at Sunday lunch in the only authentically Chinese restaurant in London in the 1970s. When travelling, if you eat whatever the locals eat at the time the locals eat, you can't go wrong. Well, maybe I'd hesitate to revisit certain fermented fish preparations – Swedish *sürstroming*, Mexico's salt-dried lake fish, Norwegian *lutefisk* – and I remember a particularly slithery tripe dish at the English Market in Cork. Otherwise – well – if anyone else can eat it, why not me? Meanwhile, Endele continues with his task, capitalising for emphasis.

'*INJEERA is made with special flour called TEFF. W'ETT is made from beef but also with chicken, lamb or cheese in stew.*'

I check the little piles of stew for cheese and find little squares of close-packed curds, salty and white.

'ALICHA *is same as* w'ett *but has no* berbere, *which is chilli.*'

Endele pushes the notebook across the table. 'This is also correct?'

'Very correct. Please continue.'

'*Injeera is eaten every day but not always with meat. On fast-days it is eaten with vegetables. On Wednesday we fast because Jesus is born and again on Friday because Jesus is dead.*'

Endele lays down the pen. 'I think we have some things alike, your country and mine. Is it not true that Friday is fish-and-chips and on Wednesday shops close early?'

This is so, and provides proof that our two nations, historically linked by mutual admiration and the stories of Rider Haggard and John Buchan, have much in common.

In celebration of nation-to-nation compatibility, Endele orders a bottle of Ethiopia's favourite alcoholic refreshment, *t'ej*, mildly alcoholic honey beer flavoured with hops. The taste is dry and clean and pleasantly bitter. The hops were brought to Ethiopia by an Englishman, says Endele, which is another good reason to drink a toast.

Compatibilities are piling up thick and fast. Another is the patron saint of both nations, St George, depicted in full glory on the church opposite in the very act of rescuing a beautiful damsel from the fire-breathing dragon.

This calls for more toasting with fresh supplies of *t'ej* that arrive in a recycled Johnnie Walker whisky bottle, further encouragement to celebrate friendship between our nations. After the second bottle, Endele is inspired to continue his notes.

'*We are all WASHING OUR HANDS before we come to table. We are eating with RIGHT HAND only and because this hand must remain perfectly CLEAN and we are not shaking hands with FRIENDS who are Muslim or Christian when they stop at our table to greet us. We are all eating the same food and there is no difference between us except when it concerns ERITREA.*'

Endele lifts the lid on a little pot that's just arrived on the table and is provided with a little brazier to keep it hot, inhales appreciatively – releasing the scent of cardamom, cumin and hot butter – and returns to his task.

'*We are also eating BOSENA SHO W'ETT, which is stew made with chilli, PEAS and butter prepared in the Christian style.*'

While Ethiopia's Muslim, Christian and Jewish populations all follow the same dietary rules by avoiding pork, there are subtle variations in texture, colour and flavourings in the preparation of *w'ett*, observable by those in the know. Among these differences, Endele explains, is the choice of the moment at which the butter is stirred in – at the beginning or at the end. Some brown the butter first for depth of flavour, while others allow it to soften to smooth creaminess in the sauce. There is also the balance between garlic and chilli in the finishing paste – some like more of one than the other and some replace the chilli with crushed peppercorns and grains-of-paradise.

Another pot arrives and is subject to even closer inspection.

'*We are also eating* w'ett *made with POTATO cooked in sauce which is prepared in the Christian style.*'

The difference between Muslim and Christian styles of cooking, Endele continues, is that Christians cook in earthenware on a controlled heat source, whereas Muslims cook on hot metal. There are other minor differences to be explored, but Endele has already had his fill of note-taking and wishes to settle down to the real business of the day.

'Now please, Missis Elisabeth, we must eat.'

The raw material of Ethiopia's daily bread, teff – otherwise identifiable as *Eragrostis abyssinica* – is harvested by hand as soon as the grain ripens and the seed-head flops earthwards. If the grain is not yet ripe, the crop will rot. If harvesting is too late, the tiny grains will vanish into the hard dry earth and the crop is lost. Teff thrives in a waterless wilderness where nothing else survives and comes to ripeness three or four times a year, when it must be gathered as soon as it's ready, an inconvenient growing habit which makes it unsuitable for machine-harvesting or commercial exploitation. As a grain food, teff is provided with its own natural yeasts that allow it to produce its own leavening when ground and mixed with water and left to ferment. Thereafter, it's ready for cooking on a heated bake-stone over a stick-fire in the yard as a poured pancake rather than a rolled or patted-out flatbread.

Prepared in such a way, the grain's nutrients are fully absorbable by the human gut – rarely the way with cultivated grain foods – since as the fermentation process gets under way, the batter develops a digestive enzyme similar to that found in yoghurt.

Ethiopian housewives prepare their own injeera at home, and it's not, Endele assures me, usually sold in the marketplace, let alone the supermarket.

Earlier that morning, on the way to the restaurant, I noticed a scattering of harvesters working low to the ground with scythes. Endele slowed the vehicle to a halt to allow photographer Rod a closer look, and myself a few minutes for a quick sketch. As I walked back to rejoin the vehicle on the road, I gathered a slender dried-out stalk and inspected the seed-head. The grains were tiny – no bigger than a poppy seed. This is important, Endele confirms, for a crop grown in poor soil under desert conditions. The smaller the grain, the less nutrients it needs and the faster it comes to maturity. This is the reason for the need for regular cropping as well as teff's ability to survive in desert conditions, as are usual in the region of Lake Tana. While the lake itself is one of the largest repositories of fresh water in Africa, when the rains fail, which they have for the last twelve years, the surrounding plain is never anything but parched and dry.

The government, Endele explains, offers grants to farmers who are prepared to abandon their independent way of life and grow exportable crops such as wheat and maize instead of teff. With the money guaranteed by the state, growers can afford to buy their bread from the bakery and there will be no need for the laborious business of preparing injeera for free. Take-up, however, has not been as enthusiastic as the government would like. The result – in the city as well as the countryside – is that Ethiopia continues to prepare injeera in the traditional way on a stick-fire in the yard, causing a shortage of firewood, which, in turn, causes degradation of arable land and desertification as the population expands.

There are no easy answers to the problem. Firewood has been in short supply in the capital since the days of Menelik II, contemporary of Queen Victoria, who imported a Swiss engineer with experience in forestry who advised the planting of eucalyptus trees, Australian natives, as reliably fast-growing and highly flammable. Rather too flammable, as it happened, since unlike Ethiopia's native trees, eucalyptus renews itself through regular spontaneous combustion, introducing a new threat to the countryside: forest fires. Lacking natural predators, the alien trees thrived under desert conditions, spreading rapidly and combusting with an enthusiasm fatal to the native tree-cover as well as the birds and mammals dependent on its shelter. This, says Endele, is a problem so far un-confronted by government.

Forest fires are one of the few hazards not identified in warnings on the Foreign Office website before Rod and I set out on our adventure. Among recent discouragements are kidnappings in Gondar, uprisings in Eritrea and trouble on the border with Somalia. Nothing to worry about on the shores of Lake Tana, however – and even had there been, the chance to travel, however briefly, in the mysterious mountain kingdom of Haggard and Buchan would have proved irresistible. In all of Africa, no place is more romantic to an enthusiastic traveller than the land of Prester John. Nineteenth-century travel writers – always my first line of enquiry when heading into the unknown – describe a tolerant and hospitable race of tall, graceful, handsome, dark-skinned men and women who practise an ancient form of Christianity, have no quarrel with their Muslim neighbours and respect the right of a small population of expatriate Israelites to follow an archaic rite of Judaism that can be traced back to the visit of the Queen of Sheba to King Solomon in the city of Jerusalem a thousand years before the birth of Christ.

There is always a certain ethical difficulty in writing about food and travel in a region better known for war and famine. But since Ethiopia is currently – in 2006 – enjoying a respite from these twin afflictions and looking to attract tourism under a democratically elected government, there is good reason to hope that peace and plenty will return and the Horn of Africa will once again be one of the most tranquil and beautiful places on the planet.

That's all very well and good, warned an old Ethiopia-hand, a diplomatic friend consulted back in London. But be careful what you say. The secret police are everywhere.

Endele is in no doubt the warning must be heeded. 'In Ethiopia we say the government owns everything, including you and me.'

Practicalities – comfort of accommodation, ease of travel, cultural and gastronomic highlights – are useful information for my readership, particularly when Rod's images are there to tell the story.

Across the road, a group of workmen are setting a kettle over a stick-fire.

'These men are making some tea,' says Endele, finishing up the last scrap of chicken stew with a final scoop of injeera.

I'm not entirely satisfied with the explanation.

'How do they make their tea?'

'You do not know how to make tea?'

When I shake my head, Endele decides to humour me.

'First they pick some leaves which are good for making tea. For this there are many different leaves you can use which grow everywhere around. Then they put the water in the pot. When the pot boils, they put in the tea and then they boil it some more. And then they put in the coffee.'

He pauses, then adds, 'I think in England perhaps you do not add coffee when you are making tea, but this is how Ethiopian workmen like their tea. I like it myself.'

Coffea arabica, the shrub whose berries deliver the world's favourite stimulant, has always grown wild on the islands of Lake Tana, but no one had thought the berries good for anything until, so the story goes, nomadic Arabian goatherds, observing their flocks were unusually lively after consuming the fresh fruit somewhere out in the desert, gathered the berries for themselves, brewed them up and made them into a stimulating drink which, unlike wine, had not been prohibited by the Prophet.

This story skips over one essential step in the development of the world's favourite beverage: fermentation, a process which happens naturally in the digestive tract of all mammals. Anything indigestible – seeds and pips – is excreted in the goats' droppings used by the nomadic herdsmen as kindling for the cooking fire, a process that delivered ready-roasted beans that, when pounded in a mortar along with the spices traditionally used to perfume goats' milk tea, delivered a beverage of such extraordinary deliciousness that its fame spread throughout Arabia and beyond.

Breakfast on the terrace in the government hotel, much to Rod's relief, includes cornflakes as well as Thermos coffee and leftover injeera. Endele spreads his injeera with ghee perfumed with aniseed, pours a cup of coffee from the hotel's Thermos, sugars it enthusiastically and adds a pinch of powder from a little bowl. 'This is how I prepare my coffee when I take it at home, with sugar and cloves and cinnamon. I like it at all times of day, middle of the day and in the evening too. Here. I will make it for you.'

Thermos coffee is never my favourite morning beverage, but the addition of a pinch of spice is a considerable improvement. Rod declines the offer, opting instead for tea-bag tea made with freshly boiled water, always a wise choice when the success of an assignment depends on not taking unnecessary gastronomic risks.

Endele has a treat in store for us, a trip to the coffee islands.

'I have spoken with my boss in Addis because we are now back in communication, and it is all arranged.'

The monastery islands where they grow the coffee, he continues, are accessible either by dugout canoe used by those who collect firewood on the islands and sell the coffee cherries for the monks, or by arrangement with the ferryman who transports stores and passengers when the need arises. The monks are members of the Ethiopian Orthodox Church who spend their lives in silent prayer and contemplation and do not mingle with the visitors who come to see the frescoes and admire the monastery. The coffee plantations support the community financially, though the monks themselves are forbidden by their vows to drink intoxicating beverages. This is good business for the people of Bahir Dar, who process and market the coffee on their behalf.

'In a little time, the canoes with the coffee beans and the firewood will be coming from the islands,' Endele announces with satisfaction. 'This will be opportunity for photograph.'

Rod heads off enthusiastically in the direction of the jetty, lugging an enormous bag of camera equipment. I follow more slowly with my paints and sketchpad. Right on cue, a flotilla of slender papyrus dhows propelled by two-man crews wielding double-ended paddles emerges through the veil of morning mist. Each dhow carries a towering load of bundled branches balanced crisscross on the prow.

The boats nose into the jetty and the paddlers unload the bundles of firewood on to the quayside. Beneath the bundles are wooden crates. Bright heaps of scarlet berries begin to blossom on sheets of sacking spread on the ground. A noisy crowd of women appear with plastic buckets. These are the coffee women, says Endele, laying in supplies of untreated berries, the raw material of the famous coffee ceremony that takes place every day in the households of Bahir Dar.

Is there by chance, I enquire, anywhere in town where ignorant *farange* such as Rod and myself might experience the drinking of a cup of real coffee with or without the ceremony? Endele looks doubtful. There is no reason for anyone to take coffee anywhere but at home, and if not at home, then the laws of hospitality in Ethiopia ensure that anyone who would like to take coffee has only to join the coffee ceremony in any household where the scent of roasting beans is an unspoken invitation.

There are other places where men may go to drink intoxicating beverages and be entertained in other ways, but these are not suitable for ladies. The coffee ceremony, on the other hand, is a family occasion to which strangers are welcome, including *farange*. This is no longer so in Addis, but in the countryside, the rules hold good. Endele has cousins in the town who would consider it an honour to welcome us and explain the importance of the ceremony as a social event.

Meanwhile, we will experience the raw material at first hand as it comes into ripeness on the coffee trees growing on the monastery islands. The monks do not socialise – their business is alone with God – but since they need money for necessities and to pay the priests who give them absolution, tours are permitted on days when there's a demand.

Today there is demand. Our expedition is to be joined by the priest from St George's church and a pair of Australian backpackers, fellow guests at the hotel.

Our transport, a rusting ferryboat bearing the logo of the World Wildlife Fund, awaits. On the way over, I fall into conversation with the backpackers, Kate and Bruce. They have travelled in the region before when they were courting. Now, as a married couple, they have left their two children behind in Sydney with grandparents, and are revisiting their days of courtship.

Back at the end of the 1990s, Ethiopia was a more dangerous place than it is now, says Kate, or they wouldn't have risked it now that they're parents themselves. Ten years ago, robbers with guns were everywhere and no one in their right mind would drive anywhere in the countryside after dark for fear of trigger-happy eighteen-year-olds looking for a fight.

Bruce takes up the story. 'There was a bunch of us from Oz travelling together in a van. We thought it'd be OK to sleep rough, even though everyone knew that a lot of the local kids out there had guns. Then one night we woke to find a bunch of people rummaging through our packs. When we told them to stop, they just shrugged and said, very politely, "We're sorry but we have to rob you."'

Kate shakes her head and frowns. 'They weren't interested in taking our money, they just wanted the kit – the jeans and jackets and boots. So we said, "Sure, take whatever you want." So they did. Even the stuff we were wearing. And then they shot out the tyres to slow us down and we had to drive on in our skivvies till we could find a garage to fix the punctures. But at least they left us the money.'

The couple look at each other and laugh. 'Maybe we were lucky. Or maybe they just needed the stuff more than we did.

After that, we felt better about what we had and they didn't. Sort of evened up the score.'

Evening up the score seems a sensible point of view.

The engines slow, leaving a slick of fossil fuel. Our transport is not planet friendly, in spite of the logo. Further along the shore, smoke rises from burnt-out grassland where a new luxury spa-hotel is under construction. The money, Endele explains enthusiastically, comes from a consortium of Ethiopia's long-distance runners, the nation's self-made millionaires. Private enterprise has its place in the new Ethiopia, particularly when the investors are national heroes.

The ferry's battered prow bobs against the wooden jetty under tall trees. The ferryman throws out a gangplank to allow his passengers to disembark, and begins to unload barrels and boxes for the monastery's stores.

One of the monks – a lay brother by the look of his boots and robe tucked into a belt – is waiting to greet the priest and lead our little party through the coffee plantations to the monastic enclave.

We follow our guide upwards along a narrow path through orderly rows of coffee trees hung with ripening berries until we reach a manicured clearing with mown grass, pruned fruit-trees, beehives and an enclave of solid stone buildings. The priest and our guide disappear together into one of the buildings. No words are spoken. This, whispers Endele, is a silent order. We proceed further up the hill until we reach the monastery church, the only building open to visitors.

The outside walls are curved to protect an inner sanctum, square in shape, in much the same way as the outer walls of a medieval castle protect the keep. This, says Endele, symbolises the womb of the Virgin Mary encircling the body of Christ. We may go no further than the perimeter since only those in holy orders may enter the inner sanctum. Unsanctified persons such as ourselves are permitted to worship in the outer sanctum, a gallery that runs round along the outer walls and is carpeted with hand-woven rugs, with every inch of wall and ceiling covered in brightly painted frescoes.

The paintings are narrative, layered one on top of the other, telling and retelling the old stories. Haloed saints and winged archangels share space with prophets and patriarchs. Over here is the beautiful Queen of Sheba dreaming in a field of lilies; over there, amid scenes of village life, Ethiopia's Seven Evangelists offer the New Testament to the descendants of King Solomon.

There are ancient vineyards where communion wine is made for the priests, exempted from the rules of sobriety imposed on the monks. Endele remembers the communion table as the first inequality of his childhood. Only the priest took wine and everyone else got just a little bit of bread and the children got none. The lesson for a hungry boy contemplating the richly robed priests in their jewel-embroidered cassocks was that if you are rich and important, you get more. If you are poor and don't matter, you get less or nothing at all.

Good news awaits our return from the coffee islands. The cousins have sent word by some mysterious form of bush telegraph, bypassing the forbidden mobile phone, that cousin Endele and his two *farange* are welcome to join the household for the coffee ceremony.

Endele announces that he doesn't need an address. This, he explains, is because Ethiopians don't need street names or follow maps because everyone knows where everyone lives. This turns out to be a little optimistic. The suburbs of Bahir Dar are arranged on a grid system, spreading outwards across the flat countryside. The streets are unpaved and lined with blank walls pierced at intervals by closed doorways. Endele drives up one way and down the other and then repeats the exercise, muttering crossly. After every intersection in the town has been explored, he finally admits defeat, coming to rest at a set of disused traffic lights beside a half-open doorway, the only sign of life in the whole town. Within can be glimpsed a few tables and chairs whose occupants are nursing bottles of what looks like whisky. A radio is playing what must surely be the latest Ethiopian pop song. At the far end, a bead curtain is looped back over to reveal another room, more dimly lit, beyond.

'This is where they serve *t'ella*, which is home-made beer, very strong, which is not suitable for ladies,' instructs Endele, disappearing within.

After a few moments he emerges, smiling broadly. Word of lost *farange* is being sent to the cousins and they will send a runner to guide us home. It is not far.

Behind every identical wall is a courtyard. Three sides of the courtyard are composed of single-room dwellings. The fourth side, the communal living room, gives access to the street. A line of tattered sofas and armchairs pushed against the walls form a public area where travellers may rest and sleep and the coffee ceremony take place after the midday meal.

Cooking and all other domestic chores are performed communally in the open courtyard, allowing a level of privacy for each family group in the one-room dwellings.

Preparations for the midday meal are already under way. While it's the duty of the women of the household to prepare the meal, the men are expected to gather firewood and light the cooking fire. Both duties are a privilege rather than a chore.

Today it's the turn of one of the newest wives, Sara, to prepare the meal. Tall and slender in a simple white cotton shift embroidered at neck and wrist with multicoloured beadwork, Sara settles herself on a step at the entrance to one of the single-room dwellings with a shallow earthenware bowl in her lap.

I place my hands together and bow, smiling. Smiling in return, Sara indicates with a graceful gesture of the hand that

I should settle myself on a stool beside her. From a close-woven basket set ready to hand, she fills the bowl with tiny golden grains, picks up a smooth stone and begins to work with a smooth circular movement of the wrist until the grains are reduced to a fine powder.

The grindstone, a simple pestle and mortar, is the maid-of-all-work in the Ethiopian kitchen, used for crushing lentils, powdering spices and milling nuts for oil. A new bride, Endele explains as I unpack my paint box to record the scene, brings her grindstone with her as part of her dowry when she marries.

If it were me, I answer with a laugh, I would have to bring my sketchbooks and paints instead of mortar and pestle, though perhaps they wouldn't be so useful. Once translated, my contribution is greeted with general merriment and the atmosphere lightens. The *farange*, it seems, is human after all. While Rod's camera equipment is treated with circumspection and a level of mistrust, no one feels threatened by paper and paint. The very reverse, since the purpose is clear for everyone to see. Advice can be offered, explanations exchanged, opinions delivered – and all without the need for spoken language, a method of communication as familiar to my audience as it must have been to their ancestors who painted the history of the pharaohs on the walls of the pyramids.

Sara, her work with the grindstone completed, sets it carefully aside on the stoop and turns her attention to a round-bellied earthenware jar set ready to hand in a corner, and begins to stir the contents with a peeled stick forked at the tip like a miniature whisk. Beside it, propped against the wall, is what must surely be a clay bake-stone and a pouring gourd. The bake-stone is a full arm's length in diameter and the gourd, Endele explains, is of the exact size required for pouring the right amount of batter to cover the bake-stone.

Sara dips the gourd into the batter and shows me the contents – so much and no more, adding an explanation for translation by her cousin. Her voice is low and gentle, as if she were instructing a favourite child. The batter, translates Endele, has been fermenting for three days and is now ready for the bake-stone. Once the jar is empty and the injeera has all been cooked, a new batch of batter will be started with freshly ground flour and will be ready in three days, when today's supplies have all been finished. The jar will not be rinsed before the new batch is mixed so the fermentation can start without delay. On Sara's instruction, I add a few strokes of the brush to my sketch – the shape of the gourd, the roundness of the bake-stone – in confirmation that I have understood.

The kindling is lit and branches arranged round the edge like the spokes of a wheel so that the ends can be pushed inwards to catch the flame. When there are sufficient glowing coals to make a bed of the same width as the bake-stone, the cooking can begin.

Sara tests the temperature with a hand held palm downwards over the surface. Once satisfied, she pours the batter smoothly and steadily on to the hot bake-stone in decreasing circles from outside to middle. I know from my own experience of bake-stone cooking – the technique is much the same wherever the tradition is for cooking on top heat, including Wales – that the heat is higher in the middle because that's where the embers are hottest. The skill in handling such a large bake-stone – three times the width of a Welsh griddle – lies in pouring smoothly and evenly without hesitation so that the batter sets in an even layer.

An appreciative audience gathers round to watch what is clearly a master class in injeera-making. Not everyone, Endele confirms, has the skill and confidence that Sara demonstrates. As soon as the air rises to make bubbles in the dough and the edges begin to curl and brown, Sara transfers the finished pancake to a bleached cloth on a basketwork tray, covering it immediately with a matching dome. The performance continues in tranquillity as the pile of pancakes grows.

When the batter is nearly finished, Sara rises gracefully, refills the gourd and holds it out to me with an encouraging smile.

The invitation needs no translation. But still, I hesitate. While I'm usually happy to try my hand at a new skill, this is dexterity of a different order.

Endele watches me with a smile. 'Have no fear. Children and *farange* are always forgiven when they make mistakes.'

The audience gathers closer. The pouring of injeera is not for the unsteady of hand or eye. While *farange* may well be forgiven, an ill-made injeera is not a risk I am anxious to take. Refusal, however, would clearly be a discourtesy. The die is cast and I cannot escape.

Taking a deep breath and holding the gourd firmly in my right hand, I do the best I can to pour the batter in decreasing circles, as instructed, from the outer edge of the bake-stone towards a triumphant finish in the middle. Gaps appear between the rings. I mend the gaps with an extra trickle. The audience sighs in sympathy as the batter belches, bubbles and rises in wavy furrows and a single wart-like blister.

The *farange* needs all the forgiveness she can muster.

'Never mind,' says Endele.

The audience disperses, chattering and laughing.

Sara continues calmly with her preparations. A long-handled wire basket is used to transfer coals from the fire to a brazier set ready with charcoal. Today's dish – the accompaniment for the freshly baked injeera – is a potato stew prepared in a cooking pot of unglazed earthenware, round-bellied with a wide mouth and a domed lid so that, as is evident from the shape, the steam condenses in the lid and drops back into the pot so that none of the moisture is lost.

The finished dish, Endele explains, is known as a *w'ett*, and is distinguished from other traditional dishes by the presence of onion. These are already being sliced into half-moons on a wooden board with a cut-throat knife by Sara. When all are prepared, the onions are set to fry gently in a little oil and covered with the lid. Meanwhile, potatoes are scrubbed and chunked. When the scent of gently caramelised onion rises, the potatoes are added to the pot with just enough water to cover the pieces. Salt is added and the lid replaced. The heat of the charcoal is gentle and the pot simmers at an even temperature.

Meanwhile Sara, working patiently with her pestle and grindstone, prepares a soft paste of green chilli, fresh ginger root and garlic cloves crushed with salt. As soon as the potatoes are soft and the moisture evaporated, the paste is stirred in and the fragrance intensifies, drawing back the onlookers who have drifted away, and the dish is ready.

As his cousin works and I record the scene, Endele provides an educational commentary. Certain things, he informs me, are important in the Ethiopian kitchen. When preparing a chicken *w'ett* for feast days, the onions should not first be fried, as Sara has done today, but pounded to a paste with chilli and garlic and sometimes with other spices such as cinnamon, turmeric and cumin. If there are many people to feed and only one small chicken, vegetables may be added. If there is sauce left over from a *w'ett*, this can be eaten with flaked and dried injeera for breakfast. To prepare injeera for storage as flakes, tear it into small pieces and set these to dry in the sun until completely dehydrated. To temper an earthenware cooking utensil so it will last for at least three years, cook split peas in the pot until soft, tip them out and replace with oil seeds such as linseed, sesame, sunflower or mustard, then heat the pot again and rub until the surface is coated and smooth.

By the end of the lecture, Sara is ready to serve the meal,

spreading a clean cloth directly on the beaten earth of the courtyard and setting the injeera basket and the pot in the middle. Those who wish to eat take their places in a circle round the cloth and eat rapidly and cleanly, without ceremony or conversation, ceding their place to others as soon as they finish. No one speaks and the meal is over in a trice.

'It is good manners to eat quickly and make room for others,' Endele informs me. 'This is for reasons of family harmony.'

Family harmony also dictates the conduct of the coffee ceremony, a more leisurely affair that takes place in the comfort of the communal living room. Sara has already done her work and the honour of preparing the coffee falls to the latest addition to the family, a tall young beauty also dressed from head to toe in white but without the exquisite beadwork at neck and wrists that distinguishes the senior ladies of the household.

Inviting a new daughter-in-law to prepare the coffee is a sign of acceptance of a bride into her husband's household.

Settling herself on a low stool beside a casket, the beauty begins to unload small bowls and implements on to a rickety little table.

'This is my cousin's newly wedded wife,' whispers Endele. 'I do not yet know her so I cannot tell you her name.'

The nameless young woman fills one of the larger bowls with green unroasted coffee beans and fills another with what looks like popping corn. Beside these she sets a round-bellied black earthenware coffee pot with a silvery sheen, followed by a handful of charcoal, a small bundle of dried grass, a metal coat-hook, a flint stone, a double-handled copper toasting-pan and a small brass pestle and mortar.

Set ready beside her on a tripod is the heat source, a shallow bowl in unglazed earthenware to which the nameless beauty adds a handful of charcoal and a wisp of dried grass, before igniting the pile with a single spark struck from the flint stone using the coat-hook.

The charcoal begins to glow. By this time the room is filling up from the street with silent observers, children among them.

'Children are allowed to join their parents and speak if they wish,' says Endele. 'This is a time when important questions can be asked and answered.'

The demonstration proceeds at a leisurely pace. First the beans are toasted in the copper pan and stirred with the coat-hook over a gentle heat until they are evenly mahogany brown, releasing a delicious fragrance that curls through the open door and draws in more of the neighbours.

The word has already gone round of *farange* present at the coffee ceremony, and people are curious. Any child staring too hard is reprimanded with a tap on the shoulder and a frown. Children are extraordinarily well behaved at the coffee ceremony, says Endele, for which Emperor Menelik is to be thanked.

Once judged perfectly roasted, the beans are pounded in the mortar until ground to the finest of powders. Meanwhile, the coffee pot is set over the brazier, half filled with water and brought to the boil. Two generous handfuls of coffee are added; sufficient, says Endele, for twelve persons.

'There will be three washings of the coffee. The first is good, the second less good and the third is taken for politeness. On the third washing, children may address their elders.'

As soon as the pot returns to the boil, more water is added. When the pot re-boils, sugar is added. On the third boiling, the coffee is ready for pouring into twelve little handleless cups set ready on a tin tray. With the little cups are three small bowls, one with sugar, one with salt and another with coffee beans for the children.

'You may add more sugar if you like, or you might prefer

salt,' says Endele. 'No one will think less of you if you choose salt, but they might think there's been a time when you couldn't afford the sugar.'

I choose sugar. Endele nods approvingly. Later he tells me that if my choice had been salt, that might have meant I thought the cousins too poor to afford sugar, which would not have been polite.

People are sensitive about such things.

'In my own family, we never had enough money to pay for sugar. There were eleven to feed so everyone had to help. When I was five, I was proud because I was old enough to be sent out to herd the cattle. When I was seven, three of us went to live with our grandmother so she had a family to look after and wasn't lonely. It was just across the courtyard, so we weren't far away.'

It was from his grandmother that Endele learned to gather food and medicinal plants from the wooded slopes of the Rift Valley where he grew up.

'My grandmother knew many things. She liked to make a tea with the leaves of a tall tree with star-shaped flowers you could recognise because they fall in bunches like grapes. She pounded the leaves and mixed them with water and we would drink it before eating a meal so our food became easier to digest.'

Children feel valued when encouraged to contribute to the welfare of the household. This must also have been my experience when my own children were young, is this not so? Indeed it is. Tasks reserved for children in our household in Andalusia included bashing freshly picked olives with a rolling pin to allow them to absorb the pickling brine, and podding chickpeas to dry for the winter. The most fun, however, was pipping raisins, skinning almonds and separating the little globules of suet from the kidney-fat when I decided there had to be a proper English plum pudding for Christmas.

'When the palm-nuts were ripe, my sisters and I would go

into the forest with pea-shooters to annoy the monkeys so they threw the nuts from the trees. When we had enough, we would crack the shells and boil them up so the oil floated to the top and could be saved for cooking. I was proud when I could bring my family the oil.'

While the wood of the wild olive was used for building and firewood, the fruit was neither eaten nor pressed for oil.

'We knew what was useful and what was not. So if we saw an olive seedling or any other tree which was useful, we cleaned all around so it could grow.'

The family's milk animals – cow and goats – were brought indoors at night so the house was warm even in winter, and every household made butter and cheese with the milk. And there was teff to be gathered for injeera, and plenty of firewood in the forest, so all anyone had to buy was spices and salt for *w'ett*, and coffee for the coffee ceremony because there were no coffee bushes near his village.

Back in the capital, Endele unloads his reponsibilities – Rod and me – at a modest hotel in the diplomatic quarter which also serves as the red-light district on the outskirts of the city. All the magnificent four- and five-star hotels in the city centre are crammed to bursting with heads of state, government officials and politicians gathered together for an important international meeting at the presidential palace.

In the absence of catering facilities at the hotel, Endele has booked us into a nearby trattoria. All the city's best restaurants are owned and run by Italians, he explains. Italy was the colonial power until the British arrived not long before the end of World War II. There was, says Endele, no need for a word for restaurant in Amharic since no one had any use for public eating places owing to the traditions of hospitality we have already experienced.

Not all the Italians went home to Mussolini's Italy. Those who remained sent for their families and opened a trattoria in the front room, serving mama's home-cooked lasagne al forno and spaghetti bolognaise. Rod brightens at the news.

The restaurant is in a residential street with a little garden and terrace which opens out into what is still recognisably someone's front room. Most of the tables are occupied by pasta-eating locals and the menu, happily for Rod, has no mention of Assorted National Food. Rod orders lasagne al forno and a bottle of Barolo. I settle for a well-iced tumblerful of Campari-soda with a slice of orange as the prelude to a steaming plateful of perfectly sauced, al dente spaghetti bolognaise – a combination of chewiness, nuttiness and restrained richness that reminds me of a long-ago summer in Portofino, where I first discovered that spag bol as served in its land of origin is not a wet pile of overcooked grain food slathered in what might well be tomato ketchup.

Endele reappears in the morning, smiling broadly. Addis, he reports, is unusually empty and peaceful owing to the presence of many soldiers guarding the important people who are conferring together at the presidential palace.

This leaves the way open for us to spend a leisurely day exploring those parts of the city not under lockdown – the government takes care to keep its dissidents well away from contact – including Mercato, Addis's central market. This, a vast, sprawling rabbit-warren at the edge of the city centre, still carries its Italian name – perhaps because there was no need for an explanation of its function as the lifeblood of the city. Like in any medieval township, the market is divided into districts – cheesemongers in one, metalworkers in another – separated one from the other by broad streets linked together by narrow alleyways.

Within the parameters of the township, anything and everything anyone might ever need to keep body and soul together is sold or bartered or exchanged. The outer sections nearest to the countryside, our point of entry, are devoted to fresh produce brought in daily, including meat and dairy, live poultry and eggs. Here the stalls are piled high with multicoloured fruits and vegetables – pyramids of green and red tomatoes of every size and shape, towers of scarlet peppers and strings of red and green chillies, skeins of purple-blushed garlic, great bunches of bananas, glowing heaps of oranges and lemons, big boxes of odd-shaped gourds with bumpy or prickly skins, bright-green okra pods, potatoes, carrots, melons, huge bouquets of spinach-like greens, dripping bunches of leaf-coriander, parsley and mint.

More permanent needs are filled along narrow alleyways lined with rickety shelters, makeshift warehouses, tin-roofed workshops occupied by leather-workers, candle-makers, suppliers and fixers of electrical goods, weavers, cotton-spinners, pot-throwers, knife-grinders, tile-makers, carpenters, jewellery-makers, wood-carvers and pot-menders.

The spice-merchants – suppliers to all Africa of the perfumes of the East – have a whole alleyway to themselves: purveyors of ginger root and grains-of-paradise, dealers in powdered orchid-root and attar-of-roses, sellers of potions to cure all ills. Arranged with perfect precision in drawers and boxes are rolls of cinnamon bark and curls of cassia, knobbly roots of turmeric, fiery little bird's-eye chillies, white and black peppercorns, allspice berries, cloves, black and green cardamom pods, whiskery heaps of cumin, poppy and nigella seeds sold by the scoopful, fenugreek, Madagascan vanilla, Turkish saffron, mastic for sweetening the breath, liquorice root for chewing, sage for the digestion.

Sheltered under canvas awnings are heaps of snow-white slush prepared with the root and stem of *ensete*, false banana. *Ensete* looks like a palm tree but is actually a grass, a relative of the true banana, and is grown by every household in the city that has a square metre of ground in which to plant it. Endele's

landlady grows it outside the kitchen window. As a backyard crop, *ensete* is planted twice yearly and takes six months to reach maturity. A single plant will feed husband, wife and two children for half a year. Its food value and digestibility is greatly increased, however, if the pulp is buried and left to ferment underground for up to six months, long enough for another tree to come to maturity. When the pulp is dug up, boiled and strained, the solids are dried in the sun and used to make bread. When freshly cropped, if the leaves are stripped and the stem peeled and chunked and crushed, it can be eaten immediately.

At the thought of *ensete* in any form at all, Endele wrinkles his nose and shakes his head. While nourishing – no question – *ensete* tastes of nothing at all, not even with honey or a scraping of palm sugar.

Perhaps, he continues thoughtfully, it is the same with the Scottish oatmeal porridge of which Endele has heard tell from a previous group of visitors? Oats are fed to horses rather than people.

Not at all, I explain. Oatmeal porridge is what my Scottish grandmother made for breakfast every morning and it tastes nutty and grainy and is delicious with a pinch of salt, a trickle of cream and a spoonful of treacle.

Endele absorbs this information in silence, then offers it up in translation for consideration by the *ensete* merchants. This is followed by merriment and an animated discussion of the identity and uses of treacle. In order to bring the discussion to a satisfactory conclusion, I am obliged to demonstrate the preparation of oatmeal porridge by my grandmother, with suitable accompaniments, through paint on paper – gathering, in the course of the demonstration, the usual audience of raggedy children and idle passers-by, allowing Rod a little space to make use of his camera. The price of goodwill is the sketch itself – proudly pinned up on a beam above the stall – but since I have by now a whole sketchbook full of market activities, the sacrifice is not hard to make.

While injeera is more desirable as food for adults, false-banana bread is good for babies and old people. It is, however, bland and flavourless – the food of necessity rather than choice.

The weavers and spinners have a whole street to themselves. The cotton-spinners are all women. Seated on rickety chairs in gossipy groups, they work rapidly and with remarkable dexterity, pulling fine threads from sacks between their knees. Seeds and twigs are winnowed out without a downward glance as they chatter and laugh and greet. And all the while their fingers twist and roll, passing the thread with miraculous accuracy through a miniature spindle, finishing each hank with a twist.

The dairy alley next door is protected from the sun with a canvas awning. In the dim light, trestle tables covered with white tablecloths are loaded with big blocks of pale butter and earthenware bowls filled with snowy curds of salty white cheese. Those in charge of these good things – brawny men and women – are wielding scimitar-shaped knives. None of them look friendly.

Unfriendliness, explains Endele, is because Rod's professional camera equipment is expensive, an indication that we might be government spies disguised as tourists.

Spies are everywhere in the market. The dairy industry is particularly sensitive as production is traditional and there can be disguising of rancidity, mixing with cheaper fats such as palm oil, and other ways to make goods go further. Government interference is resented because the fines are higher than honest tradesmen can afford, so the honest tradesman goes out of business and the cheating trader who makes money because he cheats pays the fine and stays.

Endele inspects the goods with a practised eye. 'Whenever my mother is asked why her cooking tastes so good the answer is always butter. Did your mother tell you nothing?'

My mother, I have to admit, told me nothing so useful.

'And your grandmother? Did she not teach you how to use berries from the woods and herbs to cure you when you were ill?'

My grandmother was a pampered belle from Baltimore, friend of the woman who stole the Prince of Wales, and had never boiled so much as an egg in her life.

Endele shakes his head in disbelief. How could this be so when the properties of so many good things – leaves, berries, herbs and fungi – are cheaper and better understood than doctor's medicines?

Take *chat*, for instance, sold fresh from a nearby stall as bundles of bright-green leaves bunched like spinach.

'Ethiopian coca leaf. Very good to stop hunger when working in the fields. There is talk of a government ban.'

Rod expresses a keen interest. Endele negotiates a purchase and rolls a neat little plug for Rod and another for me.

'Chew and spit.'

Rod chews and spits. I chew but am too ladylike to spit. The flavour is grassy and peppery and my heart is beating a little faster than it should. My tolerance for mind-altering substances is embarrassingly low.

I transfer the half-chewed plug to a tissue and hide it in my pocket.

Mention of hunger reminds everyone of the need for lunch.

'Today what we are eating is *kurt*,' says Endele with unusual firmness. '*Kurt* is Ethiopian fast food like McDonald's only better. We must hurry or the best cuts will be gone.'

Rod continues to chew happily. Unlike me, he is excused from experimental gastronomy owing to the need to keep both hands available and unpolluted for operating the camera.

Kurt, Endele explains as we follow him through the labyrinth, is beef from young male animals, grass-fed, walked to market at dawn, expertly slaughtered, butchered and on sale from the hook by midday. The meat is eaten raw and by three o'clock all the best cuts will be gone. By sundown in a tropical climate such as that of Ethiopia, meat is no longer fit to be eaten raw but must be cooked. Cooking facilities are available in the cook-shops who provide service for those who wish to eat their meat raw but don't want to eat it standing up at the butcher's counter.

Ethiopians are cattle herdsmen by tradition, relying on their herds for milk and meat. Slaughter is the business of profes-sional butchers accustomed to handling their animals gently and without fear. If the animals are frightened, the meat will not be good and the butcher will have no customers. Customers in a hurry can choose the piece they want, hold it between their teeth and slice it close to the lips with a sharp knife.

This can be considered a good way to eat *kurt* but is, I agree, not very ladylike.

Trade is brisk at the butcher's and the queue impatient.

The choice is fatty or lean and the butcher needs to know if the meat is for eating raw or cooked. Once this is established, the seller decides the cut and sets the price, an egalitarian way of doing business which satisfies the needs of both parties.

Endele orders and pays. We find a table in the restaurant and Endele unwraps our package. The meat is dark, firm and velvety with a deep margin of buttery yellow fat. No need for a menu, says Endele, as the cooks will know exactly what's wanted by the cut.

The package disappears and reappears with the meat cut into bite-sized pieces arranged on a wooden board with a curved knife and a lemon stuck on the point. With it comes a small bowl of roughly crushed salt crystals, another of *awaᶎe*, chilli sauce, and a roll of injeera for wrapping.

Endele slices off a translucent ruby-red sliver, wraps it in injeera, dips it in the chilli, pops it in his mouth and chews appreciatively.

Rod and I follow suit. The combination of tender meat, grainy salt, fiery chilli and soft yeasty wrapper is unexpectedly good. If this is Ethiopia's version of hamburger in a bun, I'm hooked.

'This is not only for the men,' says Endele anxiously. 'You will see two respectable ladies eating in the back. There will be more ladies later, when the men have gone. Ladies do not like to eat in public without their men.'

We are to take coffee in Moka, the most famous coffee emporium in Addis and one of the few places it's possible to drink coffee in public.

The shop is long and narrow with chest-high counters where customers can take an espresso on the way to work. Plain cake is also available, cut in squares. Most of the business, however, is in coffee beans roasted to order, chosen from a blackboard chalked up with provenance and price. The customer chooses depth of roasting, variety is decided by the vendor, and the beans are taken home for the coffee ceremony.

'This is important even in Addis,' says Endele. 'It is in these things that we remember who we are, a family joined with other families no matter who they are. Let us hope that those who decide our future in the presidential palace observe our customs.'

One last visit, a moment to keep company with a pearly little skeleton curled on black velvet in a glass case in the basement of Ethiopia's National Museum. Those who lifted her fragile bones from the red earth of the Rift Valley, uncertain if she was truly human, named her *Australopithicus afarensis*.

'I come here to remind myself of who we are and how we came to be,' says Endele quietly. 'Remember us when you return to your homeland.'

For those who accept her for who she might be and what she represents, she's Lucy-in-the-sky-with-diamonds, last of her kind, first of ours.

NIT'IR QIBE (SPICED BUTTER)

Aromatised ghee – fresh butter heated with spices and strained for storage – is used in all recipes that call for butter as an enrichment. Stirred in at the finish, it delivers the authentic flavour of Ethiopian cooking.

(recipe continued overleaf)

Makes about 750 g

1 kg unsalted butter
1 teaspoon finely chopped fresh ginger
1 teaspoon finely chopped garlic
1 teaspoon finely chopped red onion
1 teaspoon ground fenugreek
1 teaspoon dried oregano
½ teaspoon ground cumin
½ teaspoon ground cardamom
¼ teaspoon ground turmeric

Melt the butter gently in a heavy pan and skim off the foam as soon as it rises. When the butter has lost all its moisture and stopped foaming, stir in the ginger, garlic and onion. Simmer for 15 minutes over a low heat without allowing the vegetables to brown. Stir in the remaining ingredients, continue simmering for another 5 minutes, remove from the heat and leave for the solids to settle. Strain the butter into a clean jar, seal and store.

INJEERA WITH TEFF

Injeera, the daily bread of Ethiopia, is a large, soft-crumbed, yeast-raised griddle-bread which serves as both plate and scoop, and is eaten in much the same way as India's chapatti, with small amounts of some-thing good, even if just a sprinkle of flavoured salt. In any Ethiopian meal, whatever the accompaniments, injeera is the central element.

Makes 12–15
1 kg teff flour
Walnut-sized piece fresh yeast, crumbled,
  or 1 x 7 g packet dried yeast
2 litres mineral water

Sift the flour and yeast into a large mixing bowl, rubbing it between your fingers to avoid lumps. Using a wooden spoon, gradually work in enough water to make a smooth batter like runny cream.

Cover and leave in a warm place for 2 or 3 days until the yeast is fully developed and water has risen to the top. Pour off the water.

Bring 500 ml of fresh water to the boil in a large pan and mix in 250 ml of the dough. Turn down the heat and beat the mixture until smooth and thick. Allow to cool and stir it back into the dough in the bowl. Beat in enough water to make a smooth pouring batter, cover and leave to stand for an hour or two until bubbles form.

Preheat a wide iron pan or griddle. Scoop up three-quarters of a cup of the batter and pour it clockwise in circles from the outside to the middle. Cover for 2–3 minutes until the surface is dry and the edges curl. Transfer to a cloth and cover to keep warm. Repeat and continue until all the mixture is used up.

Serve dotted with little heaps of fiery chicken curry, plain-cooked dhal, any vegetable curry flavoured with ginger, hard-boiled egg and a little dab of soft white curd cheese.

INJEERA WITH WHEAT

Wheat-flour injeera, a thin wholemeal crumpet made with a slow-rise sourdough, is the most convenient and reliable substitute for injeera made with teff. Alternative flours are barley, maize, millet, rice and sorghum, mixed fifty-fifty with wheat-flour. Allow 2 days for the initial starter to ferment. Once you have your starter, it will work as a leavening for any bread dough, not just injeera.

Makes 12–15

For the sponge/starter (day 1)
3 g fresh yeast (just a pinch, if using dried)
150 ml warm water (at 30°C)
75 g strong white flour
75 g stoneground wholemeal flour

For the final dough (day 2 or 3)
225 g sponge (from above – keep the rest as a starter)
150 g strong white flour
75 g stoneground wholemeal flour
½ teaspoon salt
about 100 ml warm water

To finish
50 ml warm water
oil or butter for greasing

Mix the sponge/starter ingredients in a jug and leave to ferment at room temperature for 24 hours until frothy and spongy – this is the sponge or starter dough. Leave it for another 24 hours if the weather is cold.

Measure out 225 g of the sponge/starter dough and work it with the two flours, salt and enough warm water to make a soft dough. Work it with your fists until it is stretchy and silky. Cover and leave to rise for an hour or two in a warm place, until doubled in volume. Beat in another 50 ml of warm water – you may need more – until you have a pouring batter the consistency of runny cream. Leave to froth and ferment for another 1–2 hours.

Preheat a wide iron pan or griddle and grease with the oil or butter. Scoop up three-quarters of a cup of the batter and pour it clockwise in circles from the outside to the middle. Cover for 2–3 minutes until the surface is dry and the edges curl. Transfer to a cloth and cover to keep warm. Repeat and continue until all the mixture is used up.

Provide each person with one bread to serve as a plate and another, rolled up into a little bolster, to serve as a scoop. Serve dotted with little heaps of fiery chicken curry, plain-cooked dhal, any vegetable curry flavoured with ginger, hard-boiled egg and a little dab of soft white curd cheese.

The pancakes will keep in the fridge in a plastic bag for 3–4 days. Reheat if necessary under foil in a low oven. Alternatively, tear into small pieces and dry out in the oven.

BUNNA QELA (ROASTED BUTTERED COFFEE BEANS)

Salted, buttered, spiced coffee beans are a little treat for nibbling after a meal as a digestif if hot coffee is not available. Children like them. The alternative is popcorn, given the same treatment.

Enough for 4–6
150 g green coffee beans
2 tablespoons spiced butter (see page 365)
1 teaspoon crushed rock salt

Roast the beans over a gentle flame in a small pan, stirring all the time, until evenly browned. Remove and reserve. Melt the butter with the salt. Stir in the beans, turning them until well coated.

AWAZE (SPICED CHILLI SAUCE)

This is a fiery dip to eat with raw meat or stir into anything else that is all the better for a little heat.

Makes about 350 g
200 g dried red chillies, de-seeded and torn
4 garlic cloves, peeled and chopped
1 small red onion, peeled and finely chopped
1 walnut-sized piece of ginger, peeled and roughly chopped
1 tablespoon rock salt
1 tablespoon dried oregano
1 teaspoon ground cumin
1 teaspoon ground cinnamon
1 teaspoon ground cardamom
½ teaspoon ground cloves
150 ml red wine vinegar

Pound the chillies, garlic, onion, ginger and salt using a pestle and mortar (or in the food processor) until you have a smooth paste. Work in the spices and pack the mixture into a clean jar.

Boil up the vinegar and pour it over the chilli paste in the jar. Seal tightly and leave the flavours to develop in a cool dark corner for a day or two. It will be better in a week, even better in a month.

DORO W'ETT (SLOW-BRAISED CHILLI CHICKEN)

This fiery chicken stew, flavoured with ginger and pepper and enriched with butter, is a party dish, served at weddings, betrothals and to welcome a traveller.

Serves 6–8 as an accompaniment to injeera
1 small free-range chicken, skinned and jointed
1 lime or ½ lemon, skin and flesh roughly chopped
2–3 dried chillies, de-seeded and torn
2–3 garlic cloves, peeled and crushed

1 walnut-sized piece of fresh ginger, peeled and finely chopped
1 tablespoon dried oregano
1 level teaspoon ground cardamom
1 level teaspoon coarsely ground black pepper
2–3 mild red onions, peeled and finely chopped
175 g unsalted butter
1 red pepper, de-seeded and diced
1 glass honey beer or white wine (optional)
salt

Chop the chicken joints into bite-sized pieces (use a heavy knife and tap through the bones with a hammer). Put the chicken pieces in a bowl with the chopped lime or lemon, chilli, garlic, ginger, oregano, cardamom and pepper. Turn to mix well, cover and leave for an hour or two to take on the flavours.

Heat a heavy casserole, add the onion and a tablespoon of water, and cook very gently until the onion softens and turns golden brown – don't let it burn, just add a little water to cool it down.

Add the butter to melt and heat until it froths. Add the diced red pepper and the chicken pieces with their spicy juices, and turn them over the heat for a minute or two (don't let them brown). Add the honey beer or wine (if using) and bring to the boil to evaporate the alcohol. Add enough water to just cover the chicken pieces, return to the boil, turn down the heat, cover with a tight-fitting lid and leave to simmer gently for 40–60 minutes, until the meat is almost dropping off the bone. Remove the lid, add salt and return to the boil until the sauce is thick and shiny. Taste and correct the seasoning.

Serve with injeera or plain-cooked rice accompanied with quartered hard-boiled eggs and a mildly spiced vegetable stew.

BOZENA SHIRO (SPICED SPLIT-PEA PURÉE WITH BUTTER)

This soft scooping purée made with dried split peas or fava beans is eaten with injeera in much the same way as chickpea or bean purées are eaten with pitta breads throughout the Middle East. Similar dishes have been found in the grave-food provided for Egypt's pharaohs on their journey to immortality, so you'll be keeping good company.

Serves 6–8 as an accompaniment
350 g dried split peas, soaked overnight
2–3 red onions, peeled and finely chopped
150 g ghee or clarified butter
1 teaspoon chilli powder
½ teaspoon ground ginger
½ teaspoon ground cardamom
salt

Drain the soaked split peas and reserve.

Fry the chopped onion in the ghee gently until lightly caramelised. Sprinkle in the spices and let them fry for a moment. Put all the ingredients into a large saucepan with enough water to cover generously and bring everything to the boil. Cover with a lid and simmer for 30–40 minutes, until perfectly tender and collapsed into a purée. Add more boiling water if it looks like drying out and give it a stir now and then. The dish should be soft and juicy, almost soupy (it will thicken as it cools).

Taste and add salt. Serve warm as a scooping purée with hard-boiled eggs – or not, as you please – along with injeera and a spicy stew such as *Doro w'ett* (see page 370).

T'IBS ALICHA (BRAISED BEEF AND ONIONS)

This beef stew flavoured with turmeric and ginger, mild rather than hot, is enriched with butter, the characteristic of a dish for a special occasion. Beef is eaten on the day of slaughter, either cooked or raw, with shelf life extended by cutting the meat in strips and drying it in the sun, a form in which, after soaking, it can be prepared exactly as fresh.

Serves 6–8, with other dishes
2–3 mild red onions, peeled and finely chopped
250 g spiced butter (see page 365)
1 kg lean beef, diced
1–2 garlic cloves, peeled and finely chopped
1 teaspoon ground ginger
½ teaspoon ground black pepper
½ teaspoon ground tumeric
salt

To finish
2 green peppers, de-seeded and cut into strips

Gently cook the onions in an earthenware casserole over a low heat with a splash of water until they soften – about 10–15 minutes – don't let them stick and burn. Stir in the butter and let it melt.

At the same time, in a separate pot, cook the meat very gently in its own juices with the garlic and a splash of water for 10–15 minutes, until the meat is beginning to soften.

Combine the meat with the onions and butter, sprinkle in the spices and turn everything together over a gentle heat. Add 500 ml water – enough to submerge everything – bring to the boil, turn down the heat, cover with a lid and simmer gently for another 15–20 minutes, until the meat is perfectly tender and the sauce is thick and rich. Taste for seasoning and add salt if necessary.

Finish scattered with the strips of green pepper and serve hot with injeera or plain-cooked rice.

ACKNOWLEDGEMENTS

Thanks are due first to the friends, guides and companions, especially the late Dun Gifford, and Sara Baer of Oldways Preservation Trust, who have helped, enlightened and advised me on my travels, allowing me to make the most of the experiences from which these stories are drawn. In addition, I am grateful for the support and patience of my agent Caspian Dennis, and for the tireless energy and enthusiasm of all at Bloomsbury, but most particularly editors Natalie Bellos, Alison Cowan, Gillian Stern and Emily Sweet. Others who've guided the book from inception to production and beyond include Richard Atkinson, Alison Glossop, Lena Hall, David Mann, Francesca Sturiale, Ellen Williams, Tess Viljoen, Jane Barringer and Hilary Bird. Among the magazines and newspapers whose editors have sent me to faraway places, providing the raw material for my traveller's tales, are *House & Garden*, *Country Living*, the *Oldie*, the *Field*, the *Scotsman* and *Food and Travel*.

But above all I am indebted to my predecessors, the diarists, travellers, historians, naturalists and anthropologists whose writings continue to inspire, educate and delight all those fortunate enough to find their work on the shelves of our great libraries, particularly the iron stacks of the London Library. Even the most assiduous explorations on the internet are no substitute for works on paper. Among these (in no particular order): *Stalking the Wild Asparagus* by Euell Gibbons (1962), D.H. Lawrence's *Sea and Sardinia* (1921), *Through Many Lands by Water* by J.E. Pryde-Hughes (1930), *The Balkan Trail* by Frederick Moore

(1906), *Balkan Ghosts* by Robert Kaplan (1993), C.L. Sulzberger's *A Long Row of Candles* (1969), Sacheverell Sitwell's *Roumanian Journey* (1938), Walter Starkie's *Raggle-Taggle* (1935), Eric Ambler's *The Mask of Dimitrios* (1939), Henry Miller's *The Colossus of Maroussi* (1941), diplomat Sir Harry Luke's *Islands of the South Pacific* (1962), Roderick Cameron's *The Golden Haze* (1964), Douglas L. Oliver's *The Pacific Islands* (1951), *America's Founding Food: The Story of New England Cooking* by Keith Stavely and Kathleen Fitzgerald (2004) and *Northern Bounty*, edited by Jo Marie Powers and Anita Stewart (1995).

For insights into daily life on the islands of the Mediterranean: Louis Golding's *Goodbye to Ithaca* (1955), Lawrence Durrell's *Prospero's Cell* (1945) and D.T. Ansted's *The Ionian Islands* (1863). For guidance to the Mountain Kingdom: *Ethiopia, The Unknown Land,* by Stuart Munro-Hay (2002), John Buchan's *Prester John* (1910) and *In Ethiopia with a Mule* by Dervla Murphy (1968). When it comes to Iberia, Richard Ford's *Gatherings from Spain* (1846) has never been bettered. And finally, among those whose work extends the imagination far beyond a traveller's tales: Louis, Mary and Richard Leakey's extraordinary documentations of our African beginnings; Michael Pollan's *The Botany of Desire* (2001), Yuval Noah Harari's *Sapiens: A Brief History of Humankind* (2014), *Cities and the Wealth of Nations* by Jane Jacobs (1984) and Jared Diamond's *Guns, Germs and Steel* (1997).

INDEX

NOTE ON THE AUTHOR

Elisabeth Luard is an award-winning food writer, journalist and broadcaster. Her cookbooks include *A Cook's Year in a Welsh Farmhouse*, *European Peasant Cookery* and *The Food of Spain and Portugal*. She has written three memoirs, *Family Life*, *Still Life* and *My Life as a Wife*. She has a monthly column in the *Oldie*, is a Trustee of the *Oxford Symposium on Food and Cookery* and writes for *Country Living*, *Country Life*, the *Daily Telegraph* and the *Daily Mail*.

NOTE ON THE TYPE

The text of this book is set in Fournier. Fournier is derived from the *romain du roi*, which was created towards the end of the seventeenth century from designs made by a committee of the Académie of Sciences for the exclusive use of the Imprimerie Royale. The original Fournier types were cut by the famous Paris founder Pierre Simon Fournier in about 1742. These types were some of the most influential designs of the eight and are counted among the earliest examples of the 'transitional' style of typeface. This Monotype version dates from 1924. Fournier is a light, clear face whose distinctive features are capital letters that are quite tall and bold in relation to the lower-case letters, and *decorative italics, which show the influence of the calligraphy of Fournier's time.*